Counselling Supervision in Organisations

Professional and ethical dilemmas explored

Sue Copeland

Routledge
Taylor & Francis Group

LONDON AND NEW YORK

First published 2005
by Routledge
27 Church Road, Hove, East Sussex BN3 2FA

Simultaneously published in the USA and Canada
by Routledge
270 Madison Avenue, New York NY 10016

Routledge is an imprint of the Taylor & Francis Group

Copyright © 2005 Sue Copeland

Typeset in Times by RefineCatch Ltd, Bungay, Suffolk
Printed and bound in Great Britain by
TJ International Ltd, Padstow, Cornwall
Paperback cover design by Anú Design

This publication has been produced with paper manufactured to
strict environmental standards and with pulp derived from
sustainable forests.

British Library Cataloguing in Publication Data
A catalogue record for this book is available from the British Library

Library of Congress Cataloging-in-Publication Data
Copeland, Sue.
   Counselling supervision in organisations / Sue Copeland. – 1st ed.
      p. cm.
   Includes bibliographical references and index.
   ISBN 1-58391-196-0 (hardcover) – ISBN 1-58391-197-9 (pbk.)
1. Counselors–Supervision of.   2. Corporate culture.   I. Title.
   BF637.C6C5724 2005
   658.3'02–dc22   2005001548

ISBN 1-58391-196-0 (hbk)
ISBN 1-58391-197-9 (pbk)

To Jeff, Emma and Rachel

Contents

Foreword

Bateson's famous dictum, 'the context gives meaning', is at the basis of the book you are about to read. Sue Copeland has taken the organisational context in which counselling supervision occurs and made it the focus of her work. Like Bateson she is arguing strongly for making sense of counselling supervision by understanding the organisational context behind it, beside it, beneath it, above it – all around it.

We know little of the organisational impact on helping within various contexts whether that helping is counselling, coaching, consultancy or supervision. There is little research to inform us of the influence of organisations on counsellors and supervisors and little literature on how we manage that influence when we are informed about it. Organisations, be they voluntary, religious, health, education or industrial/workplace, are not machines but living communities of people. As such they have their own identities, their cultures, their influences, their underlying myths and their ways of making meaning. There is no question about whether organisations impact and influence their employees, their environment and those who work within the helping professions either as in-house or external helpers – the key question is about how much they impact and how much they influence and how that impact and influence takes place.

That organisations are powerful arenas of power, values, politics and interpersonal dynamics is not in doubt. They can save us and swamp us, energise and de-energise us, invigorate with life or destroy. People catch the aura of an organisation and live out its dictates without even knowing they do so. Organisations face us with the best in us and the worst in us, pull us to the limits of our potential and challenge us to face our own demons (and angels) as we face theirs.

Ignore organisations at your peril. They will reach out imperceptibly and pull you into their depths, they will make you do what you would never do on your own, and they will push you to the cutting edge of your potential, bring out the best and bring out the worst. They will revive what you thought was over and forgotten, re-ignite fires from embers that are covered with ashes. They will own and disown you, be honest and dishonest with you, love you and hate you, beguile you, seduce you, promise you and betray you. They will over promise and under deliver. In good times they will be generous, in bad times they will abandon. This is the world where Sue Copeland nests her counselling supervision – what a challenging task.

There is little on counselling supervision in organisations to guide us. It is far too easy for counsellors in workplaces, health settings, religious groups, educational institutions to get sucked into the organisational dynamics without knowing what is happening. Few counselling supervisors who have already pioneered the territory have left us road maps or strategies to help us manage this difficult terrain. As a result many counsellors work as if there were no context outside the individual. They work with the internal world of the client. Counsellors in organisations have no such narrowness – for them it is all too obvious that the external world of the client is vastly important to their physical, mental, moral, emotional and spiritual well-being. Sometimes the organisation is the problem – how can we blame the individual?

Sue Copeland's book creates a model for thinking about supervision in organisations. It goes further and suggests that supervisors can have impacts on organisations in ways that hitherto they have not considered. While we know, and have known for some time, that the focus of supervision is the work of the supervisee, we are becoming more conscious that that work is not just about what happens in the counselling room. The counselling room, when that room is physically or metaphorically situated within an organisation, is bombarded with all sorts of vibrations from the organisation. Clients bring their organisation into the counselling room; counsellors bring their clients and their organisations into the supervision room.

For many years counsellors and psychotherapists went inwards to investigate the causes of human distress and problems. They worked on the principle that mental illness, emotional distress and psychological problems had their origins inside the individual. While external events triggered off problems, solutions were discovered within the human psyche. Individuals held solutions to their lives within themselves and the counselling journey was inward to realise those solutions. There is a more contemporary view, championed by Sue Copeland in this book, suggesting that this may be one-sided and that many of the roots of human misery are as much external as internal. We cannot make the child responsible for its abuse or the employee the cause of his being bullied, or burden the patient with the negligence of the doctor or nurse. Upstream (rather than downstream) helping asks helpers to recognise that systems, organisations, institutions and groups create dysfunction and that solutions to these issues lie outside individuals within the contexts in which they occur.

Sue Copeland is eager to stress the need for proactivity on the part of supervisors in organisations and feels they have the skills and knowledge to contribute much more than they do to the organisations that employ them or that they work within. She sees their role as holding together the needs of the organisation, the counsellor and the clients/employees and working back 'upstream' to define and work with the unhealthy systems that wound individuals in the first place. Clients are always kept at the forefront of the work while the behind-the-scenes dynamics are unearthed, articulated and tackled. Helping organisations to become more emotionally intelligent is part of this process.

I hope you enjoy reading this book as much as I have. I hope, also, that you will see what Sue Copeland has done as the beginning of a learning journey or search for even deeper understanding of how the world of organisations connects to and influences and is influenced by the world of counselling supervision.

Michael Carroll
February 2005

Acknowledgements

I would like to acknowledge the work of the following people for their help and support at all stages of the writing and production of this book:

- My colleagues at York St John College, especially Alan Dunnett, Val Wosket and Jill Burns for their ideas and reading of draft copies of the manuscript and Alison Perry for her attention to detail in editing and producing the final manuscript.
- My colleagues in the counselling profession for their help with ideas and for their encouragement when the going got tough. They include; Michael Carroll, Barbara Lawton, Jackie Emmott, Pat Barnes, Andrew Kinder, Gabriel Syme and Peter Cook.
- To Lesley Murphy, my past supervisee, for her permission to use the case study of our work together which appears in Chapter 1.
- All my current and past supervisees who have provided a wealth of experience to draw on when writing this book.
- The editorial and production teams at Routledge for their support and efficiency in the production of this book.
- And last but not least my husband Jeff and daughters Emma and Rachel without whose support this book would not have been written.

Introduction

I have always found organisations exciting and challenging places to work. Practising as a supervisor within an organisational context is similarly challenging but rewarding. My interest in supervision within organisational contexts began over a decade ago when I was formally employed by a large national organisation to supervise a team of counsellors in a designated geographical area. I was assigned to the team by the organisation and all the counsellors had to attend the supervision sessions, they had no other choice. They were required to present casework to myself and seven of their peers. Additionally, I was required to produce a report on their work after each supervisory session, and to sign to say that I considered them to be working within the level of their professional capabilities. Initially I agreed to be involved with this work but I was not sure how the supervisory process would operate in a climate of coercion. I felt as if I was working in uncharted waters. Yet the organisation did create professional and ethical boundaries in which to work. They required their supervisors to be accountable to the organisation for their own, and their supervisee's work. Without the full support of the organisation and the willingness of the team to work within the parameters set, my work with them would have been impossible. My formal employment contract with the organisation was vital to my successful supervisory work.

It took me over a year to build up a sufficient level of trust in the group for supervision to be successful. At times I despaired. Gradually, however, the supervisees began to trust themselves with one another and with me. The work became productive. At the same time I also began to have a wider role within the organisation, helping managers to assess counsellors as they trained to work in a time-limited way. I came to understand the organisation culture and the continual change processes that my supervisees were coping with on a daily basis. Having this wider role meant that I was using my knowledge and skills for the benefit of the whole organisation. However, most supervisors will not be in that role yet unless they are formally employed by the organisation.

My interest in the employee status of supervisors within organisations and the extent of responsibility they have for the effectiveness of their supervisee's work was fuelled by this experience. The research carried out for my M.Phil into the dilemmas faced by supervisors working in diverse organisational contexts, confirmed my thoughts that supervisors, in the main, are not formally employed by their supervisee's organisation. As a result they have minimal contact with that organisation and no lines of communication other than through their supervisee. Supervisors working for counselling agencies were in a slightly better position, as they were usually internal employees and an integral part of the organisation. Nevertheless, they still faced the continual struggle, as did all supervisors, to assert their value when economic strictures were endemic within the organisation. Having little or no voice within an organisation made supervisors invisible and powerless. Yet they had so much knowledge and skill to offer the organisation that was not recognised or acknowledged. Some of this knowledge involved an understanding of the organisational culture in which the supervisee and their clients operated and an even deeper understanding of their own profession's culture. Yet the lack of formal employment status meant that their skills and knowledge were limited to working with individual client cases rather than expanding into the impact of organisational dynamics on the work and being able to feed this back, through the supervisee, to their line manager.

Millions of words have been written about the supervisory process, the working alliance between the supervisor and supervisee that is the lynch pin of the work. Yet the way in which that working alliance originates can be informal and often happens through networking. Over the years the employment of counsellors within organisational contexts has become more professional; job advertisements are clear and the posts set out specific requirements both in terms of a job and person specification. BACP/UKCP or similar accreditation is often asked for as a minimum recognition for an experienced practitioner. Interviews are held and, especially for full-time posts, there is often fierce competition. Organisations are very often aware that employing a counsellor is a big responsibility and so they need to adhere to employment law. Nevertheless, many employers will rely on the counsellor themselves to be conversant with the needs of their own profession concerning supervision and its frequency. Therefore, the employment of a counselling supervisor is often left to the counsellor to arrange, hence the informality of the process.

When supervising counsellors who work in an organisational context, I have gained employment in numerous ways. The most common way has been for the counsellor to approach me and ask if I will be their supervisor. They have worked in a health service setting as a staff counsellor in a hospital, as a counsellor in a GP surgery, as a counsellor in a further education college or as a staff counsellor in a social services setting. Similarly, counsellors have approached me who work in a commercial organisation or in the voluntary sector. On all these occasions, except for the commercial organisation, it was the organisation itself which agreed to pay my fee, yet the counsellor them-selves agreed the terms of my employment. At the time I did not think that this process of employment was problematic and it still remains the most widespread method for organisations to employ counselling supervisors today. Indeed, I chose my own current supervisor for my work in a university counselling service in this way even though the university pays some of the supervision fee. However, as we will see in later discussions, there are dis-advantages to this method of employment and supervisors need to be aware of the need to safeguard their own rights when working for diverse organisa-tions. Similarly, organisations need to safeguard their rights when paying for their counsellor's supervision, hence the need for the supervisor to be more formally embedded in the organisation.

Being invited by an organisation to supervise a counsellor or team of counsellors is another way of being employed as a supervisor and this is how I gained work supervising a group of counsellors/employee support workers in a commercial organisation. However, for an organisation to employ a supervisor in this way, the manager of the counselling or welfare service needs to be familiar with the counselling and supervisory process as well as formal employment procedures. In this way they will be able to systematically choose the right supervisor for the work needed by the organisation. This does mean that the manager, rather than the counsellors themselves, chooses the supervisor and in my experience this can cause problems when the initial working relationship is being established. This can also have ramifications for the organisation and the supervisor in terms of their accountability and responsibility towards each other.

Within organisational contexts counsellors may be asked to take on the additional post of supervisor within their working remit. This will mean that they then have a dual role within the organisation. From an employer's point of view this could be an easy way of employing a supervisor whose work is already known to managers and who is familiar with the client work under-taken. The supervisor role can then be added to their job description and the counsellor/supervisor can be paid in the normal way.

Similarly, a counsellor can find work as a supervisor by applying for an internally advertised position. In doing so they may be competing with other internal candidates and so the organisation will need to use the normal employment procedures for filling this internal post. In this way the supervisor will be deemed to be the best internal candidate for the work.

Lastly, a supervisor can find work by applying for an externally advertised post. This advertisement could be found in a professional journal or in a local or national newspaper. Usually, supervision posts are not full time however, and therefore when applying for an externally advertised post a supervisor will be deciding how far they are prepared to travel for the work. There will be open competition for the post and the organisation itself will need to decide who is to be involved in the selection process. Therefore, the myriad of ways that a supervisor can be chosen to work in an organisation diminishes the work being valued, except on an individual basis between supervisor and supervisee. Consequently it is vital that the supervisor views their role as an integral part of the organisational dynamics.

I sense that supervisors themselves are not proactive enough in promoting their services within the organisation. Perhaps they do not want to undermine their supervisee? As supervisors in my research study maintained, they wanted to empower their supervisees to use their own authority within their organisations. Yet two forces for change are more powerful than one. When the supervisory relationship is strong, supervisor and supervisee can work together to affect community solutions to problems rather than personal, private solutions for their clients and themselves within the organisational context of their work. However, to do this they both need to have a secure position in the organisation. This means formality of tenure. They also need to be valued by managers and trusted by their colleagues and clients alike. This position is not won easily. Nevertheless, when the supervisor is a trusted part of the counselling team they have the authority to use their knowledge and skills wisely for the benefit of the service and the organisation as a whole.

Consequently, in this book I am advocating a more proactive role for supervisors working within organisations. If an organisation is not offering employee status, supervisors can address this with the supervisee's line manager. Similarly, employment contracts are vital so that all parties in the working alliance understand their responsibilities to one another. When these are clear the supervisor is able to add value to the organisation by reporting back, not only on the supervisory process and its outcomes but also on the organisational dynamics that affect the psychological health of employees. In order for the supervisor to be able to fulfil this role the organisation will need to be open and ready to embrace the knowledge and skills that the supervisor brings with their role. Therefore, I am promoting a more developmental approach so that supervisors, working initially through the supervisee and their line manager, can influence processes and systems that will not only benefit the clients but the organisation too.

This book is divided into three parts for ease of reference. Part I examines the roles and responsibilities of the supervisor working in diverse organisational settings. It examines the definition of the supervisory role and compares the role to that of mentor, coach and consultant. Part II explores the management of the cultural fit between a counselling and supervision culture and the culture of the organisation and the dilemmas that originate from cultural warfare. Finally, Part III explores the working relationships within the supervisory rhombus. This includes chapters on securing a supervisory position, contracting for the work, exploring working relationships within the organisation, doing the supervisory work, reporting back to the organisation, evaluation, assessment and accreditation processes as well as a chapter on endings and new beginnings in supervision. All these processes are vital to ensure that the supervisor is recognised and employed as an important and integral member of the counselling team who brings with them the experience, knowledge and skills needed, not only for the individual supervisee but also for their line manager and the organisation as a whole. When the formal employment of counselling supervisors becomes standard practice within organisations they will be ready, in position, to take on the wider, organisational role that their knowledge and skills demand.

Part I

Supervision in organisations

Roles and responsibilities

Chapter 1

Mentor, coach, consultant or supervisor?: defining the role

> Receptive presence is hard, active work. We are not simply nodding and smiling, holding and comforting. We do demand.
>
> (Daloz 1999:246)

INTRODUCTION

Sitting opposite Lesley in the small committee room, I watch as her eyes filled with tears. My own sadness mirrored hers. This was the end of our journey together as supervisor and supervisee. Lesley was skilful in her role as work-place counsellor. She had worked for the company for many years as her role evolved into that of qualified counsellor. Within that role she was trusted to have influence with line managers when a client was stressed with an issue that emanated from their role at work. Additionally, she was renowned for helping those who were harassed at work. At any one time she could be dealing with many similar cases that tested her allegiance to the client, the organisation and also her emotional stamina. As her supervisor I worked with support and challenge to help her gain clarity when boundary issues threatened ethical practice.

However, increasingly I was aware that she was becoming disillusioned with the organisational culture, the pattern of change and its impact on both her clients and herself. She no longer felt valued by the organisation and was becoming burnt out. With her permission, I talked to her clinical manager about my concern for her psychological health during a period of leave from work due to stress. In this way I was able to work with the organisation, in my role as supervisor, to help them understand the pressures Lesley was encountering in her practice. Subsequently, Lesley and I worked together, during parts of our sessions, to plan a strategy that would enable her to leave the organisation for work that would be more fulfilling. In this part of our work I was a life coach, helping her to identify her unused potential and the possibilities for a change of career. My other role as a senior lecturer in higher education enabled me to have an insight into educational routes that might help Lesley to gain more personal and professional fulfilment. Therefore, I was working both as a consultant and mentor, sharing my knowledge and experience of educational routes. As a result she undertook a course of study and was successful. Consequently, she gained employment as a lecturer in further education, a job that has given her a new outlet for her energy and still enables her to use counselling skills to facilitate the learning process in others.

My work with Lesley highlights the multi-faceted role of the supervisor within organisations. During our work together, had I been a mentor, coach, consultant or supervisor? It is clear that I was employed by the organisation to be her supervisor and the client work was not lost during those supervisory sessions, but to ignore the supervisee's psychological health and unfulfilled potential would have been folly. It could be argued that career development is the domain of the supervisee's therapist but I would argue otherwise in this case. From our work over many years together I knew her well, her strengths and areas for development. She also trusted me to be challenging and supportive in my feedback. I was also employed by the organisation and worked with three other supervisees within the same organisation. Therefore, I was aware of how the culture was impacting on her levels of stress. I was in a position to be mentor, coach and even consultant, alongside my role as counselling supervisor. At times it would have been easy to ignore the other roles and concentrate solely on the role of supervisor. However, this would have been counter-productive for Lesley, her clients and the organisation. A burnt out and dispirited counsellor will not do their best client work and neither will they add value to the organisational culture. So I had a duty of care towards Lesley, her clients and the organisation to help her to find alternative ways of regenerating herself. In this case that meant leaving the organisation for a different role in a new organisation, but it could also have led to leaving the organisation and working, as a counsellor, in a new setting. Alternatively, it could have led to Lesley remaining in the same organisation, in the same role but with renewed interest and energy for her work gained through more development and training and perhaps a move to a new team in a different geographical area.

In our discussions recently we deliberated over our past work together and came to the conclusion that as a mentor I had guided her along the path to further study and encouraged her to continue in order to gain more fulfilling employment. As a coach I had helped her to see the possibilities for the future based on divergent thinking. As a consultant I was able to give advice based on my own previous experience of working as a teacher-trainer in further education. In fact, even the day we talked I shared information about a book that would be useful for her work and study at Masters' level. However, during our work together as Lesley's supervisor, the clients were never lost and the therapeutic alliance was always at the forefront of our work. Professional boundaries were not crossed. It was only when she ceased to be my supervisee that we became friends, able to share our professional lives and delight in one another's successes. Whilst we had been working together I knew I was her supervisor and the welfare of her clients was uppermost in my mind during our sessions. Nevertheless, looking back on our work, the role of consultant, coach and mentor were evident.

Therefore, in this chapter the three roles of mentor, coach and consultant will be considered in relation to the role of supervision within the organisation. The similarities and differences will be highlighted in order to work towards a more composite understanding of the supervisory role and how it can add value to an organisation. Initially this will be by helping the supervisee to work more effectively within the organisation, however, as the supervisor's profile increases they will find that managers acknowledge and use their skills more widely within the organisation.

THE SUPERVISOR AS MENTOR

The concept of a supervisor as mentor is plausible. Mentors have always been around in all walks of life yet recently they have become more visible. Mentors transmit wisdom. They take us on a journey through our lives and act as our guide. They help us to grow up and develop our identity (Daloz 1999). There is also a sense that mentors, as our guide, arrive at the right moment in our lives to assist us on the journey that we need to take (Coelho 1997). They may not be officially called a mentor but we recognise them as such by their ability to give us guidance on our developmental journey. Connor (1997:17) describes a mentor as a trusted and faithful guide who at different times may be called upon to be 'A facilitator; coach; counsellor; sounding board; critical friend; net worker; or role model.'

She was writing here about the mentoring role in the Health Service; the mentoring of young doctors to facilitate their journey through a challenging career. Mentoring is common in all professions and in education the role features strongly. As a new member of staff in my current post I was given a mentor who guided me on my journey through the labyrinth of organisational politics and the intricacies of assessment procedures. But he also provided a shoulder to cry on when I had a close bereavement and encouragement when my confidence faltered in my new role. Our joint understanding of the role of a mentor was clear. He was my guide when I needed him most but is now a trusted colleague and friend. Therefore, I have recognised my mentors in various aspects of my life by their ability to inspire, guide and aid my growth, both personally and professionally. I know that I have also become a mentor to others and this has often happened without me consciously having that title. It was not until I read the following acknowledgement in a book that one of my counselling skills students wrote, that I was aware of my mentoring role: 'I owe a debt of gratitude to Sue Copeland on whose course I gained the confidence to do so many things including writing this story' (Creese 2002).

We later talked about our working relationship and I felt immense humility that I was seen as a role model and mentor by a talented, black grandmother who herself had so much wisdom to offer. I anticipate that she will become a mentor herself, to those people who follow in her footsteps.

Mentoring is akin to supervising. A supervisor could consider becoming a mentor to the organisation. They would offer their knowledge, insight and perspective or wisdom, giving an overall picture of problem areas within the department or the organisation as a whole. Playing this role within the organisation would not be without its dangers. The possibility of confidentiality being broken, at various levels, would be there. However, a supervisor, in the role of mentor to the organisation, holds the collective information that organisations need to change and grow. When one departmental manager is the source of many clients' stress, a supervisor will be in a position to work with the organisation, guiding them to make changes within the department that will reduce the stress levels. The supervisor will have the knowledge, experience and skills to engage in this role whilst also maintaining ethical boundaries. The counsellor could also be in the position to engage in this mentoring role with the organisation, especially if they are very experienced.

This modern mentoring relationship, whether at a one-to-one or organisational level, is based on mutual, equal and collaborative learning. These features also apply to the coaching relationship and there are similarities between mentoring and coaching.

THE SUPERVISOR AS COACH

Currently, coaching is in vogue. In December 2003, the *Counselling and Psychotherapy Journal* (BACP) proclaimed on its front cover: Life coaching. The new kid on the block? The fashion for coaching extends to training for supervisors of coaches and I have a therapist/coach on my Diploma in Counsellor Supervision course. The word comes from all directions; life coach; executive coach; business coach, but what is it and what has it got to do with counselling, supervision and organisations?

Coaching is defined as many things: a conversation which is productive and results orientated; a learning experience in which patterns are observed and the stage set for new actions; asking the right questions rather than providing the right answers; finally it is about change and transformation. Zeus and Skiffington (2002:18) provide a useful comparison between coaching and mentoring (Table 1.1) which seeks to tease out the similarities and differences. However, the differences seem to be very small in comparison to the similarities of each role. Coaches work with emotions. In sports coaching much is made of the psychological mind-set of the sports person. Anyone watching a tennis player prepare for the crucial shot will observe the facial expression that indicates the schooling of the emotions to psychologically prepare for

Table 1.1   Similarities and differences between mentor and coach

Similarities	Differences
• Both require well-developed interpersonal skills	• Mentoring invents a future based on the expertise and wisdom of another, whereas coaching is about inventing a future from the individual's own possibilities
• Both require the ability to generate trust, to support commitment and to generate new actions through the use of listening and speaking skills	• Mentors are recognised as experts in their field
• Both shorten the learning curve	
	• Mentoring is usually more specifically career-focused in terms of career advancement
• Both aim for the individual to improve his or her performance and be more productive	• Mentors usually have experience at senior management level, and have a broad knowledge of organisational structure, policies, power and culture
• Both encourage the individual to stretch, but can provide support if the person falters or gets out of his or her depth	• Mentors freely give advice and opinions regarding strategies and policies, whereas coaching is about evoking answers from the individual
• Both provide support without removing responsibility	• Mentors have considerable power and influence to advance the individual's career and advocate promotion
• Both require a degree of organisational know-how	• Mentors convey and instil the standards, norms and values of the profession/ organisation. Coaching is more about exploring and developing the individual's own values, vision and standards
• Both focus on learning and development to enhance skills and competencies	
• Both stimulate personal growth to develop new expertise	
• Both can function as a career guide to review career goals and identify values, vision and career strengths	
• Both are role models	

Source: Zeus and Skiffington (2002:18).

the shot. Similarly, a footballer getting ready to take the vital penalty can be seen in comparable psychological preparation. Therefore, although coaching is about skill acquisition, there is also an attitudinal stance needed for transformation to take place in a person's life. So coaching is about learning in the widest sense of the word. Adult learners need an environment that is safe and nurturing so that they can work towards their own strategies and solutions. Here we could also be defining the environment of counselling. My first counselling teaching experience was on a course entitled: Counselling Skills in the Development of Learning. In its purest form this course recognised the link between the use of counselling skills to enable learners to unlock their potential, to overcome their anxieties and old childhood messages concerning their ability to achieve. This is where some of the work of a coach lies. It is also embedded in the work of a counsellor.

Carroll (2003) is eloquent in his exploration of the similarities and differences between counselling and coaching. Williams and Davis (2002:5) also outline some of the reasons why they think that therapists are uniquely qualified to make the transition into life coaching. These include:

- being a skilful listener
- having the gift of reframing
- being able to suspend judgement
- having experience with confidentiality and ethics
- having the ability to seek solutions and think of possibilities.

So they also see the similarities between coaching and counselling and it is the skills needed in both roles where the biggest similarity lies. Zeus and Skiffington (2002:12) also outline the similarities and differences (Table 1.2). However, when exploring the similarities and differences between counselling and coaching, there is a gap that the role of the supervisor can fill in many subtle ways. As in coaching the power differential is less in supervision than it may be in counselling. The supervisor can also give advice in the role of teacher. Similarly, as in coaching, supervisors do not engage in therapy with their supervisees, but they focus on enhancing counselling practice. Supervisors also work with the future development of the counsellor.

So individually, supervisors can act as a coach to their supervisee when individual guidance is needed over professional development. However, the supervisor can also operate as a coach to the organisation. Supervisors are in a good position to engage in this role as they have information about the organisational culture gleaned from working with the supervisee and their clients. They also have the facilitation skills to ask the right question of managers who are open to change in the organisation. Working organisationally also needs courage and confidence. Good relationships are not forged over night. The supervisor needs to have a high profile within the organisation in order to engage in a coaching role. They need to be formally employed and have a tripartite relationship with the supervisee and their line manager. In this way the supervisor will gain a reputation for being skilled and ethical in their practice and a person who can add value to organisational processes, especially to the change process.

Therefore, organisations will notice that there is less difference between a coach and a supervisor than there is between a coach and a counsellor. This means that they will be valuable to an organisation. However, the supervisor

Table 1.2   Similarities and differences between therapist and coach

Similarities	Differences
• Both use assessment	• Therapists are less self-disclosing than coaches, so the power differential is less in a coaching relationship
• Both investigate and clarify values	• Therapists rarely give advice, whereas coaches are free to make suggestions, advise, make requests and confront the individual
• Both are client centred	• Therapists tend to focus on the resolution of old pains and old issues, whereas coaches acknowledge their historical impact but do not explore these in depth. Coaches are more inclined to reflect pro-active behaviours and move the person forward out of their feelings and into action
• Both listen and reflect	• Therapy tends to deal with dysfunction, either vague or specific, whereas coaching moves a functional person on to greater success and refers clients on for clinical issues
• Both help individuals recognise the potential destructiveness of their actions and feelings	• Therapy tends to focus on past-related feelings, whereas coaching is about setting goals and forward action
• Both recognise strengths and weaknesses	• Therapy explores resistance and negative transference, whereas coaching attempts to rephrase complaints into goals
• Both seek to situate the individual in a context of adult development	• Therapy is about progress, whereas coaching is about performance

Source: Zeus and Skiffington (2002:12).

as consultant also needs to be considered and this role links with the role of the coach within organisations.

THE SUPERVISOR AS CONSULTANT

The supervisor as consultant is consistent with working at an organisational level. Management consultants are known to originate from many backgrounds including human resources, training and development and organisational psychology. Consultants support organisational change. Yet they also help to solve problems, set goals and design organisational action plans. They are parachuted into organisations to engender a quick fix rather than work on problems that are deep seated. They do not engage in building more permanent relationships within the organisation but engage at a level that is about 'making it happen' (Harvey-Jones 1988:28). Increasingly, consultants are being required to operate at a more individual level within the organisation. This type of role overlaps with a coaching role and once again Zeus and Skiffington (2002:16) usefully outline the similarities and differences between the role of coach and consultant (Table 1.3). Therefore, in the role of consultant to their supervisee, the supervisor will be engaged in a process that is similar to the teaching aspect of supervision. Indeed, in one organisation my supervisory work was labelled as 'consultative support'.

Yet a supervisor is well placed to operate as a consultant to an organisation especially if they have an in-depth knowledge of organisational culture and

Table 1.3   Similarities and differences between consultant and coach

Similarities	Differences
• Both aim to support organisational change	• Coaching can be conducted outside of a consulting relationship
• Both solve problems, set goals and design an action plan	• Consultants tend to be experts within a specific industry or business, whereas a coach's expertise is in the domain of conversation, communication, interpersonal skills and emotions. The coach does not have to be an expert in the business field
• Both can design and facilitate workshops and work with teams	• Consultants' services are information based, whereas coaching revolves around relationships
• Both can be seen as a quick-fix, remedial intervention for a targeted individual, rather than for a problem that is deep-seated in an organisation	• Consultants are frequently expected to provide answers, whereas coaches evoke answers from the individual
	• Consultants gather and analyse data, write reports and make recommendations that are frequently systemic and based on the needs of the organisation. They are rarely employed to deal with individuals during the period of transition and change. On the other hand, coaches work with individuals during and after organisational change
	• Consultants can tend to prescribe 'canned' or 'commercial' solutions, whereas coaching is more personalised and concerned with the individual's needs, values and goals
	• Consultants generally focus on work aspects, whereas coaching is more holistic and considers other aspects of an individual's life. Consultants tend to deal with specific problems, whereas coaches are more forward looking and always ready to create and take advantage of opportunities

Source: Zeus and Skiffington (2002:16).

an understanding of which department is resistant to change. They will straddle the line between mentor, coach and consultant, whilst still keeping their professional identity. That professional identity is important so that the focus of the work is not lost and currently the supervisory process, within the counselling profession, has a specific definition that could be open to interpretation.

DEFINING THE SUPERVISORY ROLE

The definition of the word supervision is controversial within the counselling and psychotherapy profession. Outside of the profession a supervisor is someone who has a hierarchical and managerial authority over others. There is a structured power differential and often the role has an appraisal function in line with the managerial function that it describes (Proctor 1997a, Carroll 1996). This is the primary meaning of the process of supervision as the general public understands it. Therefore, it corresponds to the dictionary definition (Williams 1992). Within the context of other helping professions such as social work, nursing, youth work, etc., the process of supervision does follow the dictionary definition as there is often a line management function embedded within the role. Similarly, in different professions within an industrial setting, a supervisor would certainly be someone who had a line management function that would include a disciplinary function when necessary. So, the different understanding of the supervisory role within an organisational setting can cause confusion to line managers outside the profession.

Within the counselling and psychotherapy profession the definition of the word supervisor differs from the dictionary definition and the common understanding of the word in an organisational context. Here supervision is an activity used to describe the process by which a counsellor gains support and guidance in order to ensure that the clients' needs are met appropriately (Edwards 1997) and that they receive at least a minimum quality of care (Coll 1995). The British Association for Counselling and Psychotherapy (BACP) gives its own definition:

> Counselling supervision is a formal and mutually agreed arrangement for counsellors to discuss their work regularly with someone who is normally an experienced and competent counsellor and familiar with the process of counselling supervision. The task is to work together to ensure and develop the efficacy of the supervisee's practice . . . It should take account of the setting within which the supervisee practices . . . is intended to ensure that the needs of clients are being addressed and to monitor the effectiveness of . . . intervention.

> (BAC 1996:2.3)

This is a comprehensive definition including consideration of the context in which supervision takes place. This consideration of the context is important because it will inevitably influence the counselling process. The supervisor will need to be able to identify any organisational transference that is evident and help the supervisee to work with this effectively. Similarly, it is important that this definition outlines the experience and competence needed by the supervisor within this role. This signals to the organisation the standards necessary for anyone applying for this position.

Inskipp and Proctor (1995:1) also give a definition of counselling supervision as

> A working alliance between a supervisor and a counsellor in which the counsellor can offer an account or recording of her work; reflect on it; receive feedback, and where appropriate, guidance. The object of this alliance is to enable the counsellor to gain in ethical competence, confidence and creativity so as to give her best possible service to her clients.

This definition clearly states the collaborative nature of the supervisory alliance and the importance that alliance has in maintaining the counsellor's ethical practice. Therefore, any line manager who employs a counselling supervisor will be aware that, from this definition, part of the role of the supervisor is to ensure that the counsellor's practice is ethical.

The definition that Stoltenberg and Delworth (1987:34) provide is shorter and more allied to a training role for the supervisor, 'An intensive, interpersonally focused, one-to-one relationship in which one person is designated to facilitate the development of therapeutic competence in the other person.' The educative function of supervision is part of the role of supervisor. However, from this definition a line manager may be confused, especially when employing an experienced counsellor, about the current competence of their employee.

Holloway's (1995:1) definition of the supervision process is more encompassing when she sees the process as: 'To oversee, to view another's work with the eye of an experienced clinician, the sensitive teacher, the discriminating professional.' Yet this definition is also allied to a training role for the supervisor, the role of a supervisor to counsellors in training. However, like the BAC definition, it ensures that the supervisor is a designated 'experienced clinician'. Thus, it is the organisation's role to ensure that the supervisor appointed for any trainee counsellor fits that description.

Definitions of counselling supervision abound and for an even more comprehensive exploration of definition see Tudor and Worrell (2004:43–48). Yet a definition that fully encompasses the organisational context of the work is needed. This ensures that a counsellor's line manager is clear about why they are employing the supervisor and the type of experience the supervisor needs to fulfil the role within the organisation.

THE ROLE OF THE SUPERVISOR
WITHIN ORGANISATIONS

The organisational context of the therapeutic work can be where confusion exists amongst other professionals such as doctors, teachers and business people, when they seek to understand the nature of counselling supervision, especially when supervision is being 'marketed' (Proctor 1997a). Creating a succinct definition of counselling supervision within an organisational context is a difficult task. It needs to include a description of the supervision process and also give attention to the influence of the dynamics of the wider context upon the counselling work. So the following definition attempts to satisfy that criteria:

> A working partnership/alliance in which a skilled and experienced counsellor regularly facilitates the other's growth in professional and ethical counselling competence. This takes place through contracting and working creatively with the client/counsellor/line manager dynamic, which is embedded within the organisational culture.

Such a definition will help counsellors to convince their line managers (if they are not counsellors) that supervision is a mandatory requirement for continuing ethical practice and therefore needs to be given priority each month. Counsellors have no choice, if they are a member of BACP, as to whether they engage in this process or not. It is not a luxury but a necessity, for life. However, the very word supervision suggests that the counsellor's work needs to be monitored, that even when qualified, they cannot be trusted to practise ethically without a more experienced person overseeing their work. It might seem that there is a surveillance culture within the profession and this will be discussed more fully in Chapter 3; nevertheless, mandatory, life-long supervision for all counsellors who are members of BACP is a fact of life.

Clear definitions help those people outside the counselling profession to understand the supervision process. They enable understanding to be established when the dictionary definition of the word is different to the profession's understanding of the role of the supervisor. This is essential when counselling and supervision is embedded within host organisations or when the trustees of counselling agencies are not counsellors themselves and therefore need to understand what they are paying for within their financial constraints.

From the discussion above it is clear that there is a difficulty around the definition of the word supervisor when it is used within a counselling context within organisations. So perhaps there is a need to use another word to describe the process?

IS SUPERVISION THE RIGHT WORD?

As discussed in the previous section, there is some agreement within the counselling profession that supervision is not the correct word to describe the process by which a counsellor or psychotherapist gets support and professional guidance (Proctor 1997b, Williams 1992, Zinkin 1995, Edwards 1997) and therefore some preference is given to the title 'consultative support'.

Increasingly there appears to be a move to use words such as consultative support, non-managerial supervision, facilitation, mentoring or coaching to describe the supervision process (Proctor 1997a, Edwards 1997, Carroll 2003). Such descriptions may be more easily understood in an organisational context but each one singly may not encapsulate any more than the word supervisor, the essence of the tasks that supervisors perform.

In any role, the title of the person performing that role carries with it not only the status, but also a basic understanding of what the person does within that role. As discussed earlier, the difficulty with the word supervisor is the hierarchical understanding of the word in organisational contexts. Yet in counselling and psychotherapy the supervisor is responsible for helping the counsellor to maintain competent standards of client work. How far they can take that responsibility depends on the practitioner themselves and their contract with the employing organisation. The organisation can decide to call the supervision process consultative support and therefore the supervisor and their supervisee have a dilemma; do they still refer informally to that process as supervision? Similarly, do the supervisors prefer to think of themselves as consultants? The answer lies with the supervisor themselves and their own view of their status within the organisation. The title consultant will give them more authority in an organisation that values 'expert' power. Additionally, the title consultant will help them to be more accepted within an organisational culture that views any outsider with suspicion and counsellors and their supervisor with even more scepticism than usual. Therefore, the supervisor can be proactive and give themselves a title that they know will be readily understood and respected within the organisational context of their work.

Counsellors, and by default, supervisors, are often seen as self-effacing individuals who do not pursue power for themselves but seek to empower their clients and supervisees instead. Yet this position is almost impossible to maintain if they are to survive in organisations where a source of power is equated with availability of resources. Even organisations whose sole purpose is to deliver counselling services to the public, will be managed by trustees who have to ensure that the organisation remains economically viable. So if supervisors are to be effective in gaining resources for themselves and their supervisees, they will need to consider their title carefully. The resources may be as simple as being paid for the supervision each month. Alternatively, it may be helping their supervisee to be paid an economic rate for the work that they do. Being paid just over the basic minimum rate of hourly pay for counselling sessions belittles the work and undermines the counsellor's confidence in their role within the organisation. Therefore, for the supervisor to have any influence in a situation such as this, their title is important and will differ according to the nature of the employing organisation. For example, in a health service setting the title clinical supervisor would fit with the medical model prevalent in that type of organisation. Similarly, in a workplace setting a title which is an amalgamation of consultant, mentor or coach would fit with ease. In a voluntary counselling agency the title counselling supervisor would be appropriate for the work where there was an understanding of the counselling and supervision process that might also involve supervising trainee counsellors. However, there is a problem with a supervisor using a different title for each organisational context in which they work. They will need to be sure that the process they are engaged in with all supervisees, regardless of the organisational context, is consistent and could be described by the profession as counselling supervision. Even within counselling supervision there can be different types of supervision offered to both trainees and counsellors.

DIFFERENT TYPES OF SUPERVISION

Hawkins and Shohet (2000:53) outline four types of supervision as:

- **Tutorial Supervision**: In some settings the supervisor may have more of a tutor role, concentrating almost entirely on the educative function, helping a trainee on a course to explore his or her work with clients.
- **Training Supervision**: Here the supervision also emphasised the educative function and the supervisees will be in some form of trainee or apprenticeship role ... The difference from tutorial supervision is that here the supervisor will have some responsibility for the work being done with the clients and therefore carry a clear managerial or normative role.
- **Managerial Supervision**: This term is used where the supervisor is also the line manager of the supervisees. As in training supervision the supervisor has some clear responsibility for the work being done with the clients, but supervisor and supervisee will be in a manager–subordinate relationship. Rather than a trainer–trainee relationship.
- **Consultancy Supervision**: Here the supervisees keep the responsibility for the work they do with their clients, but consult with their supervisor, who is neither their trainer nor their manager, on those issues they wish to explore. This form of supervision is for experienced and qualified practitioners.

It is clear from these descriptions that the type of supervision on offer to a supervisee will influence their perspective of what the process means to them. Elsewhere in this book I advocate that it is not good practice to combine the role of managerial and casework supervision (Chapter 7) yet Valentine (2004) maintains that to split both managerial and professional (case-work) supervision would be counter-productive within an organisational context. Whilst acknowledging the position of BACP on this point, Valentine upholds the view that:

> the management supervisor has a responsibility to ensure that the organisation's duty of care to its clients is carried out, and that they therefore have a specific responsibility to ensure that employees are enabled to fulfil this responsibility. This gives them a right and a responsibility to observe or review the practice of their team members.
>
> (Valentine 2004:119)

She goes on to stress that to add a secondary mandatory level of supervision creates another financial burden on the organisation. Nevertheless, research has shown (Copeland 2000a) that for line managers who are also supervisors within the same organisation, this dual relationship is constrictive.

CONCLUSION

New thinking is needed around defining the role of supervisor within an organisational context. Whilst a definition that is confined to the counselling profession will suit some supervisors who do not want to work organisationally, there is a need to widen the horizons of the work. The supervisor who is prepared to work with a wider definition of their role both with their individual supervisee and also with the supervisee's organisation will benefit all parties in the working alliance. The exploration of the role of mentor, coach and consultant has identified both similarities and differences with the role of counsellor and supervisor within an organisation. However, each supervisory dyad will need to decide what role their work will play within the organisation. If the supervisee becomes more aware of the impact of organisational culture on their client work, they will be useful, in a much wider sense, to the organisation. Similarly, if the supervisor is employed by the organisation on a formal basis they will eventually be in a position to offer their knowledge and skills to the organisation itself. However, this will need to be a gradual process as their profile within the organisation increases. Before that can happen there will need to be an understanding of the multi-faceted role of the supervisor by managers within the organisation.

Chapter 2

Supervising in organisations: a multi-faceted role

> Working within organisations can feel like a struggling octopus where each of the eight arms grapples with a different problem.
>
> (Coles 2003:95–96)

INTRODUCTION

In Chapter 1 the role of the supervisor was explored. Links were made between supervision and the roles of mentor, coach and consultant and it was argued that supervisors are an under-used resource within organisations. In a changing labour market they have knowledge and skills which organisations need. Yet they remain hidden, an untapped source of wisdom that is not utilised sufficiently within organisational structures that are rapidly changing in the twenty-first century. However, in this book I am advocating that a gradual approach to supervisory involvement is taken so that organisations become clear about the supervisory role. There is a need for a formal employment process to take place so that an understanding emerges of how the supervisor's knowledge and skills can benefit the wider organisation in the future.

Organisations are becoming less hierarchical, with structures that are flatter and more fluid. As the lines of authority become less clear, much more falls to the individual employee to negotiate, influence and persuade. Clearly, this work requires empathy, intuition and persuasion. In an individualistic society, the consumer wants to be recognised, and for the service to be personalised. This is especially evident in organisations like call centres where there is a need to be emotionally available to customers on the end of the phone every minute of the day. This is a relationship economy where the defining characteristic is ambiguity that requires immense skill to navigate. Employees and their managers need a level of interpersonal and listening skills to help them work with this ambiguity in order to avoid the stress that it inevitably generates.

In this chapter the nature of stress in all types of employment, whether paid or voluntary, will be explored in order to understand, firstly the role of the counsellor within an organisation and secondly to outline the importance of supervisors within organisations and their need for formal employment status. Finally, a model of supervision in organisations will be outlined before a full exploration of each aspect of the model is discussed in Parts II and III of the book.

STRESS AT WORK

Stress has become an inescapable part of working life and a culture of overwork exacerbates the problem. Bunting (2004:177), in her exploration of the overwork culture, argues that:

> Human beings have finite resources, physical and emotional and the overwork culture eats into them. For many, the result is illness: either debilitating mental conditions such as work related stress and depression, or life-threatening conditions such as heart disease. The health of the overworked employee is hit twice – first by working too hard, and second by not having the time to develop relationships, take exercise and pursue outside interests, all of which strengthen resilience to pressure. The cost to an increasing number of individuals is evident in the explosion in the number of days at work lost to stress, not to mention all those workers below the statistical radar, who resort to anti-depressants to keep going and whose lives are a frantic effort to cope.

In this type of culture there is the need for employees to be able to recharge their emotional batteries either within the work environment or outside with family and friends. Additionally, the emotional demands of work have increased dramatically over the last few decades. Counsellors and supervisors are not the only employees in organisations who are engaged in emotional labour; teachers, nurses, social workers, call centres employees and even the receptionist at the gym are engaged in emotional labour.

As I walked into the gym the receptionist was being harangued by a customer who was threatening to report her to the manager for incompetence and mismanagement of many aspects of the facilities within the centre. The customer was raging and threatening, both verbally and non-verbally. The receptionist was cool, calm and listening carefully, her face did not show her internal feelings. When leaving the gym I spoke to the receptionist and commented on her skilful handling of the situation I had witnessed earlier. She remarked that it was all in a day's work but her eyes filled with tears. I was struck by the emotional demands this exchange had made on the young

receptionist who was expected to subjugate her own emotions whilst the
customer was allowed to vent her own emotions freely.

In the scenario above, I was a customer, not a counsellor or supervisor, yet I
was aware of the skills needed by the receptionist to deal with the situation in
order to ensure that the customer went away happy. In this situation she had
no rights, only a responsibility to the customer on behalf of her employing
organisation. Nevertheless, the situation had been stressful and no doubt she
would be reliving it for the rest of the day, perhaps even recounting it to her
partner at home that night. Therefore, the emotional costs of the encounter
for this employee were high. Yet many other jobs are far more emotionally
stressful and have always been so. The medical profession, teaching, the
emergency services, to name but a few professions, have always been subject
to high emotional demands on their workers. But when employees leave and
are not replaced, the burden becomes even higher. There is little time for
empathic responses as the practical demands of the role increase. As a result
stress levels rise and line managers fear the worst, they are pushed from
above and below. Their managers want increased productivity and their
employees want to work in a less stressful environment; an environment
where they have time to sit and talk to their patients or work with smaller
student groups, giving individual attention when emotional blocks to learning are evident. In a service economy, employees want to be able to make a
difference to people's lives. This includes counsellors too, yet often they are
the employee who is brought in to reduce the stress levels within the
organisation.

COUNSELLORS IN ORGANISATIONS

Organisations increasingly recognise that all employees need emotional support for the work that they do. Sometimes that recognition is driven by the
fear of litigation, especially if the work is stressful, at other times it is driven
by a genuine concern for the welfare of their employees. Therefore, a counselling service is instigated either by employing a counsellor directly or by
engaging an Employee Assistance Programme (EAP) to provide a range of
services, from debt advice to stress management courses, but which also
includes the services of a counsellor. So counsellors become part of the emotional labour force. They have particular skills in enabling employees to
become more emotionally intelligent and the cornerstones of emotional intelligence are self-awareness and empathy. Consequently, emotional intelligence
can be defined as an array of non-cognitive skills, capabilities and competencies that influence a person's ability to cope with environmental demands
and pressures. Emotional intelligence underpins many of the best decisions,
most dynamic organisations and the most satisfying and successful lives

(Johnson and Indvik 1999). The requirements to raising emotional intelligence include:

- A desire to change;
- Self reflection (if a person does not know what is going on inside him/herself, it is unlikely he/she knows what is going on inside of others);
- Listen to the internal script that plays continuously;
- Develop emotional control;
- Practice empathy and practice active listening skills; and
- Validate the emotions of others.

(McGarvey 1997, cited in Johnson and Indvik 1999:85)

This list of requirements to change will be familiar to counsellors and within organisations their clients will have been developing the first three or four points in the list. The last two points on the list will be modelled by the counsellor as they engage with others within the organisation because emotional intelligence is often learnt by example as well as by experience.

Therefore, counsellors bring the particular skills of their profession that are useful in helping the organisation to become more emotionally intelligent. However, to fully utilise these skills it is important that counsellors integrate and become accepted as an equal member of the working community. Integration is vital. Without it counsellors will provide an individual service that does not give added value to the organisation. Nevertheless, integration into multi-disciplinary teams can be hard won for counsellors, when cultures clash. Organisations that rely on IQ rather than EQ will find that the counsellor cannot add value to their organisation because EQ is not regarded as a valuable commodity. But organisations that recognise the value of both types of intelligence will succeed.

In the early nineties I was a trained counsellor also working part-time in the capacity of an outdoor management development trainer with a large multi-national IT company. My task was to lead my team of managers in orienteering and outdoor tasks designed to develop the participants' skills in teamwork. In their organisation they were a team of highly intelligent employees who worked individually, solving complex IT problems. They did not integrate with one another during the working week. However, as the course progressed they had to learn how to interact effectively in order to fulfil their aim of becoming the winning team of the week's course.

Competition was a driving force, yet they could not jettison the team members who could not perform effectively in the wild as all team members needed to arrive at the final destination each day intact. Therefore, they soon realised that they needed to use skills of persuasion, empathy and active listening in order to enable all members of the team to perform each task successfully. When one of the team stormed off (I was to learn later that he was the line manager, having stipulated that I did not want to know which person in the team held this role), they all pooled their collective persuasive skills to get him back on track. At that time the term emotional intelligence was not in vogue, nevertheless, my team members were learning how to access their emotions and to engage with one another on an affective rather than purely cognitive level. This led to their success; they were the winning team on the course. But before celebrating with the well-deserved glass of champagne they asked to have individual feedback about their emotional development during the course. We sat in the sunshine, cross-legged in a circle on the lawn. I gave them all feedback on their strengths and areas for development in maintaining their emotional engagement with one another in future work. I felt emotional during this process and showed it. My counselling work enabled me to be comfortable in this role and to model emotional intelligence at work. I was confident that this team would be more productive in future weeks and months and hoped that they would be able to use the organisation's counsellor for their further emotional development both individually and as a team.

Over a decade ago, as a counsellor and a trainer, I knew that developing self-awareness would enable employees to become more confident in their role at work. This is a task that counsellors now need to embrace with enthusiasm. Coming out of the counselling room and working organisationally rather than individually is vital if they are to be an added resource for the organisation.

SUPERVISORS IN ORGANISATIONS

Similarly, counselling supervisors can add value to an organisation if they are prepared to use their knowledge, skills and authority for the benefit of individual counsellors and also the organisation. For supervisors to use their authority there is a need for them to be aware of the types of authority available to them. Hughes and Pengelly (1997) outline three types of authority that mirror the types of power available to individuals working within an organisational context. First, role authority is an authority delegated to a position within an organisation so that the person in that position can do the work and meet the responsibilities of that position. A supervisor needs to have this formal position within the organisation in order to have role authority. Second, professional authority is based on competence within the role and can be gained through training. However, it is only manifested and recognised by being practised. Within an organisational context, the supervisee will recognise their supervisor's professional authority but their line manager may not. The manager is often unfamiliar with the competencies of a different profession to their own, especially if counselling and supervision is embedded within a 'host' organisation. Third, personal authority is the way a supervisor establishes their natural authority within their supervisory role and communicates it to others. Therefore, all three types of authority are available to supervisors when they are formally employed within the organisation. How a supervisor exerts their authority, both individually and organisationally, will depend both on their personal style of working and its impact on the culture of the organisation.

Organisational cultures can be restrictive or enabling, a force for stagnation or growth. Supervisors are increasingly employed to work in organisational cultures and to be cognisant of their impact on the supervisory process. Additionally, they need to be aware of the impact of the culture on employees in general and line managers in particular. Along with their supervisee they will have information about how each department functions and the impact of the culture upon the employee's psychological health. This is information that organisations need to help them to grow and to develop a workforce that is both productive and emotionally secure. Counsellors and supervisors who have a high profile within the organisation can help to shape the culture. This is essential if they are to be an integral part of that culture. The scenario below illustrates this point.

A counsellor I talked to recently was engaged in a multi-faceted role that added value within a boarding school setting. She was engaged, not only in counselling on a one-to-one basis, but also as an academic tutor and targeted teaching tutor. She was also actively involved with the induction programme and with advising other tutors concerning student welfare. Additionally she was consulted on all pastoral matters within the school. Similarly, this counsellor was a member of a school committee that determined the developing culture of the organisation. Therefore, she was a valued member of an enlightened organisation that recognised the importance of her skills outside the counselling room. She was adding value, not only to individual pupils but also helping to shape the culture within the organisation. In doing so she was working actively in a preventative role, a role that enabled colleagues to understand the influence that organisational culture has on the well-being of the pupils. Additionally, she was modelling the skills and attitudes in all of the roles occupied within the school, promoting respect for others and a willingness to work with all the emotional aspects of institutional life. Her supervisor was assisting her to hold the boundaries between the roles and encouraging her to be actively engaged in committee work that shaped the culture for the future. The supervisor was not afraid to be actively engaged in this role because his formal employment by the organisation safeguarded his rights whilst also giving him responsibilities within that role.

Forward thinking organisations will be able to embrace the ethos of the counselling profession and use counsellors and supervisors to help shape a culture that enables all those within it to flourish. When the professional culture of counselling and supervision clashes with the organisational culture dilemmas can occur which will need to be managed. A full discussion of this issue can be found in Part II. If a counsellor and their supervisor are encouraged to step out of the counselling room and be equal members of the community of employees, they will develop too. They will learn how to negotiate and not be afraid of the power of their emotional intelligence in organisations where emotions remain unacknowledged, buried in the debris of paperwork and deadlines.

In public and commercial sectors formal employment of supervisors is already occurring and systems are in place for auditing the quality of their work. Therefore, there is a need for formal systems of employment (discussed in Chapters 5 and 6) to become more extensive, leading to a management of the supervisory work (discussed in Chapters 7 and 8) that includes reporting back to the organisation (discussed in Chapter 9) and assessing the work that is undertaken (discussed in Chapter 10). Additionally, there is a need for formal termination of contracts of employment and new beginning for supervisors in organisations (discussed in Chapter 11). This process is ongoing in some organisations, but all organisations need to embrace this process with their counselling supervisors so that they become a valuable resource within the organisation. In this way the supervisor can exert all aspects of their legitimate authority in adding value to the organisation.

Formality in the appointment of a supervisor within an organisation is essential even for just one and a half hours a month. The process of securing this position will dictate the tenor of the work that follows. This means that the process needs to be significant for all parties in the working alliance: the supervisor, supervisee and their line manager. In many instances, however, when a supervisor is chosen, often only two out of the three parties in this working alliance are involved in the selection process. This can be either the supervisee and the supervisor or the supervisor and the supervisee's line manager. The best option is for all three parties to be involved, whether the process is formal or informal. A formal process of employment will fit organisations that are more corporate in nature and have stringent internal and external quality audit procedures. Less formal processes will suit organisations where collaboration and co-operative working are the norm. Whichever process is chosen for employing a supervisor, it needs to be fair and a detailed job description and person specification should be readily available for the prospective supervisor. When this happens, the possibilities for misunderstanding of the supervisory role in the future are decreased. When the post of supervisor is being advertised or offered within an organisation, the responsibilities required can be tailored to the needs of the organisation. If an organisation needs the supervisor to fulfil a wider role than one-to-one supervision of counselling work, they can specify that in the job description.

For some supervisors, extending their role within the organisation to act as a mentor, consultant or coach, might be an attractive addition to one-to-one supervision. However, the supervisor's additional responsibilities may feel threatening to the supervisee especially if the supervisor is new to them and the organisation. It would be useful for an organisation that wants to make extended use of a supervisor in this way, to delay the additional work until the supervisor has developed a relationship with the supervisee first. Such duties will need to be written into the formal contract of employment forged between the supervisor and the organisation. Formal contracts are becoming more prevalent for supervisors working in organisations but it does mean that supervisors, working with many counsellors all working in different organisations, will have to contend with a plethora of contracts that could all be very different. So there is a need for a basic standard contract to be produced that can be adapted to suit individual organisations. Similarly, supervisors need to produce their own contract so that organisations know what their responsibilities are towards the supervisor. Both these contracts will form the basis of the relationships that need to be created between supervisor, supervisee and their line manager.

When a supervisor has received a contract of employment, they will be part of a supervisory rhombus that includes themselves as the supervisor, the supervisee and their line manager. Relationships within this rhombus can be complicated and will need to be fostered, along with good communication systems. For supervisees and supervisors, making such relationships with the supervisee's line manager may seem dangerous for the supervisor, with the potential for the breaking of the client's, and possibly the supervisee's, confidentiality. Nevertheless, these relationships are extremely important both to the counselling and supervisory process and also to the organisation. Counselling and supervision does not take place in a vacuum and relationships are even more complicated when the counsellor or supervisor have a dual role within the organisation. So clear systems for communication between all parties need to be developed to foster good relationships.

First of all, there needs to be commitment from all parties concerning the importance of the relationships and the part that they play in enhancing client work and organisational change. The systems by which ethical boundaries are kept need to be clear, including any reporting back procedures that are required by the organisation. Nevertheless, some supervisors will be reluctant to engage in making any relationship outside the supervisory dyad. They will be fearful that client confidentiality will be broken and they will also resent the extra time needed to undertake tripartite meetings with their supervisee and their line manager. However, this working relationship is essential if the client work is to be held safely and the organisation is to benefit from the supervisor's understanding of the impact of the organisational culture on employees.

When the supervision process encompasses the organisational context, the roles, functions and skills needed by the supervisor will expand. The formative function of supervision is concerned with the supervisee's skills, knowledge and understanding of their role as a counsellor. Therefore, within this function, it is important that the supervisor works with the supervisee to enhance their knowledge concerning the influence of the organisational context on the client work. The normative function of the supervisory work is concerned with quality control in the supervisory work. As such, the supervisor and supervisee have a responsibility to evaluate their work together and feed back any relevant information that will be useful to the organisation. Once again, this links directly with a reporting process that maintains ethical standards whilst being of use to a change process within the organisation. Finally, the supportive function within supervision helps the supervisee to alleviate the potential for burn out when working with very distressed clients. It also supports the supervisee when working within an organisational culture that can be disabling. Therefore, the functions, encompassing the organisational context of the supervisory work, are clear and the tasks of supervision are the behavioural side of those functions.

For many writers, the tasks of supervision do not include the organisational context of the work. Yet Carroll (1999) is clear that the context of the work will influence the tasks in that they will encompass the influence of the organisation on the supervisory work. This will mean that contracts need to be three cornered and the extent of the boundaries of confidentiality stated including why and how information is released into the organisation. Similarly, another task for the supervisor is to help their supervisee to manage the counselling provision if that is part of their role within the organisation. Additionally, the process of helping the supervisee to care for themselves, within an organisational culture that is demanding, is a challenge for the supervisor. Finally, the task of enabling the supervisee to understand the culture and consequent parallel processes within an organisation can be daunting for the supervisor, especially if they are employed in-house and therefore subject to the same cultural influences. Engagement in the expanded functions and tasks of supervision within an organisational context will need the supervisor to have an enhanced level of skill to manage the process effectively. They will need to be able to negotiate, assert themselves, mediate, manage group dynamics and act as mentor and coach where necessary. Supervisors may already have these skills or need to acquire them in order to fulfil their expanding role as a supervisor within the organisation. They will also need to be disposed to working in this expanded role within the organisation especially when they are required to report back concerning the supervisory work and its impact on the organisation.

Reporting back to an organisation on the supervisory work is part of the accountability process that supervisors need to encompass when working in an organisational context. Whether the organisation itself requests the report or the supervisor and supervisee decides that they want to report back, it will be a useful tool for the organisation to use in measuring the effectiveness of the counsellor. As a measurement of effectiveness, the purpose of the report will need to be clear for all parties in the working alliance. The purpose will be to provide statistical information about the frequency of supervision sessions and the therapeutic and administrative effectiveness of the counsellor. The report will also provide information about ethical and professional practice together with the supervisee's effective use of supervision. Finally, it will address the constraining influences of organisational culture and the future training needs of the supervisee. When the purpose of the report has been agreed with the organisation, mechanisms need to be developed for carrying out the process. Tripartite meeting would seem to be a good way of working in collaboration, but there will be a need for the supervisory dyad to work together initially to establish the limits of information that can be ethically divulged to the wider organisation. This information can be divulged in written form as a formal or informal report, or it can be delivered in oral form in a tripartite meeting. Whichever way is chosen, the reports need to be regular and fulfil the purposes for which they are required.

For an organisation, the evaluation, assessment and accreditation processes will be the benchmark of excellence for counsellors and supervisors. These processes will be especially important for line managers where the counselling service is embedded in a 'host' organisation, whether commercial, service or educational. They will give the line manager an indication of the standards of work provided by the counsellor and the supervisor. It is especially important for the organisation to be aware that they have employed a supervisor who is competent and will be able to feed back an accurate assessment of the work of the supervisee. Increasingly, line managers want to ensure that the supervisor is trained and accredited with a professional association in order to verify their competence. This is their assurance that they are paying for a quality supervision service, especially if they have no knowledge of counselling or supervision processes. All professional organisations are responsible for the competence of their members. They set benchmarks for all layers of membership and safeguard their ethical practice with complaints procedures that can exclude those members who no longer practise ethically. This ensures that a standard of work is maintained. How else could non-counsellors and supervisors know what to expect of practitioners they employ? If the professional standards are not maintained, the employer has the right to terminate the employment of the counsellor or supervisor.

Supervisors and counsellors are familiar with terminating relationships and making new beginnings. Nevertheless, when an organisation is involved with the process, there is an added complication that needs attention. Terminating a supervision contract can bring sadness or relief for either party in the relationship. If a counsellor is responsible for making their own beginnings and endings in the supervisory relationship, the organisation will leave the responsibility for the management of this process to them, but the organisation will need to be involved with the termination of contract of employment and payments. However, if the organisation is responsible for the direct employment of the supervisor, they will need to fully engage both the supervisor and the supervisee with helping to choose the new supervisor.

This will complete the cycle of employment. When the organisation does not involve the supervisee in this process, there can be resentment when relationships end and new supervisors are appointed without consultation. Consequently, the organisation needs to use the skills, knowledge and experience of its supervisor to add value to the organisation. The out-going supervisor will be aware of the boundary issues within the organisation that are sensitive and the relationships that cause stress for employees. This knowledge can be offered in a culture where the learning process and the development of employees is normal practice.

Figure 2.1 depicts how the model of counselling supervision is embedded firmly within organisational culture and the culture of counselling and supervision. From securing the supervisory position to ending the work and making new beginnings, the supervision work is profoundly influenced by employment procedures, relationships within the supervisory rhombus, the

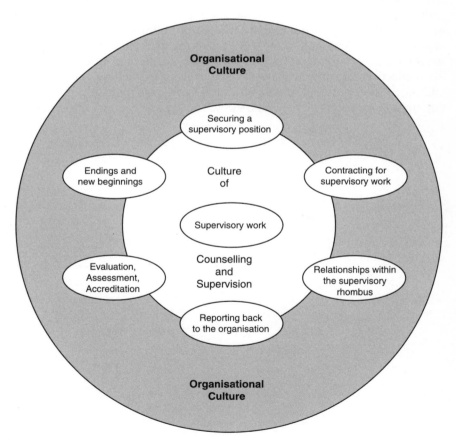

Figure 2.1 A model of counselling supervision in organisations

reporting back procedures and systems of evaluation and assessment. The supervisor who has an integrated position in the organisation will enable their supervisee to work more effectively within the organisation. Additionally they will have a higher personal profile within the organisation and so be in a position to work organisationally when the opportunity arises.

CONCLUSION

When the supervisor is an employee who is embedded fully into the organisation and its employment systems they can help the supervisee to work more effectively within the organisation. For some supervisors working in the caring sector, this will already be the norm. For others, working in diverse organisational settings, any contact with the organisation will be unfamiliar. However, supervisors need to be prepared to embrace employment status within organisations. This will enable them to feel a valued member of the working community with the rights and responsibilities that are engendered in that status. Additionally, they will need to use their emotional intelligence to foster change and development, both individually and organisationally. Their effectiveness will be enhanced when their understanding of counselling and supervision culture dovetails with their knowledge of organisational culture to produce a cultural fit. This issue will be discussed more fully in Part II.

Part II

Supervision in organisations

Managing the cultural fit

Chapter 3

Counselling, supervision and organisational cultures: what are the dilemmas?

For supervision to work well within an organisation its culture needs to be favourable. If the culture is unhealthy it is likely that the supervision will be affected accordingly.

Van Ooijen (2003:221)

INTRODUCTION

In Part I of this book the multi-faceted role of the supervisor was explored in relation to the organisation and its employees. All professionals need to be cognisant of their own professional culture and its fit within the organisation. The counselling profession, like any other profession, has its own language and norms of behaviour that are often only recognised by those who operate within that profession. When a newly qualified counsellor joins the ranks of similar workers within the profession, they will be aware of codes of ethics and norms of behaviour to which they need to adhere. Similarly, organisations have their own overt and covert patterns of behaviour, rules and regulations and communication systems. So when an employee joins an organisation they will rapidly learn what they can and cannot do within the confines of that organisation, whatever their professional role within it. Consequently, different organisations and different professions have their own cultural norms that produce dilemmas when there is a conflict between the two.

Counselling and supervision are processes with the emphasis on individual rather than corporate responsibility. So with such a fundamental difference it is not surprising that dilemmas arise within different organisational contexts, as seen in Table 3.1. Dryden (1985:2) describes a dilemma as a position of doubt or perplexity, a choice between two (or amongst several) alternatives, all of which have some unfavourable elements, and he saw dilemmas for counsellors as falling into a number of categories.

- Compromise dilemmas are those in which the counsellor holds the tension between the ideal and the pragmatic solution.

Table 3.1 Differences between counselling culture and organisational culture

Counselling culture	Organisational culture
Focus on individual	Focus on collective
Change individual behaviour	Change organisation
Physical power (bullying) not used	Bullying may be used
Resource power not available?	Resource power available
Position power (not usually?)	Position power available
Expert power in counselling	Expert power available
Personal power available	Personal power available
Humane, liberal	Ruthless management
Individual can change their life	Corporate change

- Boundary dilemmas involve choice, the choice of whether or not to cross a variety of boundaries that contain the therapeutic work.
- Dilemmas of allegiance involve decisions about allegiance to the profession or to the counsellor's own ideological frame of reference.
- Role dilemmas concern issues that may arise when a counsellor encounters role conflict.
- Dilemmas involving responsibility can occur when counsellors struggle to make decisions as to what degree they take responsibility for a client's welfare.
- Impasse dilemmas involve decisions about how the counsellor should respond when the counselling process becomes stuck.

Such dilemmas could be increased today with the emphasis on those that might be created by the organisational setting of the therapeutic work.

In Western counselling culture there is an emphasis on humane and liberal values and individual change. Each individual has personal power available and their expert power is in the counselling process. In contrast to this, organisational culture has a focus on the collective rather than the individual and regimes are often ruthless and bullying with the withholding of resources used to control individual employees, including counsellors. However, such differences are global and do not address the smaller cultural differences that exist in each individual organisation. To identify these smaller cultural differences, counsellors and their supervisor will need to look and listen to the overt and covert behavioural, social and linguistic norms within the organisation.

This chapter will define culture and the specific cultures evident in the counselling and supervision processes will be discussed. Additionally, organisational cultures will be outlined and the role of power within them discussed. The fit between counselling/supervision cultures and the myriad of cultures found in organisations will be outlined in order to tease out the dilemmas that arise when organisational cultures and the culture within counselling and supervision clash.

HOW IS CULTURE DEFINED?

In our post-modern world the word culture is familiar and it is associated with different aspects of life. For many people the word culture will be linked with ethnicity, traditions and customs. It will imply a way of life based on the mores of individual societies. Definitions of culture usually associate the concept with groups and the notion of sharing knowledge, values, laws and day-to-day ritual (Morgan 1986). With such a definition, when people from different cultures in society live side by side, there is the potential for conflict emanating from misunderstanding or intolerance of difference. Both misunderstanding and intolerance can contribute, in the final analysis, to global wars. On a smaller scale, within an organisational context, conflicting cultures can lead to dilemmas that need to be managed in a way that enables an organisation to function productively. For a more detailed discussion and definition of culture Hawkins and Shohet (2000:168) have succinctly covered this topic.

For the counsellor and supervisor working within an organisational context, the potential conflict between the organisational culture and the counselling and supervision culture needs to be managed in a way that eliminates cultural warfare and is productive rather than destructive.

DEFINING COUNSELLING CULTURE

Counselling culture has not been widely discussed in current literature. It is clear for those who work in the profession that certain indicators, especially the language used and the norms of behaviour evident, define the culture clearly. Therefore, the following scenario will be familiar.

A troubled person sits talking to an attentive listener. They are in a room alone, sitting on chairs of equal height, facing one another diagonally. There is a clock in the room and the meeting will last for approximately fifty minutes. During that time the troubled person will talk for about seventy per cent of the time, whilst the listener will talk for the remainder of the time. The listener will start and end the session and will be paid for their time either by the talker or by the organisation that employs them to listen. The meetings will be regular, either once or twice a week. They will take place on the same day of the week and at the same time and the telephone will be used to book these appointments. The listener will have contact details for the talker and

will learn a great deal about their life both present and possible past. How-
ever, the talker will know little about the listener's personal life and will not
seek overtly to find out this information.

The scenario presented here will be familiar to all counsellors at least in some of the detail. Even when practitioners subscribe to different theoretical models, the practicalities of the work will be recognised. Those people employed in different professions will not recognise the cultural norms embedded in the behaviours and environmental details outlined above, yet for counsellors it is one of the ways of defining their professional culture.

Another way that counsellors can define their professional culture is through adherence to the fundamental values of counselling and psychotherapy outlined in the BACP Ethical Framework for Good Practice (BACP 2002:2). These include a commitment to:

* respecting human rights and dignity
* ensuring the integrity of practitioner–client relationships
* enhancing the quality of professional knowledge and its application
* alleviating personal distress and suffering
* fostering a sense of self that is meaningful to the person(s) concerned
* increasing personal effectiveness
* enhancing the quality of relationships between people
* appreciating the variety of human experience and culture
* striving for the fair and adequate provision of counselling and psychotherapy services.

These values are enshrined in the work of all counsellors, supervisors and counselling trainers. They provide the bedrock of good practice and are a way of expressing the practitioner's ethical commitment. Whilst other workers might subscribe to some of the values outlined above, others are more specific to the world of psychotherapy. The commitment to alleviating personal distress and suffering and to increasing personal effectiveness are more likely to be found in the culture of counselling and psychotherapy. Within this culture the quality of the relationship between all parties in the working alliance is of paramount importance as is equality of opportunity. Additionally, the BACP values emphasise the importance of the individual and the fostering of their sense of self as a way of enhancing their life experience. Therefore, when a counselling and psychotherapy culture is viewed through these professional values, the importance of the individual and their development is clear.

Similarly, McLeod (1999), when defining counselling culture, views counselling as a social process. He sees it as designed to enhance a person's satisfaction with life, but increasingly the role of the counsellor is to act as a bridge back into participation in the social world. However, this may mean that counselling becomes a vehicle for leaving one social world or identity and entering another. For example, a person, by engaging in the counselling process, may choose to leave one career and enter another one that is more satisfying. So from the

Table 3.2 Counselling culture

The individual in counselling

- The primary focus is individual
- The individual has primary responsibility for themselves
- Individual independence and autonomy are highly valued (however this concept is biased towards Western European culture)
- Individual problems are intra-psychic and rooted in childhood and family

Action orientation

- Clients can master and control their own life and environment
- The client needs to take action to resolve their own problems
- There is a bias against passivity or inaction

Status and power

- Credentials for the counsellor are essential
- Counselling can be expensive

Processes (communication)

- Communication is verbal and talk orientated
- There is self disclosure by the client
- Direct eye contact is essential
- Reflective listening is used

Goals of counselling

- The goals of counselling are to increase self awareness and personal growth
- Improved social and personal efficiency is an outcome of counselling
- Individual behaviour is changed
- It increases a person's ability to cope
- A person is more adapted to society's values

Protestant work ethic

- Counselling works if the client works hard at the process

Goal orientation and progress

- Goals are set in counselling

Emphasis on scientific method

- The counsellor is objective and neutral
- Thought patterns are rational and logical
- Importance is placed on the expression of feelings

Time

- Appointments are scheduled and strict time is kept

Source: Adapted from Katz (1985:620).

concept of counselling as a social process, it is clear that the use of counselling within an organisational context will enable the client to live and work more effectively within that organisational culture. Therefore, a counselling culture allows people the freedom to speak about and work with their emotions rather than having them under tight control. There is no stigma attached to engaging in this process within the counselling room, it is a safe haven from the external cultures that people inhabit. Its exclusivity is freeing and normalises thoughts, feelings and behaviours that are not allowed elsewhere (McLeod 2000). The boundaries set within such a culture enable healing to take place. As McLeod (2000:2) says, 'counselling is a place where people can go when they have been silenced within the culture they inhabit.'

Subsequently people can re-enter more alien cultures, especially within an organisational context, with some degree of confidence. Therefore, whilst the counselling process is individually orientated towards change, the resulting personal confidence will have beneficial effects on a person's relationships both socially and within a work environment.

A counselling culture can be identified by the values and beliefs outlined in Table 3.2. These behaviours can vary a little depending on the theoretical orientation of the practitioner. However, in the main, they generally apply to most counselling situations. Whilst Katz was writing about the socio-political nature of counselling and the counselling profession needing to be more responsive to the needs of multi-cultural populations, two decades later many of her categories still apply to the culture of counselling.

A counselling culture can be identified by many different ways of being with an individual. They all add up to defining the culture as *how things are done around here*. This is how culture can be identified, by social interactions, norms of behaviour, use of language and environmental factors. Yet the over-arching factor in counselling is that it sees the individual as important and to some extent this factor can also be seen in the culture of supervision.

DEFINING SUPERVISION CULTURE

Two experienced professionals meet for an hour and a half in a room every month. It might be for even longer – and there is an elaborate formula to work out how long they must meet for. One talks in detail about his or her work. Both parties know that without such a meeting they can be struck off their professional register. The one who speaks about their work may feel intimidated by the other, may talk about their work in a very careful and selective way, and may hide some aspects of their work fearing a negative reaction. If she is British she or he knows that such meetings have to continue on a regular basis for as long as she practises. Some professional bodies recommend a new supervisory partnership every three to five years, some do not. Some such meeting can occur regularly between the two parties for more than 20 years even, in some cases, ended only by the death of one party.

(West 2003:123)

Anyone reading this scenario could be forgiven for wondering which profession these two people were from and under which cultural norms they operated. Yet those professionals working as counsellors and psychotherapists would instantly recognise the above description as the supervision process. West (2003) suggests that supervision has been seen as the way the cultural norms, particular to the profession, are perpetuated. Any definition of supervision culture, therefore, will be inextricably linked with the definition of counselling culture.

Life-long supervision is mandatory for any counsellor who is a member of BACP. This is a cultural norm within this professional organisation. This mandate can present a problem for some counsellors and is seen as absolutely necessary for others. Over the years there have been frequent debates (Feltham 2002, Proctor 2002) on this subject and to date there is no consensus of opinion for either side of the debate. However, what does not seem to be disputed is that supervision is essential for trainee counsellors. It is the life-long mandate that splits the counselling community. Research shows (Lawton 2000, Kaberry 2000, Webb 2000, Landany et al. 1999) that not all supervision is satisfactory or indeed ethical. Research (Tune 2001, Gubi 2002) also shows that there are many aspects of a counsellor's work that are not addressed in supervision such as spirituality and touch which can lead to a culture of secrecy within the supervisory process. West (2003) questions the kind of supervision culture that is being co-created. In such a climate of fear and mistrust there may be a sense of being watched and judged, indeed Feltham (2002) suggests a surveillance culture exists around supervision in the UK. Yet not all supervisors feel that life-long supervision is unnecessary and 'nannying'. Research (Copeland 2000a) also suggests that counsellors find it valuable and necessary for professional and ethical competence. Supervision is also seen as being supportive yet challenging, a place to think about clients and hone professional practice. It is essential to explore the variables that change the culture of a necessary and useful process into a bureaucratic surveillance culture.

Supervision as a bureaucratic surveillance culture

Supervision is viewed by a number of professionals as a bureaucratic surveillance culture when it is associated with the life-long mandate required by BACP. This mandate, coupled with the perceived impossibility of supervising clients who may never be presented in supervision, conspires to maintain the notion of a culture of surveillance. Additionally, an unequal power dynamic in the relationship can be disabling for the supervisee, especially if it is combined with the use of supervision as a sanction through the BACP complaints procedure. So a surveillance culture is perpetuated. However, in terms of supervision culture, surveillance is only half of the picture. The other half is the depiction of supervision as a culture of life-long learning that enables a supervisee to refine and develop their practice over many years of engaging in the supervision process. Although the culture of supervision is inextricably bound up with the culture of counselling, the opposing concepts of surveillance or life-long learning add a new dimension to our understanding of supervision culture.

Supervision as a life-long learning process

Supervision can be seen as a life-long learning process. It was noted earlier that the BACP requirement for life-long supervision has been hotly debated. In contrast UKCP, as Wheeler (2000) acknowledges, expects psychotherapists to engage in continued professional development which implies more trust than the BACP requirement which infantilises its members with global supervision requirements. Perhaps there is a need for change, especially when counsellors, working within organisational settings, are viewed by their non-counselling colleagues as having special treatment because of the nature of their work. They are required to have a special relationship with another colleague which gives them time and space to reflect on their work. This may seem a real luxury to other employees who do not have the same opportunity.

Similarly, a counsellor's line manager can also resent the time and money spent on supervision, without actually understanding its purposes, process or outcomes. As discussed in Chapter 1, the title mentor, coach or consultant is familiar to those working in organisations. Therefore, a change of name could facilitate a greater understanding of supervision within an organisational context. This still does not address the issue of the life-long need for the process, but it could help the organisation to view the counselling profession in a more positive way when compared with other professions represented within the organisational structure. The life-long mandate for counsellors to engage in supervision of their work is part of the culture of supervision and yet a norm that is often misunderstood by other professionals and so does not easily transport itself into organisational contexts. There is the need for counsellors and supervisors to communicate with all levels of the organisation to ensure that there is a clear understanding of what supervision is and what it can offer organisationally. If the supervision process could offer the organisation added value there may be increasing acceptance of the process. As long as supervision continues to be narrowly focused on client work, the notion of the organisation gaining added value from supervision will be negated.

Supervision and the missing client

It has been argued that supervision is an impossible profession because a person cannot be viewed out of the context of relating to another person (Zinkin 1995). Even when tape recordings are presented in supervision a supervisor cannot put themselves in the supervisee's shoes. If the supervisor has no direct experience of the client they will be trapped within the supervisee's reality of the client (Mearns 1995). However, this argument does not call for the end to supervision, especially in training, as there is a great deal to learn in the process, from teaching technique to learning how to manage the administrative processes. There is also an opportunity to support and challenge the trainee and act as a model for good practice. Nevertheless, as Mearns (1995:427) strongly asserts at the end of his paper, 'let us not presume that supervision tells us anything about the missing client.' Yet it is the surveillance culture that assumes supervision will reveal a great deal about the way a counsellor works with their clients. This will only happen if audio-tapes are regularly used during the supervision process.

Primarily supervision is about the protection of the client. If an organisation is not paying for that function, they could provide continuing professional development for their counsellors in a different and possibly more economic way. Alternatively, if the supervision process was more broadly based, incorporating dimensions of the work that would benefit the organisation, the process might fit more easily into an organisational culture.

Supervision and the power dynamic

The power dynamic in the supervisory relationship is different to that in the counselling relationship. As we will see later in this chapter when the power dynamic within organisations is explored, power has the capacity to affect people, things, situations and decisions. Therefore, power can be used within the supervisory process as a tool for policing the work of the counsellor. The power invested by the professional body in the role of the supervisor, as the guardian of ethical standards, can be used or abused within the working relationship. Many definitions of power allude to power over something or someone. So, if supervision is viewed as a surveillance activity, this definition would be accurate as the supervisor has the power to report the supervisee to their professional body if they are perceived to be operating in an unethical manner. However, if the definition of power is seen not to control, but rather to empower individuals to exercise self-control and determination (Holloway 1995), the supervision process would be more collaborative and equal and therefore its culture would change dramatically.

The power dynamic is endemic in all cultures. Yet in both a counselling and supervision culture there is a move to equalise the power balance. However, if supervision is to be effective in monitoring ethical practice in the counselling profession, the power balance cannot be equal because the supervisor has the final control as the guardian of standards for the profession. The BACP Ethical Framework for Good Practice (2002:7) requires supervisors and managers to 'have a responsibility to maintain and enhance good practice by practitioners, to protect clients from poor practice and to acquire the attitude, skills and knowledge required by their role.' As in organisational culture, supervision culture is not a power-free zone, especially when supervision is used as a form of sanction through a complaints procedure.

Supervision as a form of sanction through the BACP complaints procedure

Supervision can be used as a form of sanction through the BACP complaints procedure and as such is a powerful course of action for the professional association. It is just one of four sanction options open to the association when a complaint has been upheld against a member. It requires a counsellor to have supervision from a named supervisor for a stipulated period of time. The supervisor needs to have expertise in the area that requires addressing and to be approved by BACP. The counsellor's regular supervisor could undertake this task but it is also possible that BACP may require another supervisor to do this work who is not involved in the counsellor's usual network of contacts (Carney 2001). There is also a requirement that the supervisor undertaking this role evaluates the counsellor's performance over a specific period of time and reports back to the sanctions panel regarding the counsellor's progress. The report needs to engage with the specific sanctions that have been identified. So when supervision is used as a form of sanction, it could be regarded as a punitive process. Therefore, there is a need for the supervisor to ensure that the process is seen as an educative one and that the power differential is addressed. A supervisor can only know what the supervisee is prepared to divulge and so the relationship needs to be developed over a period of time in order to establish the trust necessary for disclosure of sensitive material.

As we will see in Chapter 8, a good, trusting relationship between supervisor and supervisee, one which emphasises the developmental rather than policing role of supervision, is essential if supervision as a sanction within the profession is to be effective.

When teasing out the norms of supervision practice in order to define the culture embedded within it, there is a need to explore what the counselling profession demands of its supervisors. Does the profession demand surveillance or the collaboration of two or more professionals to enhance the counsellor's development? Is the demand for life-long supervision a way of protecting the client or keeping the counsellor in an infantile state? These questions will continue to be debated but the juxtaposition of these opposing indicators of a cultural norm will continue to baffle other professionals in differing organisational cultures, where counselling and supervision live with them, side by side.

DEFINING ORGANISATIONAL CULTURE

Before we begin to explore organisational culture it is necessary to define the term organisation. *The Concise Oxford Dictionary* says: 'organisation: suitable arrangements for effective work; system; structure.' So an organisation is seen as a way of organising people to work effectively, possibly using a systems approach. Morgan (1986:13) says that organisations are complex and paradoxical phenomena that can be understood in many different ways. They are complex systems of interrelated departments, processes and people. They are influenced by internal and external forces and are only able to maintain a steady state so long as they change and adapt to outside forces. Their problem is 'how to create and maintain an effective organisation in which work can be done effectively, but where at the same time the worker can exhibit and develop their essential humanity' (De Board 1978:107).

The complexity of the systems involving departments, processes and people within an organisation will define its culture. Yet organisational culture is one of the most difficult of all organisational concepts to define (Hatch 1997). When sharing with others, similarity is emphasised yet each member of the group has different, separate contributions to make, so Hatch (1997:206) maintains that 'a culture depends on both community and diversity. It allows for similarity, but also supports and relies upon difference.'

Morgan (1986) mirrors this concept and maintains that organisations have cultures and sub-cultures, are fragmented or integrated, containing norms and rituals that will influence an organisation's ability to deal with challenges and change. He asserts that to appreciate these cultural norms it is necessary to view the organisation as an outsider. In doing so the images, themes and rituals of daily routine become clear and the historical explanations for such behaviours are evident.

However, there may be a tendency for counsellors and supervisors working in organisational contexts to be so immersed in their own work together that they lose sight of the fact that they both work in interlocking systems (Dodds 1986). Alternatively, if they are trainee counsellors, they may not have adequate organisational understanding, to appreciate fully the influence on the therapeutic work (Cole et al. 1981). Systems, whether fragmented or integrated, harmonious or explosive, are dependent on how the organisational culture has developed, sometimes through varying leadership styles, but more often through everyday social interaction. Yet culture is not static but is created and recreated continually as new professions join the organisation. The challenge for them is to understand the organisation as a culture, through the mundane as well as the more dramatic aspects of organisational life. It may help them to interpret the actions of others and the impact of those actions on their work. Therefore, when a counselling service is created within a 'host' organisation they will influence that organisation, even though the culture of the profession may be diametrically opposed to the culture of the organisation it joins. However, this can lead to communication difficulties (Copeland 2000b).

If the diverse cultures of organisations are to be understood by counsellors and supervisors, it is necessary to explore some of the ways in which they are depicted in the literature. Hawkins and Shohet (1989:134–138) in the first edition of their book outline five typical cultures:

1   personal pathology culture (sees problems as emanating from the individual)
2   bureaucratic culture (high on task and low on personal relativeness)
3   'watch your back' culture (highly competitive, rife with internal politics and sacrifices individuals easily)
4   reactive/crisis-driven culture (lives and breathes by creating on-going crisis situations)
5   learning/development culture (creates an environment suitable for learning and growing).

In the second eddition of their book Hawkins and Shohet (2000) call these culture patterns cultural dynamics and they add a sixth one, the addictive organisation. They describe the four major forms of addiction as:

1   where the key person in an organisation is an addict
2   where there are a number of people in the organisation replicating their addictive or co-dependent patterns
3   where the organisation itself is an addictive substance, eliciting high degrees of dependency and work holism from its members
4   where the organisation itself is the addict.

They postulate that 'in the case of the addictive organisation the entire workforce can be either acting addictively or colluding as a co-dependent' (Hawkins and Shohet 2000:174). From the above list of cultures it could be predicted that a learning and development culture is most likely to employ counsellors and their supervisors.

The concept of the learning organisation is useful to explore in relation to counselling and supervision. Peters (1994:65) talks about a learning organisation as one in which individuals have the ability to change and learn. They also have the ability to take risks and to fail but to do so in a safe way. Although Peters is specifically talking about industrial settings, the concept of a learning organisation may be recognised within settings that embrace counselling services as part of their commitment to the welfare of their employees. Hawkins and Shohet (2000:176–178) have a useful, detailed outline of how such a culture can affect supervision and this is summarised in Table 3.3.

Hitt (1996:17) defines a learning organisation as 'an organisation striving for excellence through continual organisational renewal.' This is a paradigm shift from the more traditional concept of an organisation, moving from the bureaucratic organisation (Weber 1947) to the performance based organisation (Drucker 1964) and finally to the learning organisation (Senge 1990). Carroll (1996) warns of the difficulties of introducing counselling into an organisation where there is a contradiction between the aims and objectives of the organisation and those of the counselling profession.

This emphasises the importance of the counsellor and supervisor having some understanding of organisational theory that will help them be aware of processes that affect the counselling and supervisory work. Additionally, they will need to understand the concept of power within organisations.

POWER IN ORGANISATIONS

Moving away from the concept of a learning organisation, Harrison (1993) also proposes a model of organisational culture that is based on four orientations towards power, role, achievement and support.

Table 3.3 How culture affects supervision

- Learning and development are seen as a continuous life-long process and therefore senior managers will set a good example by having supervision for themselves.
- A learning culture emphasises the potential that all the different work situations have for learning, both individually and collectively.
- Problems and crises are seen as important opportunities for learning and development.
- Good practice emerges from staff teams and departments that are well balanced in all parts of the learning cycle which goes from action, to reflection, to new thinking, to planning and then back to action.
- This means that supervision needs to avoid rushing for quick solutions, but also needs to avoid getting lost in abstract theorising.
- Learning becomes an important value in its own right.
- Individuals and teams take time out to reflect on their effectiveness, learning and development.
- A good appraisal system will focus not just on performance, but also on what the staff member has learnt, how they have developed and how this development can be nurtured in the future.
- There should be high levels of ongoing feedback from peers and between all levels within the organisation.
- Time and attention will be given to the transition of all individuals within the organisation.
- Roles will be regularly reviewed and negotiated.
- Learning in such an organisational culture resides not just at an individual level but also at team and organisational level.

Source: Hawkins and Shohet (2000:176–178).

- Power culture is based on strength and compliance with the leader's direction and drive.
- Role culture is based on structure, on ordered work and by following rules.
- Achievement culture is based on competence and getting the job done.
- Support culture is based on relationships and the quality of harmonious person interaction.

The four orientations in this framework are a way of understanding what weighting an organisation might give to each one as it is unlikely that they will exclusively show the characteristics of just one of these orientations. However, the metaphor of the organisation as a culture may not address in sufficient depth the issue of power dynamics underlying the premise that employees can play an important part in constructing their own reality within the organisational context.

Davis (1995), in her research exploring one-to-one interventions for change in senior teams, noted that the most difficult situations experienced in organisational life were the consequence of power struggles. Morgan (1986), in viewing the organisation as a political system, sees power as an essential element in that system, and Hall (1991:108) maintains that 'organisations and power are synonymous'. Organisational politics emanate from interests, conflict, and power. However, they may not be visible to anyone but those directly involved in that process. They occur when people think differently and want to act differently. This creates a tension that has to be resolved. The political metaphor described by Morgan (1986), sees organisations as a loose network of people with divergent interests who gather together as a coalition in pursuit of desired goals. When interests collide, conflicts occur. This may be conflict over limited resources and counsellors and their supervisees may struggle to secure funds to carry on with their work. Nevertheless, if they have the power they may be able to secure funds and so resolve the conflict.

Power is the capacity to affect people, things, situations and decisions (Lee and Lawrence 1985) and Morgan (1986) maintains that power can resolve conflicts of interest. Yet counsellors and supervisors may not have any legitimate power when working in organisational contexts. However, individuals in any role, in any organisation, have some power, some capacity to exert influence because power is seldom one sided (Handy 1993). The five sources of power originally postulated by French and Raven (1959) have been the basis of discussion by many writers on organisational theory. Handy (1993) outlines them and a discussion here will clarify which sources are open to counsellors and supervisors working in organisational contexts. First, physical power would seem to be the domain of the tyrant and in most organisations employees are physically free to leave. Yet bullies are not confined to schools. Harassment policies are implemented in organisations to counteract both physical and psychological damage to employees. Therefore, all employees can be subject to a certain amount of fear from this form of power and counsellors and supervisors may have to deal with the distress this causes. They may also be subject to bullying themselves. So, physical power exists in organisations but it does not necessarily have to be used. The fact that it exists, or the belief in its existence, is enough.

The second source of power is resource power. The possession of valued resources is a useful basis for influence. For this source of power to be effective however, there must be a control of the resources and they need to be desired by the recipient. For example, managers can give promotions or pay increases. This can affect counsellors and supervisors working within organisations by making them feel undervalued. The same process may also affect the counsellor's clients. In such a situation a feeling of powerlessness may ensue. Resource power also affects the allocation of funds to the counselling service. Therefore, if a counsellor or supervisor is also the manager of the counselling service then resource power will be available to them.

The third source of power is position power. This power is the result of the employee's role or position within the organisation. Yet power resides in the position rather than the individual and gives the occupant control over invisible assets such as information, access to a variety of networks and a right to say how the work is organised. Some counsellors and supervisors may have position power combined with resource power as often power relationships involve the use of more than one form of power (Hall 1991).

The fourth source of power is expert power, that is power based on knowledge and expertise. Unlike the previous power bases, this one requires no sanctions but the expertise needs to be in demand otherwise it has no basis on which to exist. For example, supervisors working in counselling agencies are available to give the trustees of that organisation information about the supervisory process and its necessity for ethical counselling practice. In such circumstances they have the power of their expertise because it may be difficult for someone not in the profession to evaluate the work. Here the focus is on the professional and their employing organisation. Professionals are often allowed to control themselves with another professional and this provides the organisation with a system of accountability (Hall 1991). This would apply to counselling services embedded in 'host' organisations within industrial, education and health service settings. Here the supervisor would be that other professional monitoring the counsellor's practice. This does not automatically mean, however, that they will not be in conflict with the rest of the organisation; as noted earlier, their expertise needs to be in demand for it to be a source of power. Yet expert power is the form of power most readily available to counsellors and supervisors.

The fifth and final source of power is personal power. Personal power resides with the person and their personality but it can be brittle and elusive, fanned by success, but with the ability to evaporate on defeat. For counsellors and supervisors personal development and a clear sense of self in relation to others will enable them to maintain their personal power in an organisational culture that seeks to dis-empower them. Personal power is open to counsellors and supervisors in any organisational setting but will be more effective when coupled with expert power.

Sources of power within organisational contexts are diverse. If counsellors and supervisors are to have any influence within an organisation they will be more successful if they seek to understand the power network and the continuing change between people and circumstance. Frequently people are unaware of their own resources and importance, they perceive themselves to be powerless. This can be a self-fulfilling prophecy (Lee and Lawrence 1985). Counsellors and supervisors are no exception so there is a need for them to recognise and use their own sources of power to enhance their influence within the organisational context.

Although all employees may be aware that they are influenced by organisational power and politics, these are rarely discussed, hence counsellors and supervisors enter an organisation having to watch and listen to gain knowledge of systems, process and politics to know how they might influence the organisation. Many might decide that they prefer to be invisible within that organisation. Nevertheless, being aware of what is problematic and critical to an organisation will give employees an understanding of its priorities. These may be different from the organisation's publicly stated aims in annual reports and missions statements (Walton 1997). This is what Egan (1994:4) describes as the shadow side of the organisation, 'the shadow side deals with the covert, the undiscussed and unmentionable. It includes arrangements not found in organisational manuals and company documents and organisational charts.' Shadow side activities can be ethical and add value to the organisation but they can also be detrimental. For example, by providing a counselling service an organisation can reflect a 'caring' image to the public but one that does not permeate the culture of the organisation as a whole (Sugerman 1992, Carroll 1997), is split off, forming a culture of its own (Harwood 1993). Whilst sub-cultures can lead to problematic communications, differences between them can also represent sources of creativity and innovation. Cultures that are too uniform, with little internal diversity, may mean a lack of innovation and therefore have a slower response to change (McLean and Marshall 1988).

ORGANISATIONAL CULTURE AND THE COUNSELLOR/SUPERVISOR

Understanding an organisation's culture is not an easy task for counsellors and their supervisor. Carroll (1997:17) notes that there is little research into organisational culture that helps 'prepare, introduce, maintain and, where necessary terminate counselling provision in different company cultures.'

Counsellors are trained to work primarily with individuals reflecting the British individualistic society. This could conflict with the norms of the organisation that may be offering a humane and liberal set of practices known as counselling in the context of a ruthless and inhumane management regime (Cummins and Hoggett 1995). With supervision too, the policy objectives of an organisation and the personal and professional needs of the supervisee may not be compatible (Bimrose and Wilden 1994). This could lead to potential conflict between the supervisor and the organisation.

All employees shape the culture of an organisation by the way they behave and the way they communicate with one another. It may be tempting to talk as if an organisation has one culture, taking much the same form throughout, but this is seldom the case. In organisations 'there are competing value systems that create a mosaic of organisational realities, rather than a uniform corporate culture' (Morgan 1986:127).

Separate departments, however, will identify with their profession or particular client group and have a different view of the world and the nature of the organisation's business (McMahon Moughtin 1997, Morgan 1986, Walton 1997). This may result in a set of professional sub-cultures that are diametrically opposed. Morgan (1986:127) notes 'when groups with very different occupational attitudes are placed in a relation of dependence, organisations are often plagued by a kind of cultural warfare'.

CONCLUSION

Dilemmas will occur for supervisors and their supervisees working within an organisational context that are generated through cultural clashes. So what are the dilemmas that counsellors and supervisors face when they work at the interface between professional and organisational cultures that can fit or, more likely, collide? These dilemmas are embodied in the following questions that need to be asked; how can counsellors and supervisors

- educate managers within the organisation about the culture of counselling and supervision?
- work at the interface of two diametrically opposed cultures without creating 'cultural warfare'?
- keep their own personal and any other sources of power without contravening ethical codes?
- seek to influence organisational culture and change processes without breaking the boundaries of confidentiality?
- maintain their professional autonomy whilst influencing organisational processes?
- give added value to an organisation with a learning and development culture?

So dilemmas emanate from the differences between the emphasis on the individual found in counselling and supervision and the emphasis on the collective found in the different organisational cultures. These dilemmas will be addressed in the next chapter, where different organisational contexts are explored in relation to their cultural fit with counselling and supervision.

Chapter 4

Managing the dilemmas

> Dilemma: A position of doubt or perplexity. A choice between two (or among several) alternatives all of which have some unfavourable elements.
> Dryden (1985:1)

INTRODUCTION

As discussed in Chapter 3, when counselling, supervision and organisational cultures collide, dilemmas arise that need to be managed so that they do not cause distress to the supervisor, client, counsellor and their line manager. This chapter will discuss the dilemmas listed at the end of Chapter 3 in relation to the main dilemma. This is posed by the question, how can counsellors and supervisors work effectively at the interface of two diametrically opposed cultures without creating 'cultural warfare' in the different organisational contexts in which they co-exist?

MANAGING THE CULTURAL FIT

When an organisation decides to provide a counselling service it will not be a comfortable co-existence. Within any type of organisation, counselling and supervision will not transfer easily into an existing organisational culture. Innovation and change are factors that may influence an organisation in their decision to provide a counselling service for their employees. Change can often bring about uncertainty and a degree of conflict into existing work relationships (Bimrose and Wilden 1994), so organisations may view counselling as crisis intervention, a way of enabling employees to cope with change on an individual basis (McGowan 1989). Therefore, counselling is seen as an individual solution to a corporate problem, that of helping employees to acclimatise to a changing environment. Coupled with this, counselling in organisations is often viewed as being short term, seeking to deal with specific problems (Bull 1997). As Carroll and Holloway (1999:3) note trained as counsellors and then supervisors many of us have used only an individually orientated perspective for solving problems, rather than considering the specific organisational factors that might strongly influence the professional's behaviour in context.

This perspective means that there is a need to change the dyadic view of the counselling process to one that is more open, including the supervisor, counsellor and the organisation (Carroll 1996). In doing so there is an implicit recognition that the supervisor will be involved, either directly or indirectly, with organisational issues that originate from the culture within that organisation and that they will be involved in tripartite meetings that include the line manager. Just how much involvement they will have and what form it will take will depend on many factors, including:

- whether the organisation has formally employed the supervisor
- whether the supervisor is in-house or external
- who pays the supervisor, the supervisee or the organisation
- whether the supervisor has a dual or even a triple role in the organisation
- what type of organisation it is, workplace, educational, health, social services or a counselling agency
- whether the organisational culture is compatible with the counselling and supervision culture.

Each of these factors will be in or out of focus depending on the organisational setting of the work.

Organisational policy and politics and consequently its overall culture, will also have a direct influence on how the counselling service is managed and the service's management of their accessibility, accountability, confidentiality and evaluation procedures. Most organisations hosting a counselling service will need to ensure that the service adheres to their quality auditing procedures. However, this may cause a cultural clash, especially if the confidentiality of the client material is endangered. Client confidentiality is enshrined in the counselling and supervisory culture. But for statistical purposes and to ensure that the counselling service continues to be funded by the institution, such information is needed. Therefore, divulging statistical information that will justify the financing of the service, whilst keeping client confidentiality, will enable both aspects of professional and organisational culture to co-exist.

Managing the cultural fit within an educational setting

Management of the cultural clash between the existing organisational culture and the culture of counselling and supervision within an educational setting presents a unique set of challenges. Tholstrup (1999) sees these challenges as emanating from the distinct features of the organisation itself. These include:

- the preponderantly young population which presents itself for counselling;
- the seasonal fluctuation in client load;
- the academic and maturational demands imposed on the students by the educational setting;
- how organisational policy and politics are mirrored by lines of responsibility between the counselling provision and the setting, and by issues of accountability, accessibility, confidentiality and evaluation.

(Tholstrup 1999:104)

Therefore, working as a supervisor within the context of education, there is a need to understand the specific and powerful cultural influences on the counselling process and to be able to empower the counsellor to engage with some of those cultural norms. First, the age of the client population will need to be considered, especially if the students are 16 years of age or under. In educational institutions, teachers, and often lecturers, are in contact with parents for various reasons. This is a cultural norm. So counsellors and their supervisors will need to decide whether this is ever necessary and/or possible whilst still keeping the confidentiality of the client. Do they find ways to accommodate this norm or, alternatively, do they decide that it can never happen under any circumstances? If there is to be cultural fit, the supervisor, counsellor and their line manager will need to establish ways of communicating with the parents when necessary and with the client's permission, whilst still keeping the client's trust.

Sally is a counsellor working with pupils from 11 to 16 years of age within a school setting. She is supervised by Mandy who is also a school counsellor within a different geographical area. They both agree that there is a need to work closely with the head of pastoral care in the school to ensure that parental consent is gained for the pupil to work with the counsellor. There is also provision for the counsellor to work with both parent and pupil together if the need arises. This procedure is not one that is evident in all school counselling services, however, Sally's school feels that this is one way of involving parents in its work with the pupils. The culture of the school is one of openness and collaboration and therefore parental permission is regarded not with suspicion, but as the norm in all pupil transactions. Both Sally and Mandy are clear that if that permission is not granted, the pupil will not be able to work with the counsellor. This might appear to be harsh, but in such an open culture, is rarely a problem for Sally and her supervisor.

In this scenario the cultural fit with the organisation and counselling is close and does not pose too many problems, however, within schools this may be a rarity.

Second, the seasonal fluctuation in the client load is part of the culture in educational institutions and teachers/lecturers expect to have longer holiday periods than other professionals. This will mean that counsellors and their supervisors will need to work round this pattern of attendance unless they work in a higher educational establishment where some students, especially those doing postgraduate study, do not go home in the vacations. Clients will usually be seen in term time only and breaks in the counselling work will need to be managed carefully so that clients do not feel abandoned.

James works as a counsellor within a boarding school for young people between the ages of 11 and 16. The pupils live in disparate geographical regions both in the United Kingdom and abroad. Over the years he has had to work closely with his supervisor Yvonne to manage the breaks in the therapy work over extended holiday periods. The culture of the school is that pupils disappear for long periods of time during a holiday, after a phase of intensive relationships during the term. Therefore, James has had to work hard with Yvonne to establish a way of making clear contracts with the pupils that includes a way of holding the relationship, when necessary, over these periods. Clarity is needed concerning beginnings and endings of the contract, but also how support will be given during the long holidays. James is prepared to give support once a week over the telephone or by e-mail as the school is prepared to employ him for this work on a sessional basis if needed. They pride themselves on the support they give to all pupils, this is part of the culture embedded in their mission statement. Therefore, the counselling service is embedded in that culture.

It is not a cultural norm in counselling to have breaks in the process that are dictated by the organisational norms rather than the therapeutic work. However, to achieve a cultural fit, counsellors have to work round these patterns of attendance as illustrated in the scenario above.

Third, the academic and maturational demands placed on the students by the organisation can cause stress to clients over which a counsellor may feel they have no control. Working with, rather than against, the institution, will mean that the counsellor, empowered by their supervisor, needs to come out of the counselling room and engage in dialogue with the relevant members of staff if they think that a student is being subjected to undue academic pressure that is causing them to be distressed. This will mean careful negotiation with the client about what information can be disclosed. Once again a three-way meeting would be best practice, but failing that, the counsellor would need to meet with the relevant member of staff to discuss the client's stress levels.

Peter is a counsellor in a university setting, supervised by Nicole who is a freelance counsellor, tutor and supervisor. Peter is worried by one of his clients, struggling to complete a final special study, at the end of the third year of her degree course. She remembers that she failed one of her 'A' levels because she did not get a good grade in a special study for that subject. She is very afraid that the same thing will happen and that she will fail this module. Her anxiety is causing her to avoid the work. Having pursued many lines of work with her that have not been successful, he discusses with Nicole the possibility of talking to his client's tutor about the anxiety around this piece of work. Nicole helps him to be realistic about the possibilities of success with this course of action. She knows, from her work as a tutor in another university, that talking with the tutor could help them to understand the client's difficulty more clearly and enable a course of action that was unknown to Peter. However, both Peter and Nicole are aware that the client's consent is vital and an understanding tutor is important too. However, they are both hopeful about a productive outcome given the university's successful student retention rate through good relationships between the academic staff and the counselling service.

In this scenario, it is important that the counsellor can relate well to academic staff. However, this type of action could sit uneasily with the culture of counselling where the one-to-one, or one-to-couple/group process is the norm. If the clients are to work successfully within the institution and the institution, in post-compulsory education, is to retain its student numbers, such a dialogue is needed. It is the supervisor's role to help the supervisee to clarify their line of action whilst maintaining ethical practice.

Managing the cultural fit within a health service setting

Counsellors working in primary care, especially in GPs' surgeries, will find that there are cultural differences between themselves and other members of the practice. Hierarchical structures, vocational stereotyping and antiquated assumptions, which are the cultural norms in many practices, will underlie working relationships between members of a multi-disciplinary team so fostering poor communication and rivalry between members (East 1995). There is a need for counsellors to be bold enough to take the initiative and forge working relationships in this context so they become indispensable to the primary health care team (Curtis-Jenkins and Einzig 1996). This will not be an easy task. Counsellors and primary care workers will have to learn to speak one another's language, a language that holds the cultural norms of the organisation.

Language is one of the many ways a culture is transmitted and therefore, if counsellors do not lay aside their own modes of communication within their profession, they will find themselves unable to have any influence within a multi-disciplinary team. They need to learn to speak the language of illness and cure, patient management and waiting lists. Speaking the language of emotion and long-term therapy will not bridge the divide between the cultures, and counsellors and supervisors may well ask why it should be that they have to learn to speak another language. However, it is the counselling service that is entering the field of health that has already been established for the benefit of patients. Staying isolated in their counselling room will also serve to increase the gulf between themselves and their medical colleagues. Like all those who enter another culture as a minority group, counsellors and supervisors, if they are going to have any influence within the organisation, must learn that language.

Sarah is an experienced counsellor working within a large GP surgery. She has learnt how to use medical metaphors to enable members of the multidisciplinary team to understand her world of counselling. She employs the language of the medical world with the use of comparative metaphors, for example she talks about sticking plasters or major surgery to help her colleagues to understand the differences between time limited work and long-term therapy. She is comfortable when working metaphorically, it is a familiar tool that she uses in her counselling work, so it can be transferred when she needs those within other disciplines to understand the cultural world of counselling.

If supervisors are to help their supervisees to learn this language and function in this alien culture, they will need to have had at least some experience of the GP surgery setting and be aware of the unique problems faced by counsellors in primary care. This was one of the conclusions that Burton and colleagues postulated as a result of their findings from interviewing supervisees working in primary care settings. They had found that 'only 25% of supervisors actually currently worked clinically in primary care' (Burton et al. 1998:128) and although there was satisfaction, in general, with supervision the practical issues that arose within the primary care settings were discussed infrequently. This applied especially to managerial issues that arose. So although this points to the need for the supervisor to work as a counsellor in primary care themselves, it would be simpler for the supervisor to be trained to work organisationally rather then individually. This would mean that they were attuned to organisational issues in any setting.

There is also a need to protect clients from poor counselling rather than helping counsellors with the ethical dilemmas that are intrinsic to the primary care setting. The counsellor needs an understanding of the medical model and also the side effects of drugs along with a clear understanding of the role others play in medical settings. If this is so, it may follow that the supervisor also needs similar knowledge so that counsellors can be supported by supervisors as they work with the dynamic flux of roles and relationships with colleagues and clients (Henderson 1999).

Henderson (1999) is adamant that unless the supervisor is willing to work with the counsellor, helping them to understand the meaning of the triangular relationships that can occur in referral from the GP, they should avoid working in this setting. She also maintains that the culture of control which may characterise this setting can mean control is expressed by arbitrarily limiting resources irrespective of the issues presented by the clients. We have seen in Chapter 2, that the control of resources is a form of power that is not often available to counsellors or supervisors. Additionally, a counselling culture is about personal autonomy and enabling clients to be self-reliant. So a culture of control within an organisation will be difficult for a counsellor and supervisor to work within effectively. Each team within a health care setting will have a different culture depending on how the organisation developed and who manages the service.

Alison is an experienced counsellor working in two GP surgeries in different geographical areas. In the first surgery there is a single, female doctor and a manager who runs the practice like one big happy family. All the staff, including Alison, eat lunch together. Everyone is treated equally and there is the opportunity to influence the way systems are developed. Alison is aware that she is valued as an equal member of the team. In the second GP practice there are four doctors but only two of them ever refer patients to Alison for counselling. She is not involved in practice meetings despite asking to attend. Her presence is tolerated and she sees the 'heart-sink' patients that the two doctors have lost patience with. Therefore, the cultures in the two surgeries are very different. In the first surgery where Alison is valued, all the team understand the culture of counselling and the purpose of supervision. There is an opportunity to develop and grow. In the second surgery there is no will to understand the world of counselling and supervision where, as a counsellor, she is tolerated but misunderstood. Within this culture, Alison feels stifled and is considering giving up the work.

In this scenario, even though the counsellor is working in a medical setting, the cultures in the two surgeries are very different and Alison feels empowered in the first surgery and disempowered in the second.

A counsellor and their supervisor will have the personal power available to them to work at gaining resources for their work that will enable them to practise ethically. The regular use of a private room, conducive to counselling work, is part of the culture of counselling and yet a resource that often has to be fought for within a health service setting. Similarly, some counsellors may have a struggle to get their managers to agree to pay for their supervision, especially at a rate that demonstrates the importance of supervision rather than a derisory rate that demeans the process.

Supervisors need to help the counsellor to understand and work through conflicts of interest that may arise out of situations such as these. Yet it is clear that supervisors, mainly, have no direct contact with the GP who is employing the counsellor (Henderson 1999). Indeed 47 per cent of counsellors in the study of Primary Care Counsellor's Experience of Supervision (Burton et al. 1998) were found to be paying for their own supervision, whilst 6 per cent were funded jointly by the health authorities and GP practices, 29 per cent funded by health authorities and 20 per cent by GP practices themselves. This highlights the difficulty that supervisors face in terms of their invisibility within an organisational context in which the counselling and supervisory processes may sit uneasily within a culture where a medical model prevails.

Managing the cultural fit within a workplace setting

In workplace settings, the counselling and supervisory processes may sit uneasily. The rapid expansion of employee counselling services or employee assistance programmes (EAPs) has occurred to help employees with personal, family and work-related problems. The cause of this expansion has been twofold, first as a recognition of stress within the workplace and second because of the increased likelihood of litigation relating to stress caused by workplace factors (Curtis-Jenkins and Einzig 1996). Inherent in this approach to workplace counselling is the concept that the organisational culture will not change easily or rapidly, therefore the individual has to learn ways of coping with it. So the notion of short term 'sticking-plaster' solutions was postulated, indicating that workplace counselling provided just such a service (Curtis-Jenkins and Einzig 1996, Arnold et al. 1995). Nevertheless this does not always have to be so if counsellors and supervisors are willing to work with, rather than against, the organisation (Carroll 1999), especially if the organisation is funding the counselling provision.

Carroll (1996) notes that when the organisation pays for counselling provision for its employees, it creates a dynamic between the organisation, the client and the counsellor. This dynamic is evident in both in-house and EAP counselling provision and therefore it is important that counsellors and supervisors learn to work with the organisational culture rather than retain a private practice perspective. Nevertheless, it is easier for counsellors and supervisors, working within a strong, disabling culture within the organisation, to discount that influence and work as though they were in private practice. Some models of counselling will work more effectively from this perspective. For example a cognitive behavioural model working in a time limited way will empower clients to change their thought patterns and become less stressed by the work environment. Alternatively, it will allow them to develop new personal goals that enable them to find more suitable employment. Yet a model of counselling that needs the same room and time each week, which works with successful attachment and subsequent disengagement in long-term work, will not be suitable for an organisation that wants the counselling service to get employees back to work after a period of stress-related illness. Theoretical rigidity on the part of the counsellor will inevitably fail the employee and their organisation. Adaptation and flexibility are needed to enable all parties in the working alliance to maximise their strengths for the benefit of all individuals working within the organisation. This includes client, counsellor and their supervisor. Therefore, as Coles (2003:137) says

> gone are the days of the small consulting room with the door firmly shut against the external world, and the deliberate concentration on the inner world of the client. In workplace counselling, therapy has to come out of the consulting room to face up to the exigencies of people's working lives and the strengths and weaknesses of commercial organisations.

The main dilemma for counsellor and supervisor when working within workplace counselling is to reconcile their need to work within a counselling culture with its inherent focus on the individual and their emotional world and yet also become a counsellor and supervisor to the organisation. Of necessity, this shift in role will mean engagement with the unique culture within the organisation and the need to speak its language. It has been noted that to speak the language of the organisation is vital when working within a health service setting and the workplace context is no exception. Some cultures will be easier to work with than others, especially if the organisation has a culture of learning and development where the managers will be more inclined to listen and learn from others' perspectives. However, as discussed in Chapter 7, there is a need for counsellors and their supervisor to communicate effectively with the managers within their organisation. Sitting behind closed doors in their supervisory dyad will not benefit the client or the organisation. If a clash of cultures is inevitable, it will need to be faced. Once good communication systems have been created, there will be the opportunity to enter into dialogue that will enable all parties in the working alliance to influence each other. Neither party holds the moral high ground. Each has things to learn from the other. Whether counsellors like it or not, they are involved with the organisational culture. They are an integral part of it.

Managing the cultural fit within voluntary counselling agencies

Managing the cultural fit within voluntary counselling agencies can initially appear an easier task than in other organisational settings. This is because line managers in counselling agencies are often counsellors themselves. In marital counselling organisations such as Relate they will be an integral part of the structure of the organisation (Lewis et al. 1992), familiar with the prevailing culture and an integral part of it. However the voluntary sector is dynamic, innovative and ever changing so practice and standards in counselling can vary greatly (Tyndall 1993). There is often a mixture of paid and unpaid voluntary workers and funds may come from a variety of sources such as government grants, fund-raising activities, sponsorship, or National Lottery money. This means that resources may not be reliable and so the services offered will be constrained by this factor (Wallbank 1997). In voluntary counselling agencies, client work may have to be curtailed abruptly because funding has been withdrawn from the project. This means that, although clients can be referred on to another agency, the culture of therapy ending at a set, planned time, however short-term the work, cannot be met.

> Helen has worked for the same voluntary counselling agency for the past three years and during that time the funding for the agency has been under threat annually. The agency relies on sources of funding that have to be applied for every year with no guarantee of success. Whilst the client group has no knowledge of the annual funding crisis, it takes its toll on the counsellors and especially on the manager of the agency. Therefore, Helen relies on her supervisor Carol, for support during these precarious times. They both know that if the funding bids are unsuccessful, the clients will have to be referred on to another agency and the culture of counselling broken because of organisational constraints.

In cases such as these, financial constraint will dictate a chain of events that might run counter to a counselling culture. In fact financial constraints belong in the cultural world of organisations. They indicate where the resource power lies. This will often mean that counsellors are paid very little for their work and that their supervision is not paid for by the organisation. However, in counselling agencies this is less likely to happen than in commercial organisations because counsellors and supervisors have more influence from within the organisation.

Nevertheless, this may be only one source of tension in a voluntary counselling agency organisation where there is a mixture of professionals and volunteers, a tension between practitioners and managerial staff, education and training and most of all between the regions and the national centre (Lewis et al. 1992).

> *Tina is a supervisor for a national counselling agency with responsibility for the supervision of a group of counsellors in one geographical area. The national office tells her that the name of the group is to be changed from case discussion groups to case supervision groups. She relays this information to her group of counsellors. On hearing the news they are upset because they fear that the change of name means that it takes authority away from them. Tina is at pains to explain that the functioning of the group has not changed despite its change of name but as there are no written guidelines concerning the function of the group, there is no official way of allaying those fears.*

Tensions within voluntary counselling agencies such as this example, highlight the differing cultures within one organisation that has national and regional centres. The supervisor has to bridge the gap between both centres and allay fears and explain misunderstandings.

Many voluntary organisations, however, have inherited cultures and traditions that may no longer be appropriate to the present task (Handy 1985) and many voluntary organisations of long standing, may, in part, be in this position. In the last decade counselling has grown and developed, becoming much more professional with a highly trained workforce. The standards expected from counsellors and supervisors in the twenty-first century will not fit with some voluntary counselling agencies. They still train their workers to a minimum standard because they are constrained by their precarious funding arrangements. Additionally, they are managed by volunteers who have expertise in their field but who may have little knowledge of counselling and supervisory processes. So the counselling culture clashes with a culture within the organisation of 'doing their best' with the little finances they have. In this respect they are similar to commercial organisations where the managers need to be educated to understand the needs of the counsellors and supervisors. There is more of a possibility of the supervisors having personal and expert power to influence policies and procedures in such organisations. For example:

> *Charlotte is a counsellor and supervisor for a small voluntary counselling agency that works with victims of childhood sexual abuse. She is aware that she has been fully trained as a counsellor and is accredited by BACP. However, she is conscious that some of the counsellors are only trained to certificate skills level. When supervising them she is acutely aware that they need to have more training in order to be more effective in their work with clients. In*

her position as supervisor and counsellor within the organisation she is able
to talk to the line manager and outline her concerns. As a result the manager
is able to find a small amount of money to assist at least one counsellor per
year to continue their counsellor training to diploma level.

In this case study it can be seen that when the supervisor is embedded in the organisation, often having a dual role, they have influence with all levels of management. They are able to influence 'the way we do things around here' which will contribute to the changing face of the organisation and its culture.

Larger, national organisations such as Relate have a commitment to research; it is one of their stated objectives and is a way of regularly monitoring the service that is provided to the public. As far back as 1974 research was carried out into why counsellors resigned from the organisation (Heisler 1974). Conflict with supervisors was the highest category response and supervisors, as a group, were said to have too fixed a view of what was acceptable practice within the organisation, making few allowances for individual differences. This would accord with Tyndall's (1993) assertion that when a supervisory system is developed within an agency it may foster an approach in counsellors that is too uniform. Yet uniformity, to counsellors and supervisors working within a very different culture to their own, might be a welcome relief. A well established supervisory system does have the advantage that supervisors have supervision for their supervision and Lewis et al. (1992) note that some local centres in Relate also buy in extra supervision. As the biggest and most dispersed agency for marital problems it still struggles not only for resources but also for prestige and legitimacy. Internally too, the tensions between the counsellors and administrators in the agency can be a cause for concern (McLeod 1993). An organisation cannot operate effectively without clear objectives, communication, record keeping and lines of accountability, but from a counsellor's point of view management rules can get in the way of client work. Yet the management committee carries out a boundary function, mediating between conflicting interests within an agency (Tyndall 1993). This may mean that the supervisor is in the middle of a conflict between the administrator/manager and the counsellor.

Adrian is a supervisor for a national counselling agency and works in two
different regional centres. He has found that the counsellors imbue him with
more power than he legitimately has within the organisation. When there is a
problem with a client complaint he finds that the counsellors are using him as
their first point of contact when in fact it should be their line manager in the
regional centre they contact first. Despite constant reminding the counsellors
still always contact him first when there is a problem of any sort concerning
their work.

In a situation like this, there is the need for the organisation to clarify the different responsibilities inherent within each role, that of line manager within the centre and the supervisor of clinical practice. Within an agency such as this it should be easy for a tripartite meeting to take place so that clarity of role is established. However, both the counsellor and their line manager need to have the will to clarify the situation, if there is tension between them the supervisor can act as mediator.

CONCLUSION

In responding productively to the dilemmas that arise from a clash of different cultures, counsellors and supervisors will help organisations to expand and grow, enabling the counselling service to be productive both on an individual and organisational level.

To ensure a cultural fit, both counsellors and supervisors are jointly responsible for ensuring that:

- The line manager within the organisation fully understands the culture of counselling and supervision and is aware of how this culture merges or diverges from the culture within the department or organisation. This will mean that tripartite meetings are essential so that perceptions can be shared in a non-threatening way, where both cultures are understood and accepted.
- They both work with the line manager to manage the dynamic between possible diametrically opposed cultures. This will mean that all parties need to be non-defensive and open to the others' way of thinking for the benefit of the department or organisation as a whole.
- They keep their own source of personal power when the organisational culture threatens to engulf their position and demean it. This is the one source of power that is open to all counsellors and supervisors and therefore, counsellors and supervisors can help one another to ensure that it is not eroded. This can be done by support and challenge and in ensuring that they encourage each other to speak out in the organisation when appropriate.
- They are aware of organisational change processes and how they affect the client work. Feeding such information back to line managers ethically is not always easy and will need client permission if the information is likely to break their confidentiality in any way. However, this process is essential for effective cultural fit.
- They meet regularly with line managers to ensure that any collective information they have can influence organisational policies whilst still maintaining ethical practice and the credibility of the counselling service.
- Where a learning and development culture exists, counsellors and

supervisors can contribute actively to both their own and the organisation's development through clear, open and ethical communication systems and through the appraisal process.

In Part III, systems will be discussed which will enable all parties in the working alliance to communicate effectively and so address the points above for the benefit of the organisation and its employees.

Supervision in organisations

Working with the supervisory rhombus

Chapter 5

Securing a supervisory position

> We need to be much more wary of organisations which have developed a
> fine rhetoric of sloughing off their responsibilities while at the same time
> increasing those of their employees.
>
> (Bunting 2004:324)

INTRODUCTION

In the introductory chapter it was noted that in the past the working alliance
between counsellor and supervisor often originated through very informal
processes. In recent years, however, some supervisory posts have been advertised in professional journals. Nevertheless, such advertisements are quite rare
and it would be good to see more of them, indicating that organisations are
taking the responsibility for the appointment of supervisors more seriously. In
numerous ways the different methods used by counsellors to choose their
supervisor have both advantages and disadvantages. However, what is not in
dispute is that however they are employed, supervisors need to be embedded in
the working life of the organisation. In this way they can help the counsellor
work more effectively within the organisation. Therefore, in this chapter the
various ways of being appointed as a supervisor within an organisation will be
outlined and the advantages and disadvantages of each mode discussed.

A COUNSELLOR CHOOSES THEIR OWN SUPERVISOR

When a counsellor chooses their own supervisor, without the organisation
becoming involved, it is a straightforward procedure involving two people in
the same profession.

*Andrea is a counsellor with ten years' experience working both as a private
practitioner and also as a counsellor in various types of organisation. Her
working week consists of:*

- *two days a week in two different GP surgeries that are geographically close to one another;*
- *one day a week as a sessional counsellor in a university counselling service;*
- *two days a week as a counsellor in private practice.*

She has had various supervisors in her career and is now looking to change to one who can fulfil her needs both in her private practice and also organisationally. Andrea is also conscious that geographically she is only prepared to travel for an hour at the most because of her busy work schedule.

Andrea is also aware of her individual needs in supervision. She wants support and challenge and yet she also needs a collegiate relationship in which ideas can be shared and dilemmas explored.

For Andrea, choosing a supervisor to meet the needs that arise from her work in three very different settings is a challenge. First, in her primary health care setting, she is aware that there is a move to ensure that any supervisor she chooses will need to have experience of working in primary health care themselves. This is not mandatory; however, Henderson (1997:9) notes that 'supervision of counselling in primary care is more than a reflective process, there is a need to ask systematic questions and attend to the context of Primary Health Care', and also that 'supervisors need to be prepared to support counsellors in their negotiations with the GP about appropriateness of referral to them' (Henderson 1997:10).

Andrea is conscious that having a supervisor who also works in a primary health care setting can have advantages that centre on the supervisor's ability to understand the medical culture of the GP surgery and the tensions that can occur when working in a multi-disciplinary team. Additionally, if a supervisor has also experienced working in such a setting, they will have a good working knowledge of medical conditions, prescription and illegal drugs and how to find psychiatric input when required. In all probability they will also be working from a broadly similar clinical methodology and orientation, working in a time-limited way through choice rather than necessity. They will both also have assessment skills and so be aware of the warning signs which indicate possible psychiatric problems, eating and other associated disorders and personality problems, all of which will need referral back to the GP. However, there are also disadvantages to having a supervisor who works as a counsellor in a primary health care setting. The supervisor can make the supposition that the culture of one GP practice is very much like another. This can lead to assumptions being made that could adversely effect the counsellor's working relationships within the team. The supervisor will not feel the need to ask 'the idiot question' about the way work is carried out in that particular context and therefore, organisational transference will not be identified.

Andrea's work within a university counselling service also means that she faces different organisational dilemmas to those encountered in her GP work. Some of the cultural differences are noted in Chapter 4. Within this sector there is no directive for her to choose a supervisor who also works as a counsellor in the university sector. Nevertheless, she is aware that working in a time-limited manner in both organisations means that any supervisor with experience of time-limited work, in any organisational setting, will have an understanding of the issues presented by working in this way. Similarly, Andrea is aware that choosing a supervisor who counsels in both medical and educational settings will limit her choice especially as she needs to keep boundary issues to a minimum. She does not want to choose a supervisor who also works in the same medical or educational setting. She feels that this will be problematic, if she is both colleague and supervisee at the same time and within the same organisation.

The supervision for Andrea's private practice appears to be less problematic in terms of her choice of supervisor. Yet she is aware that she will want her new supervisor to take responsibility for her current clients' safety in the event of her sudden illness or death. She has no one else who could carry out this task for her.

When choosing a supervisor within a particular geographical area Andrea needs to be aware of the prospective supervisor's connections with her employing organisations. For example, a prospective supervisor, unbeknown to Andrea, may also work with the manager of the university counselling service, as their counsellor. The overlapping of boundaries can be impossible to avoid, especially in geographical areas where supervisors are limited. Nevertheless, Andrea will need to ask the right questions when choosing her supervisor, to ensure that the overlapping of boundaries is avoided as far as possible. She will also need to decide what compromises she is prepared to make concerning her travel time and at what cost to her physical health.

For Andrea, her individual needs in supervision are extremely important. She has been practising for ten years and has had three different supervisors during that time. She has learnt what works for her in supervision and is not prepared to compromise on her need for support and challenge in equal measure but also for a relationship that is collegiate and equal in terms of the balance of power. However, these needs do have to be balanced with her organisational needs and the time constraints in terms of travel. So Andrea is faced with a complex set of criteria when choosing her new supervisor. The task is made a little easier by the fact that both her employers have not yet said that they need to approve her new supervisor. As an experienced practitioner they trust her judgement and have agreed to pay a proportion of her supervision costs without being involved with the selection of the supervisor.

Andrea faces a number of dilemmas in choosing a supervisor. Her employers are not making demands that need to influence her choice, yet the variety of her work settings, including her private practice and also the limitation on her travel time means that she needs to draw up a list of questions to be answered before the choice is made. These include:

- How many years' experience does the supervisor have?
- In what types of organisations has the supervisor worked both as a counsellor and a supervisor?
- What organisations does the supervisor have connections with currently?
- Does the supervisor have knowledge of how organisations work?
- Does the supervisor have experience of working as a counsellor using time-limited counselling?
- Has the supervisor had any training as a supervisor, especially for work in organisational settings?
- How does the supervisor describe the way they work?
- How far away does the supervisor practise geographically?

All counsellors will be familiar with the questioning process used when choosing a supervisor. Yet within the different organisational settings, Andrea will need to be aware that they could put different pressures on the supervisory relationship.

Selecting a supervisor for a health service setting

When counsellors working in health service settings choose their own supervisors, managers in that context are delegating the responsibility for that choice to the counsellor. This process is not without its difficulties for both the counsellor and the supervisor. Whether within a GP surgery or a hospital staff counselling service, a supervisor can find themselves without any lines of communication with their supervisee's line manager. When the work is progressing smoothly this will not be problematic; however, when a crisis of an organisational or ethical nature arises, it will be vital that communication links are established. For example, when a counsellor is not able to develop a working environment within the GP surgery or hospital which meets ethical standards (i.e. private and sound proof) it is important that the supervisor has access to the Practice Manager or Head of Department in order to add weight to the requirements voiced by the counsellor.

When engaged in research on this topic, some supervisors were opposed to any interference by the supervisor in organisational matters (Copeland 2000a). They advocated empowering the counsellor to speak for themself on this issue. If this can be achieved, this course of action is to be endorsed. However, if it is not successful then a counsellor is left with only one course of action, which is to leave that place of employment and seek work elsewhere. Therefore, when a supervisor agrees to work with a counsellor in a health service setting where line managers do not understand the nature of the supervisory process and where appropriate resources are not available, they will need to think through carefully the ways of managing the dilemmas that arise as discussed in Chapter 4.

Selecting a supervisor for an educational setting

The educational institutions that employ counsellors are varied. Further and higher education colleges often have counselling services, as do universities. Similarly, schools, especially secondary schools, employ counsellors on a sessional basis. Where there is a designated counselling service within an institution, especially in further and higher education, it is often managed by someone who is also a counsellor. When this happens they will often ask the counsellor about their supervisor's level of experience and training. They have enough knowledge about the counselling profession to be able to make these enquiries. Yet, despite this, common practice still dictates that they do not open up lines of communication with the supervisor. However, when schools are employing sessional counsellors, there may be no one who is familiar enough with the counselling and supervisory process to be able to make a comment on the counsellor's choice of supervisor. Therefore, the counsellor and supervisor need to work together to form a framework for good practice in this setting.

Selecting a supervisor for an industrial/commercial setting

In the case study above, Andrea did not work as a counsellor in a commercial setting but from my research (Copeland 2000a) it is evident that managers in such a setting would not, in general, be involved in the selection of a counsellor's supervisor. As in the example of a secondary school, the counsellor's line manager would be confident in the counsellor's selection of supervisor. Yet there are not many professions where an employer will pay a person to do a job yet not have any idea if that job is being undertaken competently. Managers who employ people who are in a different profession will trust the practitioner to know what they need in a fellow practitioner. In commercial settings this trust is necessary when multi-disciplinary teams work together. The same point can be made about counselling and supervisory work in health service settings. However, it is also at this selection stage that counsellors can experience resistance by employers to paying for the services of a supervisor. Employers will need a thorough understanding of the supervisor's function before an agreement to fund them is reached. Therefore, at this selection stage a counsellor will have to work hard in educating their manager about the supervision process.

Selecting a supervisor for a counselling agency

In the case study, Andrea did not work for a counselling agency but had she done so, she might not have been in the position of selecting her own supervisor. As we will see when addressing other ways of selecting a supervisor, when organisations are familiar with the counselling and supervisory process, it is possible that the organisation will have a pool of in-house or external supervisors from which to select. This will mean that the counsellor has very limited choice about who their supervisor will be. When this is embedded in the culture of the organisation, there will be an acceptance of this as 'custom and practice'. Nevertheless, it will not always suit every counsellor or supervisor. Free choice is necessary when a good working relationship is at the heart of the supervisory work. Therefore, it will be the responsibility of both counsellors, supervisors and line managers in counselling agencies to ensure that there is free choice of supervisor whenever possible. This may be an ideal; however, if supervision is to be effective for client, counsellor and the organisation, it is absolutely necessary.

Each organisational setting has its own needs in terms of supervisory arrangements. When a counsellor is expected to choose their own supervisor, they have a difficult task when balancing organisational needs and their own individual needs. The advantage of the counsellor choosing their own supervisor is that they know their own needs best and additionally, they are also aware of the needs of the organisation and its client group.

BEING INVITED BY AN ORGANISATION TO SUPERVISE A TEAM OF COUNSELLORS

When a counsellor is invited by an organisation to supervise a team of counsellors, there are many issues to be considered.

Julie has been asked to apply for the post of supervisor to a team of counsellors who work for a service industry in her local geographical area. There is no formal job or person specification but she was required to fill in an application form and have an informal interview over the phone. She now has to decide if she wants the job on the terms offered by the organisation.

In the above scenario, Julie was not surprised to be asked to apply for this post. She had always had a large network of colleagues and worked on a committee with the person who contacted her about the post. Although she was not entirely happy with the concept of gaining work through word of mouth, she was aware that at least she had engaged in a semi-formal selection process through completing the application form and carrying out the telephone interview. After this interview she was sent a contract of employment and now has to decide whether she will accept the post.

When making this decision Julie has to be aware of a number of factors that need to be taken into account. It is useful for her to ask the following questions:

- How often will this supervision take place?
- Where will it take place?
- Are the counsellors/welfare officers aware that a supervisor is being chosen for them?
- What are the rates of pay?
- Are there any reporting back procedures and if so what is the purpose of them?
- In what ways is the supervisor accountable to the organisation for their work?
- What sort of contract is the supervisor required to sign?

There is a formality about being invited to supervise this team of counsellors, and the questions outlined above give an indication of the areas of concern for the supervisor. Although the head of the service in this organisation is a counsellor and supervisor himself, there is still the need for the supervisor to be concerned about the level of responsibility required of them in this role. Having been in this position myself, I was unsure about a number of issues. Maintaining confidentiality whilst reporting back to the organisation was a major concern. As we can see in Chapter 9, reporting back to an organisation needs to be carefully managed so that confidentiality is not compromised. There is also an issue here concerning the management's selection of the supervisor. In this scenario the counsellors were not consulted about the organisation's choice of supervisor and could easily feel disenfranchised. Julie would need to work very hard to overcome the counsellors' initial reluctance and engage them in the supervisory process gradually. Additionally, if she takes the job, Julie needs to decide whether she can remain neutral when the counsellors complain about the organisation and vice versa.

Therefore, whilst being chosen as a supervisor by an organisation can initially be exciting, there are questions to be asked and areas of responsibility to clarify before the work can begin.

BEING INVITED TO TAKE ON THE ADDITIONAL ROLE OF SUPERVISOR

Kevin has been a paid counsellor within an NHS Trust for eight years. He was responsible for setting up the counselling service and inducting new counsellors as the service grew. Subsequently he was asked by his manager to supervise the other counsellors within the service and the manager agreed to pay for his training as a supervisor.

Being invited to take on the additional role of supervisor whilst also counselling in the same organisation is a common way of becoming a supervisor. It can often happen within counselling agencies where the manager is familiar with both counselling and supervisory processes. However, there are traps for the unwary when acquiring a supervisory role in this way. Being invited to take on this role, without having to face open competition for the post, can set up envy within a team of counsellors. There could be other counsellors who would also have liked the role. Therefore, Kevin will need to be aware of this dynamic when considering his position within the organisation. Also, before agreeing to take on this extra role, Kevin will need to be aware of the boundary issues that arise when supervising colleagues working in the same service. Although he will not have the dual role of supervisor and manager, nevertheless, there may be a tension between the public perception of a counsellor's competence within the service and the supervisor's actual knowledge of their practice. If dissonance occurs, it will provide the supervisor with a dilemma. Do they reveal this information to the supervisee's line manager or do they keep quiet and hope that the manager finds out for themselves?

Additionally, Kevin will be a member of the team and a colleague, whilst also responsible for ensuring that clients are safely held within an ethical framework. If clients are not safely held, he will have to manage the dynamics of working in a team where he needs to ask a colleague to stop practising for a time or even to engage in more training. Whilst this scenario is extreme, it will need to be considered as a possibility before the internal post can be accepted. Similarly, if a complaint is made about the counsellor within the organisation, Kevin will need to ask himself whether, as a counsellor and supervisor, he will be able to support the counsellor and the organisation equally.

So, Kevin will need to ask himself a number of questions in order to be prepared for any ethical dilemma that could arise from the dual role of counsellor and supervisor that he now holds within the organisation.

- How can I manage the boundaries between my role as a counsellor within the team and my role as a supervisor of the other counsellors?
- Will it be ethical for me to socialise with the other counsellors whilst also being their supervisor?
- What will I do if I think that my supervisee is unfit to practise and they do not agree to stop working for a while?
- How will these difficult decisions that I have to make affect my working relationship with other members of the team?

- Will I get too involved in the organisational issues that supervisees bring because those issues also involve me as an employee in the same organisation?
- Will my style and model of supervision be compatible with the counsellors' way of working?

Although taking on the additional role of supervisor whilst working as a counsellor in the same team will generate dilemmas, organisations will often choose their supervisors this way because it is a cheaper financial option. Alternatively, a counsellor will seek out the role because they want to train as a supervisor and need supervisees to fulfil the practical element of the course. This said, securing a supervisory post in this way and fulfilling a dual role within the organisation can be productive. However, all parties in the working alliance need to agree to the selection of that particular member of staff and all parties need to be prepared to work with the dilemmas that will inevitably arise.

A COUNSELLOR MAKING INTERNAL APPLICATION FOR THE POST OF SUPERVISOR

Carol has worked for a couples counselling agency for the last seven years. During that time she has gained experience in all aspects of the work including psychosexual counselling and has been supervised internally. The supervision post is now vacant. It will mean having responsibility for six individual supervisees. Carol intends to apply for this post.

When applying for this post, Carol needs to be aware that there may be other internal candidates. Therefore, she needs to decide how she will feel about still working for the organisation if she is not successful in her application. Will it affect her work as a counsellor within the organisation if she is supervised by a colleague who she does not consider to be as competent as her? Will she feel the need to move on to another organisation if she is not chosen? Carol will need to think carefully about these issues before applying for the internal role of supervisor.

If she is successful in getting the post, Carol will be in a similar position to Kevin in the case study above. She will have the dual role of counsellor and supervisor in the team. Unlike Kevin, she will also know that she has gained the post through open competition within the team. Nevertheless, she will still have to ask herself the same questions as Kevin in attempting to avoid the ethical and professional dilemmas that could occur. Before even applying for the post she will have the opportunity of asking herself the following questions:

- How will my dual role as counsellor and supervisor affect my working relationships with the rest of the counselling team?
- Where will I find my own supervision now that it is no longer available internally?
- What would I do if I found that a supervisee was unfit to practise, even for a short length of time, and they did not agree with my judgement?
- Would I be willing to report back to the managers of the service on the performance of my supervisees?

So, once again, a supervisor who is appointed internally will face dilemmas that arise from their in-house position within the organisation. They will benefit from understanding the organisation's culture through their own experience of it, but they will encounter dilemmas that arise from having a dual role within the organisation and also having to socialise with their colleagues.

APPLYING FOR AN ADVERTISED POST AS A SUPERVISOR

John is an experienced supervisor who has completed training to diploma level both as a counsellor and supervisor. He works across a wide geographical area in his counselling and supervisory work but is seeking to consolidate his hours so that he limits some of his travelling time. He sees a post for a supervisor in an NHS Trust advertised in a national newspaper and also in a professional journal. He feels that the job description and the person specification are well thought out and it is evident that the organisation wants the best person for the job.

The post consists of having to supervise two teams of counsellors plus individual supervision of all members of the teams. This work is to be carried out for one day a week. John is aware that there may be internal candidates applying for the post but he is confident that his training and experience match the organisation's requirements.

When applying for this post, John is, in effect, applying for a job that is being offered like any other post in any other profession. There is a job advert, a job description and person specification and he knows that there will be an interview for the right candidates (see Appendix 2 for a sample application form and Appendix 1 for a sample job advertisement). This organisation has thought this task through and is appointing in a professional way. Even though it is only a job for one day a week, the organisation has decided that it must be offered openly in order to attract the best possible person for the organisation's needs. Therefore, it would seem that John has no need to worry about educating the organisation concerning counselling supervision. However, as with any job application, John will need to think about the questions he will need to ask at interview in order to decide whether this job is really what it seems on paper. He will need to ask:

- What are my contractual obligations to the organisation?
- Who am I accountable to within the organisation?
- What are my responsibilities within the organisation?
- Are there any reporting back systems that I have to follow?
- What happens if one of my supervisees refuses to have me assigned to them as their supervisor?
- Where do the boundaries lie between individual and group supervision?

Therefore, when a supervisor applies for a post that is externally advertised there will be a need to ensure that they have a good understanding of the organisational context of the work. They will need to be familiar with the individual issues that arise in specific settings. If they have not counselled or supervised in that particular setting, they will need to be aware of the skills they have that can be transferred into any organisational setting. Additionally, they will need to be aware of the effect of organisational culture on the counselling and supervisory work as outlined in Chapter 3.

CONCLUSION

There are many ways of securing a position as a supervisor within an organisation. As discussed, the usual way is for the counsellor to choose their own supervisor. This will mean that the organisation pays for supervisory work without having any choice about who they employ. Nevertheless, as the understanding of the context of counselling grows, line managers will be more inclined to contract formally with the supervisor for their work. They will want to have the added value that a skilful supervisor can bring to the organisation, someone who understands the organisational culture and has knowledge and skills that will add value, enabling the organisation to grow and develop. Unless an organisation understands the strengths that the supervisor brings to the work, they will not be able to use them to their full capacity. Supervisors need to be employed on a formal basis so that organisations understand their full potential. As a result, each party in the working alliance will have their part to play and responsibilities to discharge within the organisation.

Responsibilities of the supervisee

- Working with their line manager to devise an advertisement, job description and person specification for the post

- Ensuring that their line manager understands the supervisory process and if necessary providing the line manager with a facts sheet on the supervisory process
- Ensuring that the line manager is aware of the rates of pay expected by supervisors
- Understanding what they want from their supervisor in terms of knowledge, experience, skills and personal qualities
- Ensuring that the supervisor has understanding of different organisational settings and their culture

Responsibilities of the supervisor

- Understanding the organisational culture of the work
- Understanding the contract nature of the work including their responsibility/accountability to the organisation
- Ensuring that they have a full understanding of the reporting procedures required by the organisation
- Managing boundaries between themselves, the supervisee, line manager and any other colleagues within the organisation
- Ensuring that ethical practice is maintained within the boundaries of the organisation
- Ensuring that consultative support is available for this work

Responsibilities of the line manager

- Advertising for a suitable supervisor
- Appointing an appropriate supervisor for the organisation
- Understanding the supervisory process
- Consulting with the supervisee about the appointment of a supervisor
- Communicating with the supervisor and supervisee over ethical and practical organisational issues whilst, at the same time, maintaining confidentiality
- Contracting with the supervisor for an annual or biannual report about the effectiveness of supervisory work

Chapter 6

Contracting for the supervisory work

> The supervisor and supervisee must consider their respective legal obligations to the employing organisation as part of the process of contracting in the initial stages of commencing work together. Where conflict arises between the demands of the organisation and the nature of the counsellor's work then the supervisor must make explicit their role and obligations.
>
> (Jenkins 2001:36)

INTRODUCTION

In the previous chapter the formal employment of the supervisor was discussed so that their knowledge and skills could be used to enable their supervisees to work more effectively with organisational dynamics. The next stage in the formal employment process is for an employment contract to be agreed.

Contractual agreements are part of most professional relationships (McCarthy et al. 1995) and there is an agreement that a contract is needed when supervisors are working in organisational contexts (Bond 1990, Proctor 1994, Page and Wosket 2001, Wiener et al. 2003). Indeed, Wiener et al. (2003:144) maintain that: 'it is obviously essential that the contract made between the supervisor and supervisee and the employing institution is carefully considered if boundaries and effective supervision are to be maintained.'

Yet a supervisor can be working for an organisation without a written or even a verbal contract. Given the nature of the work and the responsibility of the supervisory role, a contract is essential. Hawkins and Shohet (2000) also agree that in most supervisory situations there are other critical stakeholders in the supervisory contract besides the direct parties. Contracts can be complicated when two or more people are involved (Tudor 1997) and so contracts for a supervisor working within an organisational context need to include the supervisor, supervisee and also their line manager.

This chapter will discuss the nature of contracts in general, including the notion of a three-cornered contract with supervisor, supervisee and their employing organisation. Dilemmas in contracting will then be considered, including the most frequent dilemmas experienced by supervisors when working in organisational contexts. Formal and informal contracts will be explored, including the advantages and disadvantages to all parties in the working alliance. Finally, the contracting responsibilities of all parties in the working alliance will be outlined.

DEFINITION OF A CONTRACT

Sills (1997) carefully identifies three levels of contract that can exist in counselling: administrative, psychological and professional. In an organisational context it is the administrative and professional contract that outlines the roles and responsibilities of the supervisor and counsellor. This also needs to include the responsibilities of the line manager. The administrative part of the contract relates to venue, fees, timing and frequency of the supervisory sessions. If the supervisor is external to the organisation these details are often left to the counsellor to negotiate with the supervisor. The professional part of the contract defines the counselling and supervision work and how it will proceed. Sills (1997) takes Bordin's (1979) model of goals, tasks and bonds to explain the professional contract and this is a useful model to use in a three-cornered contract with counsellor, supervisor and the organisation. The goal is the shared outcome of the supervisory work. The tasks are the specific activities that the supervisor and the counsellor engage in whilst investigating the counselling work. The bond is the working alliance that is expressed in the respect for one another and the commitment to the shared activity. Similarly, Carroll's (1996) emphasis on the aspects of a contract which includes the practicalities, working alliance, presenting in supervision, evaluation of the work and the organisational setting in which it occurs, helps the supervisor to formulate a clear working agreement with the counsellor. Goals and tasks are included in the professional contract and can be of interest to the supervisor, counsellor and their line manager in the notion of a three-cornered contract.

THREE-CORNERED CONTRACTS

The concept of a three-cornered contract (Hewson 1999, Towler 1999) has been developed from Ekstein's (1964:138) model of a supervisor wearing a 'three-cornered hat' to explore the supervisor's relationship between the client, psychotherapist and the organisation. He envisaged an equilateral triangle with the supervisor in the centre of the triangle, making their position the point of gravity within the triangle, whilst connecting this point with all three corners of the triangle. The idea of the supervisor serving the interests

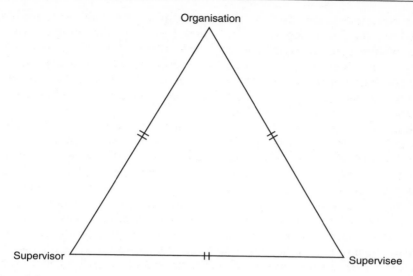

Figure 6.1

of all parties equally within this working relationship is clear. However Martin (2003), whilst applauding the concept of the clinical rhombus, sees its weakness in the assumption that the 'administration' (management) consists of one person and that they are indeed sane! Experience shows that in many organisations this is not so. Nevertheless, Hewson (1999:76) is clear that 'the equilateral triangle . . . is the ideal configuration, for in this there is equidistance between each party, showing a balance between the contract from the agency to the supervisor, from supervisory to supervisee and supervisee to agency.' Hewson's equilateral triangle is illustrated in Figure 6.1.

As with Ekstein (1964), Hewson (1999) sees that any imbalance in relationships can lead to either collusion between the organisation and the supervisor, or collusion by the supervisor and supervisee against the organisation. Therefore, carefully worded contracts for all parties in the working alliance are essential.

DILEMMAS IN CONTRACTING

Assumptions are made that all supervisors contract with their supervisee, either in written or oral form, yet often the organisation is not involved in the contract making process. Gray (1993) acknowledges that managers are afraid of the affective domain within organisations. They also assume that the counsellor will be the person best qualified to know what they need from a counselling supervisor and, additionally, who will be able to fulfil that role. Nevertheless, this does not abdicate managers from all responsibilities regarding the counselling work that is carried out under their auspices. However, within organisations managers can be in a 'no win' situation. They either have no involvement and are seen to be disinterested and lacking in any understanding of the supervisory process or, alternatively, they can be seen as too controlling when, without consultation, they appoint and allocate a supervisor to individual counsellors.

Research (Copeland 2000a) shows that in health, educational and commercial settings 37 per cent of supervisors have no contract at all with the organisation. However, within counselling agencies the percentage is much higher at 57 per cent. This indicates that line managers within counselling agencies understand the need for supervisors to have a contractual obligation for their work with their supervisees. In all settings verbal contracts were more common than written contracts. For 55 per cent of supervisors in this study their contracts were general but 14 per cent specifically addressed confidentiality and boundaries and 21 per cent addressed organisational issues. However, these results from postal questionnaires to supervisors, need to be read with caution, the response rate was low and the supervisors who did answer were clearly interested in the topic of supervision within organisational contexts as indicated by their replies to the open ended questions. These replies indicate that dilemmas presented to supervisors centred around:

- conflicts between manager and supervisee especially involving financial constraints
- the competence of the manager
- the manager's lack of understanding about the counselling process
- dual role systems within the organisation
- confidentiality issues
- client issues.

Identification of these issues testifies to the fact that if a contract with the organisation was in place for the supervisor, they would also have lines of communication in place. This would include three-way meetings to discuss such issues, safeguarding the interest of the clients whilst ensuring ethical practice.

Similarly, when experienced supervisors were interviewed for this study they all indicated that there was a need for them to have a contract with the organisation to help define their roles and responsibilities. However, only the supervisors employed by a counselling agency had any contract at all. This contract was formal and outlined conditions of service in terms of payment and what was needed from the supervisor in order to meet the organisation's requirements. In this respect it provided clarity. Despite this formal, written contract however, there was a feeling that when the organisation was in the process of change, reapplying for a current post as a supervisor felt threatening and undermining. For one supervisor, working in an educational setting, who had a verbal contract with the manager, the contract was not just about rights and responsibilities, but also about increasing the viability and competency of the service. Similarly, two other supervisors agreed that it was politic to insist that the supervisee's line manager gave the supervisor a contract. Indeed, the supervisors who did not have any contract with their supervisee's organisation would have liked one in order to:

- alert the organisation to the importance of counselling and supervision
- make it easier to complain about an incompetent counsellor
- negotiate appropriate remuneration
- clarify responsibilities.

Therefore, contracts are the key to a balanced clinical rhombus in which all parties take responsibility for their part in the working alliance. Contracts will give supervisors rights as an employee and the power to influence decisions that are made about their work. These contracts can be either formal or informal depending on the organisation and its management systems.

FORMAL CONTRACTS OF EMPLOYMENT

Formal contracts with organisations are uncommon (Copeland 2000a). However, as far back as 1997 Foster (1997:16) maintained that contracts were essential for supervisors working in primary health care. She outlined the main requirements for such a contract, over and above the usual details concerning fees, timing, etc., as being concerned with:

1 responsibility
2 performance
3 confidentiality
4 records.

This contract was essentially between the supervisor and the supervisee with no space for the supervisee's line manager to be part of the agreement.

Anecdotal evidence suggests that formal contracts can often leave supervisors feeling uncomfortable. If written in legal language, a contractual document can be ridiculed and assertions made that supervisors would not sign such a document or have anything to do with the organisation that produced it. So what is it that alienates supervisors from the very contracts of employment that they have as counsellors? Is it the legalistic jargon or the fact that they are asked to verify the supervisee's competence, either verbally or in written form, to the supervisee's line manager? Or is it that they feel slighted by the line manager's lack of trust in their supervisory role? Yet which employer in any other profession would pay an employee for work that they knew nothing about? We need to turn to the origins of counselling supervision for some of the answers to these questions.

Counselling supervision was not recognised in its own right until a decade ago. Before then it was undervalued and unnoticed, inextricably bound up with counselling but not separate from it. Currently though, supervision strives to be seen as a profession in its own right and therefore employers need to be sure that the supervisors they employ are contracted to do the work necessary to ensure that their counselling service is professional and ethical. Nevertheless, this role as 'gatekeeper' of standards in the counselling profession is not the sole responsibility of the supervisor. Both the supervisee and the manager have their part to play in the clinical rhombus.

Formal contracts are in evidence within counselling supervision, both in industrial/commercial settings and also within health service settings. Tehrani (1996) describes the contract that the Post Office (now the Royal Mail group) has developed with its supervisors and counsellors, setting out the goals and tasks expected of both parties. It acknowledges the need for confidentiality of the counsellor's own personal information but needs the supervisor to provide evidence that the counsellor is working to an acceptable level of competence. It also invites the supervisor to provide the line manager with any counselling training requirements and to inform them of any organisational issues that impact on the counselling work. Factual information is also needed from the supervisor about the number of cases brought, attendance at supervision sessions and any other information agreed by the counsellor. The supervisor is also required to have a personal liability insurance policy giving £1 million cover. This contract seeks to protect both counsellor and their clients and the interests of the supervisor and the organisation. Proctor (1997b) acknowledges that all supervisors will be familiar with the process of contract making with their supervisees that can include contextual issues. However, the Post Office contract, emanating from the organisation itself, could have the capacity to be more threatening than an informal contract and, therefore, not all supervisors would be disposed to sign it. Nevertheless, as the organisational context of supervision becomes more prominent, supervisors are aware of the need to be accountable to the organisation that pays them.

The disadvantages of formal contracts

When a supervisor, working in an organisational context, does have a formal contract with the organisation, they are clear about the extent of their responsibilities to the organisation and they are also clear about the responsibilities held by other parties in the working alliance (Copeland 2001). This clarity is important. However, the legal responsibilities of the supervisor are defined by their contractual responsibilities to another party, such as to the supervisee, or to an organisation (Jenkins 2001:28). For a contract to be legally binding it requires four conditions to apply:

1   the legal capacity of the person involved to be age 18 years or over
2   a firm offer and unequivocal acceptance
3   the clear intention of both parties to make a legally binding agreement
4   the contract is supported by 'consideration', i.e. an exchange of goods or services in return for payment.

If written, the contract needs to be signed and dated by both parties (Jenkins 2001). This type of formal contract is rarely in evidence when supervisors are working in organisational contexts and it is easy to see why from the employer's point of view. Whether or not they have thought through the implications of formally contracting with supervisors for their work within the organisation, the fact is that legal liability is defined by their formal employment status. This means that the organisation carries vicarious liability for the acts of its employees, which will include the supervisor. Therefore, if a formal, legally binding contract is to be made, an employer will need to be sure that the supervisor is a competent practitioner.

As discussed in Chapter 5, there needs to be a formal employment process that verifies the supervisor's level of training and experience necessary for the post. Without this process taking place it would seem reckless for an organisation to contract formally with a supervisor and so have vicarious liability for the supervisor's work without verifying their competence. Nevertheless, this verification process is not always easy in a young profession seeking to develop national standards of competence. As noted in future chapters, organisations such as BACP are accrediting supervisors and setting standards for competence practice within that process. Nevertheless, training courses are not subject to any accreditation processes to date. They are reliant on the validation processes within the training institution for maintaining high standards for the training of supervisors. Therefore, there are risks involved in organisations employing supervisors on a formal, contractual basis.

For the supervisor too, the costs of signing a formal contract may outweigh the benefits. If an employer has vicarious liability for their work then they will need to ensure that a reporting process is in operation to keep a check on that work. This could be an obstacle for the supervisor who needs to be ensuring that they keep the supervisee's material confidential. There are ways of complying with the reporting process whilst not breaking confidentiality. However, all parties in the working alliance, including the line manager, need to agree on a format that will ensure ethical practice along with effective communication within the organisation. If reporting systems are written into the contract without negotiation with the supervisor, the organisation will find that competent supervisors reject the work.

Theresa is a very experienced counsellor and supervisor. She was asked by a national organisation to supervise three of their counsellors in a particular geographical area. Initially, she was enthusiastic about the prospective work, especially as the organisation had a history of caring for its employees' welfare. However, when she was given a formal contract of employment to sign she found that she was required to give a sessional report to the supervisee's line manager, on the supervisee's work. The pro forma for the report was lacking in detail and there was no indication of how it was to be used by the line manager. Theresa was concerned that the report could compromise the supervisee's confidentiality concerning both themselves and their clients. She was also concerned that she was required to sign saying that she deemed the supervisee to be competent working with clients. Such a formal declaration left her directly open to complaint if the supervisee was found to be incompetent by the organisation. Therefore, reluctantly she decided to decline the work as the lack of clarity in the contractual agreement threatened her ethical standards and left her open to litigation by the organisation.

Nevertheless, with the current move towards awareness of the influence of the organisational context on the supervisory process, the likelihood of the above scenario being repeated is becoming less common. Ensuring ethical practice when the supervisory rhombus is in place does become more problematic as multiple boundaries are negotiated.

Formal, written contracts can be a liability to both organisation and supervisor, legally and professionally, if they are not managed carefully. However, the benefits of formal contracts can often outweigh the difficulties if they are worded and implemented prudently.

The advantages of formal contracts

Despite some pitfalls, formal supervisory contracts do exist and offer protection for the supervisor from exploitation by employers. Without some binding contractual agreement, a supervisor has no mechanism for negotiating a pay rise or for communicating their concerns about a supervisee's competence. It is similar to having a safety net 'just in case'. Every supervisor would like to feel that all employers are trustworthy, honest and reasonable but in reality, as many supervisors have readily said, the situation can be very different (Copeland 2000a). Negotiating for a pay rise can be especially problematic without a formal contract. Even within a formal contract there is a need for a statement to be made concerning the range of fees that are negotiable, but also for there to be an indication that the fee will be reviewed after a fixed period of time. This ensures that cost-of-living rises are possible for the supervisor, like any other employee within the organisation.

Similarly, formal contracts outline a supervisor's obligations towards the organisation. They know what they need to do and what will happen if they do not meet those obligations. Responsibilities are inherent in any role held within an organisation, yet the supervisory role is often misunderstood, as indicated in Chapter 2. A formal contract is a way of helping all parties to understand their responsibilities, and it needs to be accompanied by face-to-face discussions about its interpretation as, for instance, a reporting back procedure can be threatening until practical details are discussed.

> Keith began his work with Pat, his supervisee, who worked in an NHS setting, after she contacted him informally on her own behalf for supervision. During informal talks about payment, Pat indicated that her supervisor for the GP part of her work for the same NHS trust, had a formal contract with the organisation. On hearing this, Keith decided that this would be a good option for him too. Through Pat, a three-way meeting was arranged to discuss the proposed contract. As Pat's line manager already had experience of drawing up such contracts, discussion revolved around the issues of payment, reporting to the organisation, the responsibilities of all parties and the termination process. Face-to-face discussion enabled all parties to clarify the details in the contract so that there were no misunderstandings. It helped the process that Pat's line manager had a good understanding of the counselling and supervisory process and so was talking the same language as Pat and Keith. The whole process left Keith feeling confident that the contract protected the interests of all parties and gave him a line of communication with the organisation. He felt protected and respected.

In this scenario face-to-face discussions were essential for clarification of contractual details.

WHAT DOES A FORMAL CONTRACT LOOK LIKE?

Jenkins' (2001) four elements that make a legal contract were outlined earlier. However, contracts do not have to be written in legalistic language that can feel threatening. They can be clear, unambiguous and written in everyday language that is accessible and non-threatening. A formal contract will define the terms used in the document and will outline its duration. The responsibility of the supervisory role will be clear as will the professional standards encompassed in the role. There also needs to be clarity concerning the monitoring role played by the organisation in ensuring the supervisor's competence. The setting of fees and expenses will be an important part of the contract. Similarly, agreement concerning the limits of confidentiality within the supervisory work will be outlined together with the supervisor's need to have personal liability insurance. Finally, issues surrounding the termination of the contract and the signing of the final document will be addressed.

Defining your terms

A definition of the terms that are outlined in the contract is essential because, as noted earlier, the term 'supervisor' can have many definitions. Similarly, in some organisations the supervisee may have the title of counsellor within the organisation or they could be known by another title in the organisational structure. Therefore, if the definition of the terms is clear there will be less chance of misunderstanding when the contract is in use.

Duration

It is vital that the duration of the contract is stipulated so that the supervisor is certain when their work with the organisation begins and ends. Some contracts will indicate the date on which they expire and others will state the date on which they are due for renewal. Either way the security of such tight boundaries enables the supervisor to know how long the work will last, at least in the first instance.

Supervisor's responsibility

A supervisor's responsibility towards the organisation and their work within it, are outlined in detail in the contract. The contract will outline the tasks that the supervisor is expected to perform in return for the fee paid. First, this will mean that they need to work to a common definition outlined by a professional body responsible for counselling and supervision practice. This may be BACP or UKCP or the counselling section of the British Physiological Society. An organisation may choose to name a particular professional body in the contract or leave it open to enable flexibility in their employment of supervisors from varying theoretical perspectives. However, working to a professional definition of the role will enable organisations to know that the supervisors they employ are all conversant with the same definition.

Second, the organisation may want to stipulate that the supervisor works in a way that reflects the organisational context of their supervisee's work. For example, when a counsellor is working in a primary care trust, the trust may require the supervisor also to have some first-hand experience of working in such a setting. This will enable them to understand more fully the culture of the organisation and the issues of working with time-limited contracts. This puts the onus on the supervisor to consider the impact of the organisational context on both counsellor and client and, therefore, could also reveal the need for a careful verbal contract between supervisor, supervisee and the supervisee's line manager in order to maintain ethical practice. Any stipulation of this kind would also need a supervisor to have a high level of knowledge about the organisation's systems and cultures and their impact on the counselling work.

Third, the contract will need to stipulate that the standard of work performed by the supervisor is efficient, appropriate and satisfactory. For this point to have any validity there will need to be a manager within the organisation who can monitor the supervisory work and detect any deficiencies. Monitoring systems will also need to be in place to carry out this task. There is an indication in the next section of how this can be executed. For a supervisor this may be a new departure from the relative autonomy usually experienced in this role. They will be familiar with adhering to codes of ethics and practice but perhaps not so familiar with having their own practice scrutinised by an organisation. For this to be an amicable and developmental arrangement there needs to be a high degree of trust between the line manager, supervisor and supervisee, built up over time. The supervisor will need to be sure that the supervisee's line manager has a clear understanding of the supervisory process and that as a result, they are equiped to scrutinise the effectiveness and efficacy of the supervision work undertaken. Professional organisations such as BACP need to develop clear minimum standards for the work to help line managers in this task. Without such standards, line managers who are not counsellors and supervisors themselves will struggle to be effective in this monitoring process.

Fourth, for a contact to have any 'teeth' there needs to be the possibility of sanctions against the supervisor if any part of the contract is breached. So in this part of the contract the organisation may reserve the right to take action, after a period of time given for redress, if the services outlined are not provided adequately.

Finally, a contract may stipulate that the supervisor is responsible for reporting back to the organisation on the competency of the supervisee and additionally it might highlight any training needs. These are both contentious issues and will be discussed further in Chapter 9. However, responsibility must always be linked with accountability and in this instance the supervisor does have to be accountable for their supervisory work within the organisation.

Supervisor's standards

A supervisor's obligations, outlined above, cannot be monitored without knowing what standards are expected of them when carrying out the work. Therefore, an organisation needs to outline their criteria for the employment of a supervisor, clearly and without ambiguity. They will require the supervisor to be registered or accredited by their professional body and to have had some experience of working within an organisational context either as a counsellor or a supervisor. Similarly, if the organisation works specifically with time-limited counselling, the supervisor will be required either to be experienced at working in such or way or at least to be familiar with that type of work.

In this section of the contract supervisors will also be required to familiarise themselves with the precise role that their supervisee plays within the organisation. This is especially important if the supervisee has any dual role (e.g. nurse and counsellor, welfare officer and counsellor, etc.) in their job description. Where there is a dual role, there could be a strong possibility of ethical issues arising from blurred boundaries.

Ultimately, any employer has the right to monitor the standard of work produced by their employees and therefore, when a supervisor agrees to work within an organisational context they can expect to have their work scrutinised by the organisation in some way. This might be through the supervisee's evaluation of the supervisory process or it could be by the supervisor's 'self-reporting' to line management. If the expected monitoring process is written into the contract from the beginning of the work, they can choose actively to be subject to this evaluation, hence there are no surprises. Counselling services within organisations often enable their clients to evaluate the counselling received and therefore, it could be argued that supervision needs to be subject to a similar process. However, supervisors may feel that this process is unnecessary when the relationship between themselves and their supervisee is open and honest. But it can be argued that a manager within an organisation, who has little knowledge of the counselling process, will need this feedback from the counsellor in order to ensure supervision standards are met.

Monitoring the effectiveness of supervision

Counsellors working within an organisational context are open to scrutiny of their work through their employment contract and this is especially true in the health service where counsellors are subject to the auditing processes in place for all employees. It is reasonable to assume that supervisors will be similarly accountable for their work. The mechanisms by which this happens can be written into the formal contract. Supervisees can be required to evaluate their work with the supervisor or both parties may be required to write an annual report for the organisation. This could be open ended and free flowing, indicating the main concerns within the supervisory process and perhaps areas for development by both parties.

Alternatively, the areas for evaluation of the counsellor as a practitioner may be strictly indicated by the organisation in the form of an itemised report that is required either annually or biannually. For some supervisors a reporting back procedure may be welcomed as a way of formally acknowledging, to the organisation, the effective work achieved by the supervisee within that year. For others it will be seen as a symptom of a restrictive and distrusting organisational culture. Either way such a report will need to be written as a collaborative document, owned by both parties. This will be a demonstration of the good working relationship that exists between supervisor and the supervisee that is the lynch pin of the supervisory process as indicated in Chapter 8.

Fees and expenses

In any contract of employment there needs to be an agreement about the level of fees and expenses to be paid for services rendered, as well as an indication of when these fees will be reviewed. This is essential if supervisors are not to feel exploited by the organisation. It is important that this section of the contract is negotiated by both the supervisor and their line manager. This will provide a fair rate of pay for the responsibilities that the organisation requires of the supervisor. In many cases, however, counsellor and supervisor can be reluctant to discuss fees and a fair remuneration for services rendered. Nevertheless, if supervisors are to be accountable to the organisation for the quality of the supervisee's work, they need to be paid accordingly.

Confidentiality

This section of the contract is the lynch pin of ethical practice within the supervisory process. There have to be clear guidelines to indicate where the boundaries lie if confidentiality is to be maintained. This applies to all parties in the supervisory rhombus, so the supervisee's line manager will write themselves into this part of the contract. However, when organisations create supervisory contracts, outlining the boundaries of confidentiality, they inevitably only include the supervisor's responsibility to the supervisee and their client, omitting the line manager's part in this process. Boundaries are complicated when more than two people are involved in a therapeutic process, therefore it is vital that each boundary intersection has its own point in the contract clearly outlined. For example:

- supervisee and their line manager/professional manager
- supervisor and the supervisee's line manager
- supervisor and supervisee
- supervisor, supervisee and supervisee's line manager
- supervisor and their supervisor for their supervision work.

This will contribute to clarity when ethical dilemmas arise within the supervision work. For this process to be effective, the lines and means of communication need to be stated, and within this section there also needs to be an indication of compliance with the Data Protection Act (1998) and how this will be achieved.

Personal liability

It seems obvious that any contract for supervision work would include liability for personal injury or damage to property whilst supervising. This would mean that it is essential for a supervisor to have personal liability insurance. A counsellor working in private practice would already have this cover as a sensible precaution when working with clients at home.

Ending the contract (termination)

For both the supervisor and the organisation it is important that there is clear indication of the procedures to follow when the contract is to be terminated. This gives the organisation the right to terminate the supervisor's contract if their work is found to be unsatisfactory. It also gives the supervisor the right to terminate their contract if procedures are imposed by the organisation that compromise ethical practice or if they want to finish working with a particular supervisee. This provides a safety net for both supervisor and supervisee, whilst giving protection to the client ensuring that their counsellor is not left unsupervised. Therefore, in ending their contract, a supervisor can send a clear message to the organisation that they are unhappy with the processes and procedures that the organisation has put in place. Similarly, the organisation can terminate the supervisor's contract if their level of competence is unsatisfactory. However, this could leave the supervisee without a supervisor and so they would be in breach of their ethical code. Once again clear lines of communication are needed to put into operation this part of the contract.

Signing the contract

If contracts are to be formally binding then they need to be signed by both parties (Jenkins 2001), and it is important that this is carried out before the supervision work begins. However, it is also important that the contract has been read carefully before signing takes place to ensure that there are no potential ethical pitfalls buried within its legalistic framework. So, a supervisor needs to ask themselves, at each point of the contract, what will this mean for me in practice? Signing the contract before the work begins would be the ideal situation but sometimes it will not be practicable. A supervisee may need supervision quickly, especially when changing supervisors abruptly (see Chapter 11 on endings in supervision). Additionally, the supervision may need to be started before the content of the contract can be fully understood in a practical way. Although formal contracts can be daunting on first reading, they do provide a safeguard for the organisation and also for the supervisor and their supervisee. An example can be seen in Appendix 3.

INFORMAL CONTRACTS

Informal contracts are more common than formal contracts even when supervisors are working within organisational contexts (Copeland 2000a). As we have seen in Chapter 5, managers are often more than happy to let counsellors choose their own supervisors. This means that the normal contracting process between supervisor and supervisee is the only process by which lines of accountability and responsibility are delineated, often verbally but sometimes in written form (Copeland 2000a). Without access to the supervisee's line manager, a supervisor can only negotiate a two-way contract with the supervisee. Inskipp and Proctor (1995) and Proctor (1997b) usefully outline a working agreement for content and process that includes sharing information about the organisation/agency in which the client work is taking place. Hawkins and Shohet (2000:54) also outline the five key areas that should be covered in a contract, including:

- practicalities
- boundaries
- working alliance
- the session format
- the organisational and professional context.

They describe these key areas for negotiation in terms of two people working out how they propose to work together and it is useful to consult Hawkins and Shohet (2000) for more general details. These areas will be used below to highlight the organisational context in the negotiation process.

Practicalities

For Hawkins and Shohet (2000:54) the practicalities mean being clear about such arrangements as 'time, frequency, place, what might be allowed to interrupt or postpone the session, and clarification of any payment that is involved, etc.' However, many of these practicalities have implications for the organisation. For instance if counsellors are BACP members, there will be a minimum of one and a half hours a month of supervision, which is mandatory for counsellors. Some organisations may agree to pay for the counsellor to have more supervision if their case load is high. The supervisee will need to negotiate the *frequency* of supervision first with their line manager before discussing it with their supervisor. The question of frequency may be hard won or easily gained depending on whether the line manager is conversant with the supervisory process and its mandatory status, at least with BACP.

Similarly, agreements about the *place* where supervision is undertaken might not be open for negotiation. An organisation may want two or more supervisees to be worked with individually, but on their premises, so that no travel time is lost for their employees. If the supervisor agrees to this arrangement, there needs to be a room available that is suitable for confidential work. This could mean that a specific room has to be booked each month. Agreement also needs to be reached about what is allowed to *interrupt or postpone the session*. This will be influenced not only by how private the room is, but also by how important supervision is to the organisation. Some supervisees might be in control of their own diary so they can make sure that supervision is never cancelled when an emergency arises at work. However, for other supervisees this may not be the case. They might have to cancel supervision if for instance, they are needed to do a critical incident debriefing immediately.

Finally, payment will need to be negotiated with the organisation, either by the supervisee or the supervisor themselves. If the supervisee pays the supervisor and then claims back the money from their employer, this is less problematic than the supervisor having to invoice the organisation for services rendered.

Negotiation of the practicalities involved in the supervisory process will be much more complicated when the organisation is involved. The supervisee will need to clarify many practical details with their line manager before embarking on negotiating this part of the contract with their supervisor. In organisations where the line manager is also a counsellor, this process can be amicable and painless. However, where counselling services are embedded in a 'host' organisation, the supervisee will have to educate their line manager concerning the supervisory process before the practicalities can be agreed.

Boundaries

In any contract negotiating boundaries can involve many aspects of the supervisory process. At first glance Hawkins and Shohet's (2000) discussion of the boundary between supervision and therapy seems to have little to do with the organisational context of the work. It has more to do with the exploration of how the supervisee's personal issues impact on the counselling process. However, if those personal issues are seriously affecting the counselling work, the supervisor might need to help the supervisee to find ways of negotiating a break from work with their line manager. If the line manager understands the need for a counsellor to look after themselves, this break will be possible, however, with less management understanding more negotiation might be necessary.

When boundaries concerned with confidentiality are being negotiated, the organisation needs to be fully considered. Contractual arrangements regarding reporting back procedure and responsibilities will need to be outlined, preferably in writing, so that client confidentiality is not compromised (see Chapter 9 for details of communication patterns). Breaking client confidentiality has serious consequences for all parties in the working alliance and so the lines of communication need to be crystal clear. As Hawkins and Shohet (2000:55) state 'the supervisor should be clear what sort of information participants would need to take over the boundary of the relationship; in what circumstance; how they would do this; and to whom they would take the information.' This could necessitate the supervisor having information regarding contact points within the organisation.

Boundaries and especially confidentiality will be discussed in subsequent chapters, however, the possible complications arising from this process, especially when the organisational context is considered, cannot be overestimated.

The working alliance

Hawkins and Shohet (2000:56) maintain that 'a good working alliance is not built on a list of agreements or rules but on growing trust, respect and goodwill between both parties.' Trust, respect and goodwill are the lynch pin of the working alliance. However, if the supervisor is allocated to the supervisee by the organisation, the working alliance might take some time to become established. The supervisor has to be open and transparent about the organisational processes to which they adhere in order to earn the supervisee's trust. In some cases the relationship will never become as fully functional as it could have been if both parties had chosen each other freely. In my own experience, having been allocated to a group of supervisees within an organisation, with good will and openness from everyone, the relationship can build, over time, into one of trust and mutual respect. But contracting for what each party wants within this working alliance will necessarily include the supervisee's line manager. This can happen once the supervisor and supervisee have agreed how they want to work together; for example, what each would find helpful and unhelpful. Therefore, the working alliance is more complicated when organisational factors are taken into consideration.

Session format

This is also an area where the organisational context of the work is a factor. Decisions will need to be made on the amount of time necessary to spend on organisational issues as it is easy for these to squeeze out the client work. Perhaps it is impossible to agree upon a hard and fast ratio in the initial contract making session, but it is important to address the context of the work and the possible impact it might have on the supervisory process. It is at this stage that some supervisors may decide that the organisational context of the work is too problematic for them to embark on the supervisory work with this counsellor. It is better for this decision to be made in the contract making stages of the process rather than in the middle of any ongoing work. Additionally, the organisation might stipulate that all cases are to be brought to supervision. For an organisation, supervision can be seen as the only safeguard they have to ensure that their counsellors are working ethically and so their guidelines for supervisors may be highly structured.

The organisational and professional context

It is the emphasis on the importance of the organisational and professional context that makes Hawkins and Shohet's outline of the contents of an informal contract slightly different from other writers such as Page and Wosket (2001) and Carroll 1996. They acknowledge that 'in most supervisory situations there are other critical stakeholders in the supervisory contract besides the direct parties' (Hawkins and Shohet 2000:56).

They accept that some organisations will have their own explicit supervision policy where the organisational expectations of all parties in the working alliance are clarified. However, if this does not exist then they agree that the explicit expectations of the organisation need to be discussed. However, research (Copeland 2000a) has shown that within many organisations, where the provision of a counselling service is embedded in a 'host' organisation, there is little discussion with management about their expectations of the supervisor's role and few, if any, policies about supervision exist. Whilst writers such as Inskipp and Proctor (1995), Page and Wosket (2001), Hawkins and Shohet (2000), Carroll (1996) and Henderson (2001) advocate that supervisors have an active involvement with their supervisee's employing organisation, in a great majority of cases, this does not take place. Therefore, as essential as an informal contract is between supervisor and supervisee, without the organisation being involved, ethical dilemmas can occur for which there are no ready solutions.

CONCLUSION

It is evident that contractual arrangements, either written or verbal, between supervisor and supervisee are well documented but formal and informal contracts involving the organisation are less in evidence. However, contracting between the supervisor and the organisation, either in written form or orally, would enable responsibilities to be negotiated. This would safeguard everyone's rights within the tripartite relationship. But counsellors and supervisors would need to have negotiation skills and be robust enough to engage in this process. Nevertheless, this process is a vital one if supervision is to be seen by line managers as not just a ventilation exercise for counsellors, but an ethical necessity for the organisation. Additionally it would mean that the supervisor's responsibility within the organisation was clear.

Responsibilities of the supervisor

- Educating the supervisee and the line manager about the content of the formal supervisory contract with the organisation if all parties agree on a formal type of contract
- Negotiating the finer details of the formal contract with the supervisee's line manager
- Signing the formal contract and abiding by the details within it
- Negotiating the details of an informal contract if that is more acceptable to all parties
- Adhering to the contract of employment whether informal or formal

Responsibilities of the supervisee

- Educating their line manager about the type of contract needed by their supervisor
- Keeping themselves informed of the contract between their supervisor and the organisation
- Keeping the supervisor informed of any organisational issues that might affect either their own or their supervisor's working contract
- Adhering to their own contract of employment

Responsibilities of the line manager

- Understanding the nature of the supervisory contract needed by the supervisor
- Making decisions about the type of supervisory contract needed by the organisation
- Drawing up the supervisory contract
- Negotiating with the supervisor before finalising the contract
- Keeping all parties in the working alliance informed about the contracts
- Updating of the contract of employment on a regular basis

Relationships within the supervisory rhombus

We need to explain clearly and convincingly to NHS managers, GPs and others what supervision is and why it is so important.

(Curtis-Jenkins 2001:120)

INTRODUCTION

In the previous chapter contracts were discussed in relation to the supervisor's formal employment within the organisation. In this chapter the three-cornered working relationship between the supervisor, supervisee and their line manager will be addressed in relation to the various responsibilities and lines of communication needed for effective work. There will also be discussion of dual and triple roles that a supervisor could hold within the organisation and the ethical dilemmas that may occur as a result.

Good working relationships in any organisation are vital for productivity and a person's psychological health. However, within the counselling profession working relationships are usually between the counsellor/client(s) or counsellor(s)/supervisor. Traditionally, in most organisational contexts, they have not involved anyone else unless the counsellor is in training and the training institution employs the supervisor, or alternatively, the organisation is a counselling agency where relationships with the counsellor's line manager is the norm for a supervisor. Yet counselling supervision can no longer take place in a vacuum, ignoring the organisational context of the work. Supervisors have a responsibility to ensure that good practice is not only about the client work but also about giving the organisation feedback that enables them to make changes that benefit all parties in the working alliance, including the organisation.

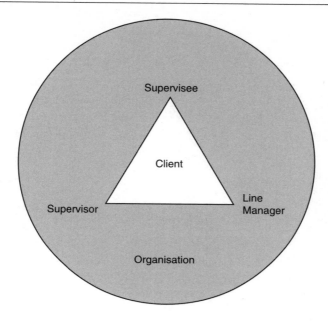

Figure 7.1

OUTLINING THE WORKING ALLIANCES

Good relationships within the working alliance in an organisation are vital. Yet the working alliance is larger than just the supervisor and their supervisee, it includes the supervisee's line manager and the organisational context of the work. Encompassed within this tripartite relationship is the client who is protected by this working alliance (Figure 7.1).

Within an organisational setting, there is a complicated set of relationships that can either enhance or harm the supervisory work with possible detrimental effects to the client. However, if the relationship between the supervisor and their supervisee is sound, this can be built upon in order to encompass the supervisee's line manager. It will then be possible for the supervisor and the supervisee's line manager to have a relationship that is trusted by the supervisee (Figure 7.2).

Yet, to some supervisors these relationships will sound complicated and there may be a risk of boundaries being transgressed. In such situations a supervisor may decide that this risk is too great and therefore they will not enter into any relationship with their supervisee's line manager (Figure 7.3).

In taking this course of action the supervisor is leaving the organisation vulnerable by not taking their responsibility towards the organisation seriously. When working as a supervisor, taking risks within an organisational setting is vital, in order to enhance the client work, support the supervisee

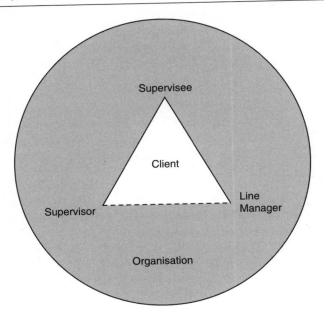

Figure 7.2

and provide an educative element for the supervisee's line manager. Therefore, it is useful to discuss the differing relationships within the working alliance in order to outline the issues that emerge and explore possible ways of managing them ethically.

THE RELATIONSHIP BETWEEN SUPERVISOR AND THEIR SUPERVISEE

A great deal has been written about the relationship between supervisor and their supervisee (Gilbert and Evans 2000, Holloway and Carroll 1999, Wiener et al. 2003, Lawton and Feltham 2000, Page and Wosket 2001, Hawkins and Shohet 2000, Carroll 1996, Holloway 1995, Inskipp and Proctor 1995). Among books, only Inskipp and Proctor, Carroll and Hawkins and Shohet in the second edition of their book expand, in any detail, to include in this relationship anyone else within the organisational setting in which the client work takes place. However, all the authors above agree that a sound working relationship is the bedrock of good supervision. Page and Wosket (2001:116) argue that if 'a sound collaborative relationship has been established between supervisor and counsellor, both can put their cards on the table and candidly explore any and all possibilities presented during the (kind of) investigative work.'

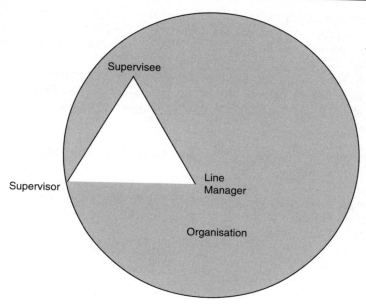

Figure 7.3

For example, one supervisee said:

> *'I want to tell you that I am sexually attracted to my client and I need to talk about this because it's the first time it's ever happened and I'm frightened. We both work in the same organisation and so there is a danger of me bumping into him and I am worried that we might engage in conversation and both of us be tempted to take our relationship further.'*

After the piece of work was completed satisfactorily she said:

> *'I would not have been able to be so honest if I had not had such a good relationship with you. You have known me for so long and you know all about my real need for a long-term relationship at the moment. I knew that this sexual attraction was something to do with that. I now feel confident to continue my work with this client, keeping boundaries firmly in place so that we do not meet "accidentally" within the building.'*

In the example above the supervisee was engaged in the restorative function of supervision that had brought the boundary between supervision and being a client very close (Inskipp and Proctor 1995). Nevertheless, the sharing of this knowledge had enabled the supervisor to work with her issue productively.

Although not all supervisors are as wide-ranging in their understanding of what is appropriate material for supervision, once a trusting relationship has been built, it will be possible for difficult material to be disclosed and discussed.

Webb (2000:64–65) also explores the issue of the supervisory relationship and which factors help or hinder the disclosure process in supervision. Her research found five factors that influence whether disclosure takes place. They are:

1   Individual versus group supervision. Disclosure is more likely to happen in individual supervision.
2   The impact of the supervisory alliance. Disclosure is more likely to happen when there is rapport between supervisor and supervisee.
3   The significance of trainee status. Disclosure was less likely to happen if the supervisee was a trainee.
4   The significance of the supervision setting. Disclosure was less likely to happen when the supervisor was external to the organisation rather than being an in-house supervisor.
5   The significance of being able to choose your own supervisor. Disclosure was more likely to happen if the supervisee had chosen their supervisor.

Within an organisational context there are factors that influence the supervisory relationship and will help or hinder the disclosure process, and therefore the effectiveness of the supervisory process.

Similarly, Wiener et al. (2003) see that the role of the supervisor is to facilitate the presentation of sensitive material in the supervision sessions, material that might include the presence or absence of anger, envy or aggression. Holloway views the dynamic supervisory relationship as the core of the work and says that

> Relationship is the dynamic element of supervision. The structure and character of the relationship embody the other factors and in turn all other factors are influenced by the relationship. . . . Understanding the relationship is understanding the process. . . . Each supervisor and supervisee brings to the relationship of supervision his or her own expectations of how the process will unfold. Some of these expectations will be the result of experience in being in supervision. Expectations will also come from other formal and informal relational experiences, and some will come from knowledge gained thorough anecdotal materials and literature. These past experiences will shape the process just as the process will contribute to the development of the relationship structure that will in turn influence uniquely the participants' engagement on the process.
>
> (Holloway 1995:41)

Therefore, the relationship in the supervisory dyad is extremely important and Holloway (1995) gives us a clue about the influences on its development. Another supervisee said:

> *'I feel so open with you. We can have a laugh and I can really be myself. I don't feel the need to censor anything I say and I look forward to our sessions as a place where I can off-load my worries and share my successes too. You help me to clarify the organisational issues, because they vary so much in all three different contexts. When I jump about you help me to anchor myself in one organisation at a time. Yet I don't feel put down or under pressure to come up with the answers. But I knew what I wanted when I came to you, my last supervisor was good for me as a trainee, but you challenge more but accept me as a person.'*

This example gives an illustration of the dynamic of the supervisory relationship and its importance in shaping the supervisory work.

However, when working in an organisational setting, as Webb (2000) asserts, one of the most important influences on the relationship is the freedom that either party had in choosing one another. The paths by which a supervisor comes to be working with any particular supervisee are discussed in Chapter 5, but the influence those paths have on the ensuing relationship can be profound.

When the organisation chooses the supervisor without consultation with the supervisee(s)

> *Emma is an experienced counsellor working in an NHS Trust in a GP surgery. In previous posts she has always been able to choose her own supervisor and has had good experiences so far. However, when starting her counselling post with the Trust she finds that she is expected to use Tom, the supervisor who has been appointed to supervise all the counsellors working for the trust across the county. In this position she feels angry that such an important decision has been taken away from her. She does not feel inclined to even begin to work with Tom, whilst feeling such anger and frustration. Therefore, she knows that their first meeting will be strained and holds out little hope for a good beginning to the working alliance.*

In a scenario like this a dynamic will be set up from the outset that could be detrimental to the working relationship between supervisee and supervisor. Emma is justified in feeling angry and frustrated when an important decision has been taken out of her hands. Therefore, at their first meeting Tom will need to enable her to express those strong feelings before a working alliance can be forged. Particular attention will need to be given to the contracting process so that Emma feels that there are real negotiations taking place. Tom will also need to be aware that Emma's feelings will not disappear overnight and that hard work will be necessary, over many sessions, in order for him to earn the right to be trusted.

In many organisations supervisors are appointed without consultation with the supervisee but this does not mean that the relationship will not work eventually. A skilled supervisor will need negotiation skills that encompass active listening and a willingness to be truly democratic. If this relationship eventually does not work, the supervisor will need to inform the organisation so that other arrangements can be made. This has to be the final outcome. If the supervisee does not actually think that this is possible, it will lead to a relationship that is not open and therefore, difficult client issues will not be brought and the client will be unprotected.

When the supervisee(s) are consulted, by their line manager in an organisation, about the kind of supervision that they want

Ewan is one of a group of counsellors working in a large, national organisation. They have been supervised by the same supervisor for many years and now that she has retired the organisation is ready to appoint someone new. Ewan's line manager consults with all the counsellors to try and get a consensus about the skills and qualities they need in the new supervisor. There is some agreement within the team of counsellors about what they need from a new supervisor, however, they are all aware that even though they have been consulted, the final decision about who is appointed will rest with their line manager.

When the new supervisor is appointed they need to be able to forge a relationship with each individual counsellor, seeing each with unique needs. This is stating the obvious, however it is harder to do in practice than when thinking about it in theoretical terms. Each relationship will be unique and the supervisor needs to be aware that every member of the team will have had different needs when being consulted about what they wanted from the new supervisor. Once again, as in the scenario with Emma, this supervisor will have been appointed by the line manager, albeit with consultation, and the supervisees will have no choice, they will have to be supervised in-house or pay for their own supervision externally. Therefore, the new supervisor will have to use the same negotiating skills as in the above scenario. The new supervisor will also hold collective information about the organisation and each counsellor's role within it. Therefore, they will need to contract carefully to ensure that information can only be disclosed and used by the organisation when it is appropriate. When counsellors have been consulted about their needs before the new appointment, they will be more disposed to forging a good working relationship.

When the supervisee's line manager is also their supervisor

Clare has just joined a counselling team within a voluntary agency. She was informed at her interview that the manager of the agency would also be her supervisor because of financial constraints within the organisation. In her previous post Clare had external supervision for her work and was hoping that she could continue with the same supervisor in her new post. Although she heard what was said at her interview about supervision arrangements, she hoped to change the situation on starting the job. However, this was harder to manage than she had envisaged.

In this scenario Clare knows that she needs to have access to an external supervisor if her line manager is going to be her in-house supervisor. She is aware that she does not want to alienate her new line manager; yet in order to practise ethically, she knows that the addition of external supervision is essential. Clare does not want to wait until there is a crisis in her work to address this issue with her line manager. In beginning their working relationship she will need to acknowledge her manager's difficulty in balancing the financial constraints with the ethical dilemma that a dual relationship role presents. The line manager may not be aware that the dual role presents any dilemmas. Therefore, she will need to discuss ways of splitting the supervision so that he is responsible for case management whilst an external supervisor works with the clinical part of the supervision process. It is not always ideal to split the organisational issues of the work off from the clinical work but this just might be a compromise that works for both the supervisee and their line manager. If Clare is to achieve a good working relationship with her line manager, this might be the best she can hope for initially.

Research does show (Copeland 2000a) that this particular dual role relationship can be problematic. Supervisors in this position noted that there was the potential for the power dynamic to affect the counselling work adversely. Initially, this was not apparent for some supervisees until the situation changed and the supervisor relinquished their line manager role for the single role of supervisor. The supervisees then found that they were free to address what was not being said when the dual role was in place. Even when the relationship between line manager and supervisee is good, the issue of the power held within the line manager role will hinder the supervision process.

In this position it is important that the supervisee is confident enough to insist on separate counselling supervision, whilst encouraging their line manager to be more creative when addressing the financial constraints.

When the supervisee chooses their own supervisor but they are paid by the organisation

Tony has been successful in being appointed as a full-time counsellor in a university student counselling service. The service has agreed to pay for his supervision and it is understood that he will retain the supervisor he worked with for the last two years in his previous post. His line manager will not have any communication with Tony's supervisor other than to process the claim for the predetermined payment of the supervision sessions.

In the scenario above Tony has already established a good working relationship with his supervisor and so his change of employment should not affect that working relationship. However, it will be useful for Tony to check out if his supervisor is comfortable with supervising this new organisational context for his work and the dilemmas that can arise within short-term work.

The relationship between supervisor and supervisee can be thwarted if the organisation has had too much control in choosing the supervisor or if the line manager also has the dual role of supervisor. In these two scenarios, it is more difficult to establish a working relationship easily and quickly for the safety of the client and the support of the supervisee. The least problematic scenario is when the supervisee can choose the supervisor with whom they have a good working relationship. However, if organisations consider the supervisor to be responsible for the client work, they do need to be sure that the supervisor has the relevant training and experience to undertake the work. This is especially true when supervisors are working with trainee counsellors within an organisation. Additionally, developing channels of communication with the supervisor will enable the organisation to feel more involved with both the client and the supervisory process.

It is vital for the protection of the client that the relationship between the supervisor and their supervisee is open, supportive and challenging. Developing this type of relationship successfully, however, will be dependent on how the supervisor was appointed and whether the supervisor has a dual role within the organisation. Once this relationship has been established, it is essential that the relationship between the supervisee and their line manager has similar qualities so that when ethical and professional dilemmas arise, they can work together to manage them within the organisation.

THE RELATIONSHIP BETWEEN THE SUPERVISEE AND THEIR LINE MANAGER

Within an organisational setting, the relationship between a counsellor and their line manager is often a source of friction, especially if the line manager is not a counsellor. This friction then emerges in the supervisory work. Copeland (2000a) found that supervisors had a strong sense of the way their supervisees' organisations viewed the counselling service and counselling supervision. Within NHS trusts, either within GP practices or staff counselling services within a hospital, supervisors found that inappropriate referrals were being made. Similarly, hospital management often did not fully understand the staff counselling service or what was needed to support that service. Within an industrial setting too, one supervisor found that sometimes, even within personnel departments, there was no clear understanding of the counselling process. This understanding was vital for counsellors to feel valued and understood rather than demeaned. It was also seen as vital if the supervision process was to be seen as part of ethical practice and paid for out of the departmental budget.

Within counselling agencies, where there might have been an expectation that managers would understand fully the counselling and supervisory process, supervisors did not find that this was necessarily so. Some trustees were not always equipped to make sensible decisions about which supervisors to employ and what supervision was all about. Although when line managers are also counsellors, it would be expected that they would have a full understanding of the supervisory process. However, it is possible for them to blur the boundaries when giving advice and support to the trainee within their organisation. A lack of understanding of the trainee's stage of development further compounds the difficulty. In cases such as these, the line manager is well meaning but misguided when they are not trained or experienced as a supervisor.

This lack of understanding around the counselling and supervisory process militates against good relationships between supervisee and their line manager. The manager will be battling to control resources allocated to the counselling service, whilst the counsellor will be trying to educate their manager about good practice and ethical requirements in the counselling profession. This educative process will mean that the counsellor has to learn how to speak the language of the organisation in order to act as an agent of change within it. For example, the counsellor will talk to their line manager about the organisation's duty of care towards its employees. They will explain that this includes the counsellor having supervision to enable them to discuss not only the clients in their care, but also their own case management and workload and their self-care regime. Managers will understand the language of litigation and its prevention.

For the supervisee and their line manager to have a good working relationship, there needs to be common understanding of the counselling and supervisory process. There also needs to be willingness on the part of both parties to listen and understand the position of the other, whilst maintaining their own professional integrity. When the relationship is one of mutual respect as professionals, there will be a good opportunity for the supervisor also to make constructive links with the supervisee's line manager.

THE RELATIONSHIP BETWEEN THE SUPERVISOR AND THE SUPERVISEE'S LINE MANAGER

At first glance the relationship between the supervisor and the supervisee's line manager seems an unlikely one and many supervisors will say that it is also one they do not welcome. Such a relationship could easily undermine the trust built up in the supervisory dyad. Yet it is a necessary and important relationship if the supervisor and the organisation are to take their responsibilities seriously. It needs to be welcomed by the supervisee. However, it is a relationship that rarely exists, especially in industrial, educational and health service settings. Within counselling agencies it is more likely to happen, especially if the supervisor has the dual role of supervisor, trainer or counsellor within the same agency. The model that does and can exist within some counselling agencies is that the supervisor, supervisee and their line manager sometimes have tripartite meetings to facilitate the sharing of information, whilst keeping confidentiality within the organisation itself. This means that the client work is held securely, whilst all parties in the working alliance have an opportunity to openly voice their concerns about the impact of the organisational culture on the counselling and supervisory work. This is the ideal scenario but it is not easily achieved in an organisation where the counselling service exists within a 'host' organisation. A counselling and supervisory culture may not sit easily within an organisation where there is a dominant, incompatible culture, as discussed in Chapter 3.

There needs to be a willingness on the part of the supervisee's line manager, the supervisor and the supervisee to acknowledge that there may be times when the supervisee will want the supervisor to talk to their line manager on their behalf. Research shows (Copeland 2000a) that this is not a common form of communication for supervisors, they prefer to empower the supervisee to talk to their line manager themselves. However, on a practical level this may not always be possible. If a supervisee is very stressed, they may want the supervisor to talk on their behalf or just to endorse the decision that they have both come to, for the supervisee to withdraw from client work for a while. This will be vital for the protection of the clients. Yet it could be left to the supervisor to instigate communication with the line manager, so long as the supervisee agrees to this course of action. In reality the line manager might welcome, or alternatively, be concerned about this type of communication, depending on how the supervisor was appointed (see Chapter 5). If the line manager was instrumental in making the appointment, this communication will be easily arranged. If the appointment is made by the supervisee, the supervisor will have to be proactive in requesting the meeting to discuss issues around the supervisory process. However, perhaps the most useful relationship will be the tripartite one between supervisor, supervisee and their line manager.

THE TRIPARTITE RELATIONSHIP BETWEEN SUPERVISOR, SUPERVISEE AND THEIR LINE MANAGER

The tripartite relationship between the supervisor, the supervisee and their line manager can be a fruitful one as discussed earlier. Three-cornered contracts were touched on earlier and an illustration is given from Hewson (1999), see Figure 6.1 in Chapter 6.

Any imbalance in the relationship within this supervisory rhombus could lead to collusion between two parties against the third party in the relationship. However, the existence of such a relationship within organisations is rare.

Within counselling agencies there are opportunities to set up communications systems, especially if all the parties work within the same building and are willing to talk on a regular basis. In larger organisations the supervisor may work in several centres and therefore any meetings will have to be agreed and planned in advance. Even when there is an agreement between all parties in the working alliance that regular communication is 'a good thing' the logistics of making space to talk in what can be a very busy working schedule can be difficult. There is a need to agree that communication is not only necessary but vital if there is a problem that needs discussion by all three parties.

Communication is necessary, and this applies especially within organisations where the supervisee's line manager is not familiar with the counselling and supervisory process. In such instances, there needs to be an agreement, at the contract stage of the relationship, as to how and in what circumstances a tripartite meeting would be necessary. It is important that the supervisor is instrumental in setting up these processes for their own protection, as well as that of the supervisee and their clients. A good, well thought out communication system will hold the client work securely rather than producing leaking boundaries where all parties are fearful of communicating at all in case confidentiality is breached. Nevertheless, it does mean that the line manager needs to be part of such a communications loop. In some organisations managers will expect supervisors to hold the ethical and professional boundaries of the client work, taking vicarious liability on behalf of the organisation, especially if they have a contract with that organisation (Jenkins 2001). If tripartite meetings are written into the contract as part of the working agreement, all parties will expect this type of communication to be the norm and they will be viewed in a positive way from the beginning of the work. Within training institutions contracts for this type of communication are more common, for the protection of the client, the organisation and the trainee.

THE RELATIONSHIP BETWEEN THE SUPERVISOR, TRAINEE COUNSELLOR, THEIR PLACEMENT AND THE TRAINING INSTITUTION

This four-fold relationship between the supervisor, trainee counsellor, their placement and the training institution is a complicated one. Clarity is needed between all parties to ensure that there is no doubt about the relationship each has with the other. If this is not clear, there will be issues that do not get dealt with by any party in the relationship that could lead to unethical practice being hidden. Ideally, all parties will meet on a regular basis to discuss their relationship with one another both individually and communally. However, whilst a trainee may have a good relationship with the line manager in their placement, their supervisor may have no relationship at all with the placement (Figure 7.4). The liaison between the two parties will be the training institution as seen in Figure 7.5. Therefore, there is a need for the training institution to instigate four-way meetings between themselves, the placement, the supervisor and the trainee to ensure that everyone in this working alliance understands their individual and collective responsibilities.

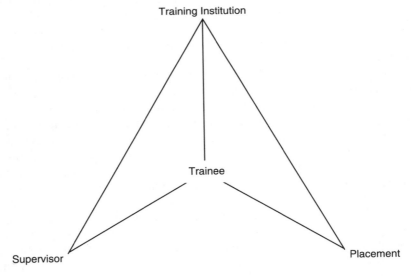

Figure 7.4

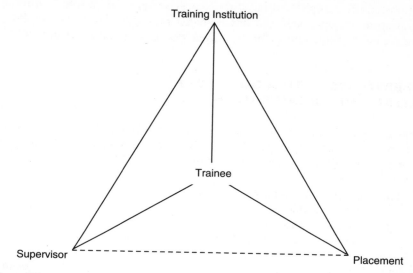

Figure 7.5

Conversely, the trainee will have a good relationship with their supervisor and also with the training institution but not with their line manager within the placement (Figure 7.6). Therefore, once again there is a need for a four-way meeting to resolve this issue. Communications within this four-way

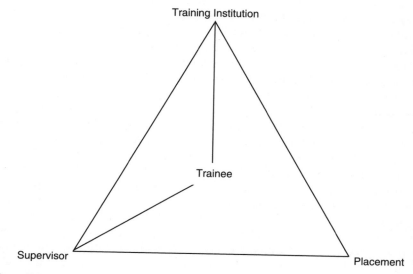

Figure 7.6

relationship are complicated but if the supervisor has a dual role within the organisation as supervisor and line manager or supervisor and counsellor, there are more opportunities for meeting to discuss issues that are difficult.

SUPERVISORS WITH A DUAL ROLE WITHIN THE ORGANISATION

In some organisational settings the supervisor, working in-house, will have a dual and sometimes triple role. Research has shown (Copeland 2000a) that within one organisation supervisors can be:

- supervisor and line manager
- supervisor and trainer
- supervisor and counsellor
- supervisor, trainer and counsellor.

Having such a position within the organisation, for some supervisors, meant that they shared a common knowledge with their supervisee about the culture and systems within the organisation, so enhancing the relationship and creating the power to make things happen. However, each of the dual or triple roles had specific advantages and disadvantages for the working relationship.

Supervisor and line manager

This is a particularly difficult dual role to hold within an organisation and one that has distinct ramifications for ethical practice. Research has shown (Copeland 2000a) that supervisors who held this dual role in a health service setting and in voluntary agencies felt that the constraints were, in the main, detrimental for the supervisory relationship. The power to 'hire and fire' meant that the supervisee was afraid of appearing incompetent when bringing difficult cases. Indeed, one supervisor who had experienced this dual role and subsequently the single role of supervisor with the same supervisees, was sure that they were 'no longer in the difficult position where I live, manage and supervise . . . no longer have to wear two hats, which was actually very, very, difficult'. With the single role as supervisor, this supervisor found it possible to be more true to themselves and go straight for what they considered to be the therapeutic concern. It enabled them to be clear about the therapeutic process rather than the management process. The power differential between manager and supervisee was the basis from which the difficulties arose for this supervisor. Subsequently the supervisees told the supervisor how much easier it felt to bring their difficulties without censoring themselves. For many organisations this dual role arises because of financial constraints and a lack of understanding about the nature of the supervisory relationship. However, if the line manager can stand firm and have the power to relinquish one or other of these roles, the supervisee will benefit in their relationship with their supervisor or their line manager.

Supervisor and trainer

Traditionally, within some counselling agencies and also in counselling training institutions, the dual role of supervisor and trainer is a common one. Research (Copeland 2000a) showed that for some supervisors there were advantages for the supervisory relationship. Supervisors working within a counselling agency could see the results of their training sessions when engaged in subsequent supervision sessions. Additionally, the role of educator was also seen, by some supervisors, as an argument for keeping this dual role. It was also seen as an advantage for supervisors and supervisees to see more of one another to 'provide a kind of bonding experience' within the relationship.

Within educational contexts in both British and American counselling training courses, supervision is an integral part of a tutor's role (Holloway 1995), but usually it is not the only supervision that a trainee counsellor receives. They will also have individual supervision for their work in their placement and can therefore take issues there, issues that may feel uncomfortable to bring to a tutor, who will also have an assessment role. Consequently, it is not surprising that tutors with this dual role, in this research, felt quite comfortable and actually saw it as a distinct advantage. It enabled them to 'have a greater knowledge of the students, to see all aspect of their work'. However, this research did not interview students, to see if it enhanced the working relationship for them to have more contact with a supervisor who was also one of their tutors. Supposition could be made that the relationship may be likened to that of supervisor and line manager. Nevertheless it cannot be disputed that the tutor/supervisor is more aware of the trainee's counselling practice when occupying this dual role. Therefore, it is up to them to build a working relationship that is open and conducive to both parties giving open and honest feedback to one another.

Supervisor and counsellor

The dual role of supervisor and counsellor within an organisational setting appears to have fewer disadvantages for the supervisory relationship. Here the supervisor will have knowledge of the client group that their supervisee is working with and they will both be working in the same organisational culture. However, they may, of necessity, share the same social space and come in contact with each other on a day-to-day basis. This means that there is the opportunity to get to know each other on a more personal level and establish good communication systems with each other and the management.

Alternatively, their close proximity could mean that boundaries are transgressed, boundaries that would not normally be a problem if they worked in separate organisational settings. For example, the supervisor could be allocated a client who had been previously working with her supervisee. This would mean that they had prior confidential information about the client that would not normally be available to them. Vigilance would be necessary if this scenario was to be avoided. Nevertheless, they would have a shared understanding of the organisational culture that would impact on their supervisory relationship. This would be helpful in understanding the impact of the organisational culture on the client material, or it could hinder the process in producing blind spots so that as an insider, the supervisor could not ask the idiot question that would enable the supervisee to see things more clearly. As ever, within the relationship, whatever organisational constraints are present, it is the supervisor and the supervisee who will need to have the will and the inclination to make this work for them.

Supervisor, trainer and counsellor

When the supervisor has a triple role within the organisational setting, the advantages and disadvantages of the dual roles discussed previously can be compounded. This triple role can often be found within counselling agencies and also in health service settings. However, the trainer role is often a small part of the work and is perhaps less intrusive upon the working relationship than the counsellor role. Nevertheless, it will mean that in their trainer role, the supervisor might be in the position of training their supervisee. Therefore, the same points will emerge as discussed earlier in the dual role of supervisor and trainer. A triple role can be managed and a good, working relationship between supervisor and supervisee maintained, but it will take hard work and an extra vigilance for both parties.

A dual or triple role for the supervisor can be managed and a productive relationship maintained within an organisational setting. However, both supervisor and supervisee will need to be aware of the possible ethical dilemmas that could arise if boundaries are crossed.

ORGANISATIONAL CULTURE AND RELATIONSHIPS

As we have seen in Chapter 3, organisational cultures are complex, paradoxical phenomena and can be understood in many different ways. The influence of such cultures on the supervisory relationship can either help or hinder its effectiveness. When both supervisor and supervisee are internal employees within an organisation, they will both be subject to the same cultural influences that could go unrecognised either within the client–counsellor or counsellor–supervisor relationship. Conversely, if the supervisor is external to the organisation, they will be able to ask questions about the way things are done in the organisation in order to tease out the cultural influences on the counselling and supervisory process. However, to be successful in this task, the supervisor and the supervisee will need to have an understanding of how organisational cultures are manifest, both overtly and covertly. Towler (1999:177) writes succinctly when he says 'Supervisors spend a considerable amount of time and energy helping supervisees field the impact of organisational culture. In this respect supervision might well be described as a "counter-cultural" activity.' Morgan (1986:127) describes this as 'cultural warfare' and in the following case study this is clearly so.

> Marion is the external supervisor to four counsellors who are working full time within a large commercial organisation. Over the years the organisation has been subject to many internal changes. Initially, the counsellors' line manager was also a counsellor and supervisor who understood the needs of the profession. He instigated on-going training for the counsellors and undertook to employ a supervisor who was well trained and experienced. Therefore, although the overall culture of the organisation was bureaucratic, the culture within the counselling service tended to be one of learning and development. However, this all changed when the line manager moved to another post and was replaced by a manager who was not a counsellor and did not subscribe to the learning and development ethos already in place. She changed the system so that much more of the counselling was done on the telephone and individual targets were set for the counsellor to see as many clients as possible in the shortest amount of time. These were published every month so that the counsellors were now in competition with one another to be top of the league table. So the learning and development culture disappeared and the counsellors became angry and unhappy. Marion, as their supervisor, was aware of the internal changes and knew that she would have to work hard to hold her supervisee's distress whilst ensuring that the client work was not curtailed unnecessarily. At times she despaired of ever being able to forge a relationship with the line manager in order to effect cultural change within the counselling department.

So, holding the tension between differing cultures in departments whilst also forging relationships that can influence the change process is a difficult task for both supervisee and supervisor. In the scenario above, where the culture is driven by results, the supervisees will need Marion to be supportive and yet also be prepared to have a meeting, jointly with themselves and their line manager so that the ethical issues can be discussed. These issues involve the inappropriate nature of targets for client numbers and the publication of those results. The line manager will need to understand the need for counsellors to work together and that the current system is divisive. So education is necessary in some organisational cultures where there is a wide gap between what happens in the organisation as custom and practice and the needs of the counselling service.

CONCLUSION

Relationships in organisations are complicated when supervisors and their supervisees step outside their supervisory dyad to encompass other employees. There could be a temptation to ignore the wider context of the work. However, to do so would mean that the opportunity for interaction between supervisor, supervisee and line manager would be lost. It would also mean that the influence of organisational culture on the client work would not be explored.

Responsibilities of the supervisor

- Developing a sound collaborative relationship with the supervisee
- Developing a clear line of communication with the supervisee's line manager
- Ensuring that, if they hold a dual role within the organisation, the boundaries of each role are kept when engaging with their supervisee
- Becoming an agent of change within the organisation

Responsibilities of the supervisee

- Developing a sound collaborative relationship with their supervisor
- Enabling the line manager and the supervisor to set up lines of communication

Responsibilities of the line manager

- Enabling the supervisee to choose their own supervisor or when this course of action is not possible, consult the supervisee on the kind of supervision they need
- Ensuring that they do not have a dual role of supervisor and line manager
- Organising regular tripartite meetings between themselves, the supervisee and their supervisor

Chapter 8

Doing the supervisory work

The supervisor is pulled in all directions – by counsellor, client and organisation. Good practice emerges in being able to hold the tension between them all.

(Towler 1999:198)

INTRODUCTION

In Chapter 7 the wider working alliance between the supervisor, supervisee and their line manager was discussed. This chapter will consider the direct working alliance between counsellor and supervisor, in relation to the heart of the supervisory process within the organisational context of the work. Wheeler (2000) maintains that there is a lack of clarity about the role and function of the supervision process. Clarity is needed to enable organisations to understand the nature of the work within the supervisory sessions. When engaging in the supervisory work, the supervisor will need to perform a number of functions and tasks. To engage in both functions and tasks, especially when working in a organisational context, supervisors and supervisees will need to have a competent level of skills and knowledge to manage the work effectively. They will also need an attitudinal way of thinking that embraces the complexities of working with organisational dynamics. So when both supervisor and supervisee have developed clarity about the way they work, the functions and tasks that need to be carried out and the skills they need to execute them, they will be a useful resource for the organisation. They will have the skills and attitudinal mindset to work with the dilemmas that the organisational culture produces in a challenging and exciting environment.

THE FUNCTIONS OF SUPERVISION

A function, as defined in the context of supervision, is an activity/ responsibility that belongs to the role of the supervisor. For example a *function* for the supervisor is that of *supporting* the supervisee in their counselling work. Many writers address the functions of supervision (Kadushin 1976, Inskipp and Proctor 1995, Holloway 1995, Hawkins and Shohet 2000) and overlap in their understanding of what they are about. Kadushin (1976, cited in Hawkins and Shohet 2000), writing about social work supervision, describes the three main functions as educative, supportive and managerial. Similarly, Inskipp and Proctor (1995) use the terms formative, restorative and normative to describe the functions of supervision. Holloway (1995) has a more expansive list that includes monitoring/evaluating, instructing/advising, modelling, supporting/sharing and consulting. However, all lists are sufficiently similar for there to be a common agreement about the functions of supervision. The instructing/advising and modelling functions from Holloway are the educative functions from Kadushin or the formative functions from Inskipp and Proctor. Likewise, Holloway's monitoring/evaluating and consulting functions are the managerial functions of Kadushin and the normative functions of Inskipp and Proctor. All writers agree that the supportive function is essential for supervisees who are affected by distress, pain and possible fragmentation of the client. However, when the supervision functions are conducted within an organisational context their scope needs to be expanded to include the effects of that context upon the therapeutic work between supervisee and client. For example if a supervisee is the sole counsellor working in a GP practice where there is a long waiting list, there might be a temptation to see six clients rather than five within each working day. Here a supervisor will need to support the supervisee in finding ways to manage the waiting list whilst also looking after their own psychological health and so avoiding burn-out.

Formative, educative or instructing/advising and modelling function

This function is concerned with a supervisee's skills, knowledge and understanding of their role as a counsellor, often within an organisational context. It is the supervisor's responsibility to ensure that first, their supervisee has the skills to work effectively with their clients. These will be the therapeutic skills that enable them to build and sustain a relationship with the client that helps them to change in a positive direction. If the supervisee is a trainee counsellor then this function will need to be at the forefront of the work. Nevertheless, even experienced counsellors will welcome working collaboratively to enhance their therapeutic skills. Essentially, in this function the focus will be on the client and Hawkins and Shohet outline the main points for exploration:

- Understand the client better
- Become more aware of their own reactions and responses to the client

- Understand the dynamics of how they and their clients were interacting
- Look at how they intervened and the consequences of their interventions
- Explore other ways of working with this and other similar client situations.

(Hawkins and Shohet 2000:50)

Didactic case discussion may, for some supervisory dyads, be the lynch pin of their work together. This function provides the opportunity to explore the efficacy of the therapeutic relationship and to find alternative interventions with present and future clients. However, when the therapeutic relationship is taking place within an organisational context, this function must include an understanding of the influence of that context on the client work.

> *Ann worked within a voluntary counselling agency as one of a team of coun-sellors who worked with women who had been sexually abused. As time went on she was increasingly aware that the agency was managed in a way that encouraged time boundaries with clients to be ignored. Clients were also encouraged to make themselves a coffee in the staff kitchen. This meant that Ann struggled to keep her own practice ethical when she might bump into her clients in the kitchen before her session.*

In the scenario above, Ann needed to discuss with her supervisor ways of keeping her own boundaries with her client, whilst not being punitive towards them. She decided that she would discuss her concerns with the agency manager, who was not a counsellor herself, and if there was no change then she must consider whether to leave the organisation. Alternatively, she could go on struggling to keep her own boundaries with her clients by having no contact with them outside the therapeutic hour even if they were in the building.

A counsellor also needs to understand their own position in the organisational structure when examining their own awareness of their reactions and responses to the client. If they are employed by the organisation directly, especially as a full-time counsellor, they too will be subject to the same cultural influences as the client.

> *Mary is a counsellor working full time in a large service organisation. She is supervised by Terry, who is paid by the organisation but external to it. Recently the organisation has been engaged in major internal structural changes that affect both Mary and her clients. Mary is feeling very vulnerable as she is required to reapply for her current post. She is counselling several clients who are also in the same position yet are also presenting with diverse*

personal problems too. When working with these clients she finds that she is drawn into their feelings of anger, frustration and impotency within the organisation and is seriously thinking of looking for another post elsewhere. Although she is trying very hard to remain detached, it is almost impossible for her to disengage from similar feelings about her position within the organisation and engage with the personal issues that her clients also bring.

In this scenario above Terry will need to be aware of Mary's situation within the organisation in order to enable them both to disentangle Mary's feelings from those of her client. When this has been achieved, they can explore more fully the dynamics of the therapeutic relationship and the interventions used in order to facilitate the growth of the client. If Terry had also been an in-house supervisor, subject to the same organisational change, it would have been very difficult for him to be detached from the dynamic engendered in the organisational culture.

Normative, managerial or monitoring, evaluating and consulting

This function is concerned with quality control in the supervisory work (Hawkins and Shohet 2000). There is an emphasis on the accountability and responsibility of the supervisee and the effects of the organisational context upon the client work. As Carroll (1996:49) maintains 'it is here that the supervisors become advocates of clients and of the counselling profession making sure that quality service is rendered and that the ethical and professional dimensions are maintained to a high level'.

Page and Wosket (2001:140) can also be seen to address this function in the *review* stage of their cyclical model of supervision. They see the review stage as 'ensuring that both supervisor and supervisee regularly reflect upon the quality of the supervisory relationship and the effectiveness of the work done in supervision.'

The words *assessment* and *evaluation* are used to emphasise the responsibility of the supervisor, either with trainee counsellors or to the profession, and these processes are discussed more fully in Chapter 10. Similarly, Holloway (1995) uses the word *evaluating* as a way of describing work with trainees. However, from both writers there is little direct reference to the supervisor's responsibility *vis-à-vis* the organisation once a counsellor has qualified. Yet if this function is about quality control, an organisation will have a vested interest in the supervisor's opinion of how the supervisee is fulfilling their role within the organisation.

Andy works as a supervisor for a large commercial organisation that employs two part-time counsellors for their large work force. As part of his contract with the organisation he is required to write an annual report on the counsellors' competence and future training needs. He is happy about this report as he writes it jointly with each supervisee and therefore, for the supervisees, it also provides an opportunity for their successes to be outlined and their training needs to be emphasised.

Research demonstrates that reports like those outlined above are more commonly required by counselling agencies than by commercial organisations (Copeland 2000a). Contracts are discussed more fully in Chapter 6.

Supportive or restorative function

This function is concerned with supporting the supervisee who is working with the pain and distress of clients often in organisational contexts that are dysfunctional and disabling. For Carroll (1996) this function provides the containment for supervisees as they find their own way to be effective as counsellors. Page and Wosket (2001:121) also use the word *containment* to describe part of the supervisory process. They maintain that

> the sense of security of the supervisor can provide a means of containment for the insecurities of the counsellor in relation to their counselling work. If the insecurities can be contained within supervision then this provides the supervisee with a safe place in which to experience and explore their doubts and anxieties, thereby, it is hoped, provide a route through and beyond those insecurities.

Page and Wosket (2001) also use the word *affirmation* in a similar way to that of Carroll (1996) and Inskipp and Proctor (1995) in that they see it as a restorative process that needs to be undertaken with seriousness and sincerity. Nevertheless, they do add that affirmation cannot be seen as an antidote to intolerable working conditions. In this way the managerial or monitoring function comes into play to ensure that long working hours or lack of appropriate resources are not tolerated, but that the supervisee is supported as they challenge the organisation to change these working conditions.

The functions embedded in the supervisory process are concerned with what needs to be done in the role of the supervisor and the tasks are about how the functions are carried out. It is to these that we must now turn.

THE TASKS OF SUPERVISION

A task, as defined in the context of supervision, is the behavioural side of the function/role, a definite piece of work expected of a supervisor when engaged in their role. For example, one *task* that a supervisor will engage in is to employ *counselling skills* when working with the supervisee. Many writers (Holloway 1995, Inskipp and Proctor 1995) have discussed the tasks of supervision. Holloway and Carroll (1999:47) have isolated seven general tasks of supervision as a result of research that was set up to elicit in what form the tasks existed and consequently to test them in reality. They are the

1   relationship task
2   teaching/learning task
3   counselling task
4   monitoring task (monitoring professional/ethical issues)
5   evaluation task
6   consultative task
7   administrative task.

Holloway (1995) also outlines the tasks in a similar way as:

1   counselling skill
2   case conceptualisation
3   professional role
4   emotional awareness
5   self-evaluation.

Other writers allude to the supervision tasks that are embedded in their models without actually naming the activities as a task. For example Page and Wosket (2001) talk about evaluation as one of the steps in the review stage of their model and in mode seven of the Hawkins and Shohet (2000) model, they allude to the evaluative task when they talk about the context of the supervisory work and its possible links with counsellor assessment.

Therefore, most writers agree about the general tasks of supervision but it is the more specific tasks within an organisational context that need addressing. Holloway and Carroll acknowledge the need for counsellors and their supervisors to:

hold in tension and in some relief polarities that emerge from the:

- Needs of the individual versus the needs of the organisation
- Values of counselling versus the values of business
- Role of counselling versus taking on other roles
- Need to look after individuals and the needs of groups.

(Holloway and Carroll 1999:143)

Carroll (1999:144) outlines eleven tasks specifically relating to supervising within organisations and I would like to expand on these in turn so that they can be clearly identified in practice and monitored by supervisor, supervisee and also their manager.

Generate clear contracts with all parties

Chapter 6 has already outlined the need for supervisors to have formal contracts with the organisation. The substance of this contract is also outlined. As discussed, an informal contract is better than no contract at all but a formal one will ensure that the supervision work is firmly on the organisation's agenda. Yet it is not the only contract that is needed when both the supervisee and their line manager are involved in the communication triangle. The supervisee will need a contract with the organisation and the supervisor and the manager will need to contract with the supervisor and the supervisee. So if all parties in the tripartite working alliance have a contract for their work, roles and responsibilities will be clarified. I am very often surprised when supervisory contracts are not in existence within organisations and it is often a crisis that prompts managers to feel they need to put one in place.

In their part of the contract it is important for the manager in the tripartite working alliance to ensure that:

- They endeavour to help both parties to maintain the counselling profession's ethical framework.
- They agree that the counsellor can choose their own supervisor within the parameters stipulated by the counselling profession for effective supervisory practice.
- They develop a policy on confidentiality within the counselling service which also prescribes the circumstances in which confidentiality can be broken.
- They require supervisors and counsellors to be accountable for their practice by writing a yearly joint report.

In organisations where the actual business is involved with offering a counselling service to the general public, the above guidelines may not be difficult for the manager to follow. However, if the counselling is in-house for the benefit of the employees, things might be very different. A manager will have to work within a culture where, for example, confidentiality might not be kept within the boundaries of two individuals but within the team as a whole. However, if they write a policy on confidentiality this could be accommodated but all parties would need to agree to it. Similarly, the purpose of writing a joint yearly report would need to be clear in terms of its remit and boundaries of confidentiality. It would be far too easy for it to be linked to any appraisal system if the guidelines for its use were not tight.

For a supervisee it is also important that they contract for their work within the organisation both with the supervisor and their line manager. They will need to work proactively with both their line manager and supervisor to identify and manage professional and ethical dilemmas that originate from organisational issues. Therefore, a supervisee will need to contract with the supervisor for these additional aspects of the supervision work outlined below, in addition to the usual contracting issues as summarised in Carroll (1995), Page and Wosket (2001) and Inskipp and Proctor (1995).

- The boundaries of what they write together in the report to the supervisee's line manager.
- The limits of confidentiality within their working relationship and the organisational parameters.
- How to manage emergencies that occur with the client work, i.e. is the supervisor or the line manager the first point of contact?
- Where the lines of responsibility and accountability lie between the supervisor, supervisee and the organisation and who holds ultimate responsibility for the client' welfare.
- Who is responsible for the payment of the supervisor.

The supervisee will also need to contract with their line manager for all of the above points that are raised with their supervisor.

It is important that all parties in the working alliance are aware of each other's contract so that information is shared and lines of communication are clear. This will mean that there are no surprises when ethical and professional dilemmas occur to which there appear to be no immediate answers.

Enable counsellors to work and live within organisations

When both counsellor and supervisor have a clear contract for their work within an organisational context the firm boundaries that are established by its existence will enable risks to be taken. If a counsellor is afraid to step outside of the counselling room for fear of breaking the confidentiality of the client, their role within the organisation will be severely restricted. They will not be able to publicise the service effectively and trust in the service will be harder to build. By being visible they will become the trusted public face of the service. Good counselling services, whether they are in-house, external or a counselling agency, exist because their public face, whether that is the manager or the counsellor, is known, trusted and understood.

> Sylvia is one of five counsellors for a big retail outlet in the UK. She has been
> with the company for seven years and serves a large geographical 'patch'. Her
> counselling sessions are held in the store where the client is based and when
> she enters the premises she is greeted on all floors by people she has worked

with over many years. She stops and speaks to those who greet her and it is clear that the trust in her levels of confidentiality are high. People update her on their current situation and want to tell her of their progress. However, she is careful to only engage in such a conversation if there is privacy, having respect for the person's confidentiality. She is able to walk this fine line between showing her public and private face because she has built up the trust in her ability to keep a client's confidentiality and yet still be human.

In the case study above Sylvia is sure of her ability to hold the boundaries of confidentially within the organisation and yet still be visible and known within the organisation. Her supervisor is confident in her ability to be gregarious within the organisation and yet still hold the boundaries needed for ethical practice. However, within the organisation she has a single role as a counsellor and does not want any involvement in the politics of the organisation on any level. She works with the client individually, not organisationally. She does not seek to explore organisational transference or the influence of management style upon the client's welfare. In closing her eyes to these possible aspects of the work she ignores the influence of the organisation and its culture on her client's welfare. However, this does make the work less complicated.

When a counsellor or supervisor has a dual or even treble role within the organisation living and working within the organisation becomes more complicated (see Chapter 7) and the need for clear contracts more vital. Dual relationships within organisations are not uncommon (Shea and Bond 1997) and Holloway (1995) maintains that dual relationships are one of the most problematic ethical issues facing supervisors within organisations. Research (Copeland 2000a) shows that dual roles are common in counselling agencies where a counsellor can also be a manager and a supervisor can also be a trainer, manager or counsellor. Similarly, in other organisational contexts counsellors can also hold the role of a nurse, a personnel officer or an administrator. In cases such as these, supervisors were adamant that they needed to help the counsellor be clear about which hat they had on at any one time. One supervisor acknowledged that the real dilemma was 'how to run the two roles together and deal with confidentiality'.

Another supervisor who was working with a supervisee who had a dual role as a nurse and counsellor within the organisation recognised that the power dynamic seemed to creep into all the client work. The counselling clients also sought her advice as a nurse and it was sometimes tempting to weave both of her roles together. Therefore, when a counsellor has a dual role within the organisation, supervisors need to recognise and manage dilemmas originating from:

1   the difficulty of keeping confidentiality; and
2   the power dynamic that could adversely effect the client work.

They must strive to enable the counsellor to maintain clarity in their dealings with employees.

Help counsellors to control the flow of information

Supervisors have a complex task to perform when working with counsellors in organisational settings as we have noted in the previous section. But counsellors who have to manage a service will need a supervisor to have a different set of skills in order to help them manage the flow of information within that organisation. All counselling services, whether in-house or external to the organisation, will need to evaluate their service in order to justify the cost of the service. Therefore, there will need to be an ethical release of information into that organisation. Once again contracts come into play, enabling the counsellor and supervisor to know where the boundaries lie around the release of any information.

> *Jeff is a staff counsellor in a large NHS Trust. He works across two hospitals and over his three years in post he has built up a high level of trust both with his clients and also with the hospital managers in many departments. He has been asked by personnel to co-facilitate a stress management workshop for staff members of one department who have requested this service. He is aware that he has already counselled four members of that department on a one-to-one basis and is about to start work with a fifth person. One member of staff has kept their counselling a secret from the other members of the department whilst the others have openly acknowledged that they see Jeff. Jeff is also aware that the management of the department is the cause of many problems presented by the clients.*

Delivering a stress management course to all departmental members could possibly present the following opportunities:

- for all members of the department to openly acknowledge their involvement with Jeff
- for everyone to discuss their unhappiness with their working environment and the management of the department
- for decisions to be made about how they might feed this information back to management.

If these opportunities were realised, through skilful facilitation by Jeff and the personnel officer, it could mean that the staff had the potential to change their stressful working environment by sharing information and feeding their concerns back to management. Jeff would no longer be holding on to individual information, gained through the counselling process, which could benefit the whole team if it were disclosed and consequently acted upon by senior management. However, this potential opportunity does also pose a threat. Jeff must tread a fine line between facilitating the process of group discussion concerning the stressful working environment and maintaining each individual's confidentiality concerning their disclosures in the counselling room. It is not an easy task. There is the threat of:

- the breaking of individual confidentiality inadvertently
- not being able to balance individual relationships (both known and unknown to the group) so disrupting group dynamics
- changing relationships back in the counselling room as a result of being seen in a training role during the course
- being seen as more powerful in the training role than in the counselling role and so raising expectations of the influence that could be brought to bear on management.

A supervisor can work towards helping the counsellor to discuss these opportunities and threats before entering into a training role within the organisation.

Help counsellors manage the counselling provision

Within organisations counsellors can find themselves managing the service, a role, in some instances, they might be ill equipped to undertake. Therefore, it will be the supervisor who needs the specialised skills and knowledge to help the counsellor with the managerial tasks.

Louise began her counselling career working with people who had eating disorders. She had a special interest in this work because she had been the main carer for her mother who was disabled by her weight. As she gained more experience in the field she decided to set up a special agency for eating disorders. She then found herself managing a service that grew rapidly. She employed several sessional counsellors and soon found that she needed managerial supervision from her existing supervisor. She was finding it difficult to manage the boundaries between her friendship with the sessional counsellors and the need to manage the service effectively. This meant refusing a pay rise when the funding was in jeopardy and being firm about time keeping when a counsellor constantly arrived late for her sessions. Her supervisor, who had been a manager in an educational institution before becoming a counsellor, was able to work through these issues with her. Eventually she was able to grow into her managerial role and accept the necessary loss of her colleagues as her friends.

In this scenario it was important that Louise's supervisor had the necessary experience to work productively on these managerial issues with her. In some instances it may be necessary for managerial and clinical supervision to be provided by separate supervisors if one supervisor does not have the necessary skills and knowledge for managerial supervision. Some organisations see that this separation is productive. However, it could lead to splitting which would be counter-productive for the supervisee, client and also the service.

When managing a service, there may also be a need to manage the work of any trainee counsellors who are given a placement within the organisation. Contracts with the training organisation and the trainee's supervisor will need to be managed carefully and supervision for this work will need a clarity of thought and an insight into multiple boundary issues, especially if all organisations are sited within a restricted geographical area. Supervisors may feel that some training is needed in order for them to have the specialist knowledge and skills to clarify any ethical dilemma that could arise in such a management situation.

Work with counsellors at the interface between the individual and the organisation

Chapter 3 explored organisational culture and what it means to employees. The culture of counselling and supervision relating to how it might clash with prevalent cultures within organisations has also been examined. Here the supervisor's role is vital in enabling the counsellor to recognise the difference between the different cultures and to find ways of working with the organisational culture that enhances rather than depletes the therapeutic work. Carroll (1999) argues that it is an advantage if the supervisor is external to the organisation so that they can help the counsellor gain the distance they need to make decisions about how to work at the interface between the client and the organisation. Many of the supervisors in my research (Copeland 2000a) agreed with this position. They maintained that it allowed them to ask 'the idiot question' about ways of working within the organisation that were taken for granted by employees, including, at times, the counsellors.

Marie was the group supervisor to four counsellors working in a voluntary counselling agency. It had been custom and practice for the manager of the service to sit in on the group supervision as an observer with the previous supervisor. Marie was not happy about this as she was given the impression that the line manager was not trusted. She decided to ask the 'idiot question' – 'why does this have to happen?' The reply was that it had always been like that since the service began five years ago. When talking to the line manager Marie found that she did not enjoy the observer role and would rather stay out of the sessions but did not want to seem unsupportive to the supervisor.

Therefore, custom and practice was changed and the supervision sessions were more effective because of a greater trust built within the group.

Also in the research, supervisors indicated that having no line management responsibility was seen as a great advantage. However, they agreed that as an external supervisor they had to listen more carefully because of the lack of background information on the organisation. The disadvantages for working externally as a supervisor were few, however, they agreed that there was a need to gain some knowledge about the organisational context of their supervisee's work. Sometimes this knowledge is accumulated over time, through experience working in different roles within an organisation during a supervisor's previous professional life. At other times the knowledge is gained by reading about organisational culture. The supervisee can also be asked questions to elicit the relevant information. For example, the supervisor might ask their supervisee about the management structure of the organisation. They might also ask how the counselling service is viewed by managers. It will also be useful to know how the service is resourced and what priority is given to the supervision process and to the continuing professional development of all employees. In this way the supervisor will gain knowledge about the shadow side of the organisation (Egan 1994) as well as the overt cultural norms within the organisation.

Joy is a supervisor working with a group of four counsellors who work in the same department within their commercial organisation. She was appointed directly by the organisation and has contact with the counsellors' line manager through annual reports written jointly by her and the group. Through case discussions she has become aware that the group is subject to the same organisational culture as its clients. That culture is unstable and abusive. After discussion with Joy the counsellors agree that they can talk to their line manager about their own experience of the organisation's abuse without having to break client confidentiality when they raise the issue.

In this scenario the supervisor's task is made easier by the fact that this is group supervision and therefore, cases are shared. The supervisor can ensure that the influence of the organisational culture can be teased out from the joint sharing of their client work. Once recognised, the counsellors can work collectively to address the issue with their line manager. However, in cases such as these, the organisation needs to be able to respond positively and make changes to such a culture. This will not always be a swift process, if indeed it happens at all. Nevertheless, the counsellors and their supervisor will have discharged their responsibility and worked at the interface between the counselling service and the organisation.

Help counsellors look after themselves as they work within the organisation

As we have seen earlier, one of the functions of a supervisor is to support the counsellor when working in an environment that may be hostile to, or uneducated about, the culture of counselling and supervision. Increasingly, counsellors are being asked to fulfil a work schedule that is aimed at cutting waiting lists and giving a service for the least possible cost (Copeland 2000a). Therefore, to keep their job in an increasingly competitive market, some counsellors may be tempted to agree to working in 30-minute sessions or to take on more clients in a day than is recommended by their professional body. They may also be asked to complete other tasks of a managerial nature that are not strictly part of their role. For example, in a voluntary counselling agency, where funding is tight, counsellors might be asked to engage in fund-raising activities. Yet to remain psychologically healthy a counsellor will need the support of their supervisor to resist these pressures. If they are newly qualified, they may be eager to please their new employers or to prove to themselves that they can do the job effectively and efficiently, but at a cost to their physical and psychological health.

> *Karen is a newly qualified counsellor who had been successful in gaining employment as a sessional counsellor in three very different organisations. She worked very hard to please the managers in all three organisations. However, six months into her work, her supervisor noticed that she was feeling tired and 'down'. Together they established that Karen was working over 20 client hours a week. In the counselling agency she was working with more clients than her contract stated because the service was inundated with clients who were in crisis and needed to be seen urgently. Similarly, the same scenario was happening in the GP practice where she was the sole counsellor desperately trying to keep the waiting list down.*

In the scenario above Karen and her supervisor worked together to find out why her work had increased. In both organisations Karen was not only trying to prove to her managers that she could do the job but she was also concerned about the time the clients had to wait before they could see a counsellor. Having established this fact, they discussed ways of managing a waiting list system in the counselling agency. In the GP surgery they established that the doctors needed to be re-educated about appropriate referrals and that they also needed to know just how heavily the service was being used in the hope that another counsellor could be employed. Therefore, the supervisor needed to be supportive as Karen talked to the doctors and also made changes to her working schedule within the counselling agency. That support was vital, especially in the GP surgery, as Karen worked alone and could not bounce ideas off anyone else. If she had worked within a team of counsellors, she might have had the support she needed within that team.

Where appropriate, work with a team of employee counsellors

Carroll (1999) acknowledges that where counsellors work in a team and are supervised together, there are tasks to be undertaken, besides the individual client work, which will enhance their effectiveness within the organisation. The supervisor will need to concentrate on the team and their individual dynamic plus the team within the organisation and finally, their relationship with the supervisor. I agree with Carroll when he says that the supervisor will also need some understanding of group and inter-group processes. From my own experience of supervising a group within an organisation, it is easier if the group are supervised together, so all information is shared and there are no secrets within the supervision session. Yet I have found that if a team of counsellors are supervised individually, there may be information divulged by one person that could benefit the whole team. For example, if one of the counsellors is working productively with the client and their manager over a harassment issue, the whole team could benefit from the sharing of that information. So the supervisor might encourage the counsellor to share, but keeping the client's identity confidential. However, if one counsellor divulges information about another counsellor in the team, this could present the supervisor with an ethical dilemma. They will have information concerning unethical practice by another of their supervisees. If the supervisee in question does not tell the supervisor, the information must remain secret. It is a difficult situation for a supervisor.

Therefore, when working individually with a team, within an organisation, it is important for the supervisor to outline the boundaries surrounding their work together so that the above scenario is avoided. Supervision of a whole team together will give far more potential for change within the organisation if, united, they present an issue to their line manager as seen by the scenario outlined above. However, individual, rather than team supervision, may be preferred if there are deep splits and rivalries within the team. Yet paradoxically, those splits and rivalries may be healed if the team dares to be supervised together by a supervisor who has experience in working with groups. Supervising a whole team takes courage and determination to succeed on the part of the supervisor and the team. It also needs time to establish a relationship especially if the supervisor has been chosen *for* the team by their line manager. For a fuller discussion of group and team supervision in general consult Proctor (2000) and Lammers (1999).

Facilitate counsellors in the management of records, statistics, reports and the communication of these to the organisation

As Carroll reports, counsellors working in organisational contexts will need to keep statistical records of the work they do in order either to justify the money spent on the service or to make a case for grant aid for the agency. There is an assumption that the counsellors may not have the required skills for this task and that the supervisor will be able to help. However, as counselling services become more prevalent within organisations, counsellors are aware, even when training, that they may be required to produce such information. The supervisor's task, therefore, is to help them to remain ethical when information is being disclosed.

> Celia is a counsellor in a GP practice and is managed by the head of the consortium of counsellors. The team of counsellors, working across GP surgeries in the county, meets once a month to share dilemmas. At one meeting the head of the consortium says that they will all need to audit one another's case notes to make sure that everyone is writing them correctly in line with the trust's guidelines on the writing of notes. He indicates that all health workers in the trust will be subject to the same auditing procedures. Celia is not happy about this process as she is aware that some of the counsellors do not hide the identity of their clients and additionally, the manager has indicated to her that he will swap his notes with hers. However, Celia does not want to be the only one to object to this internal action within the team. She decides to take the issue to her supervisor.

In the scenario above Celia is right to feel uncomfortable with the internal auditing of one another's case notes. If the identity of the client is available on the notes, there will be a breaking of confidentiality. Additionally, there could be competition in the group of counsellors concerning record-keeping techniques, or some may have a fear of getting it wrong. Auditing of case notes is becoming increasingly the norm, especially within a health service setting. The need for counsellors to be accountable to an organisation, like any other employee, can be balanced by systems that enable confidentiality to be kept and individual rivalry discussed. Once again, the supervisor's external perspective on the process is vital as they are not subject to the same team dynamics as the counsellors.

Work with counsellors to understand and manage the parallel process within the organisation

Carroll asserts that parallel process means that one part of the organisation will reflect what is happening in another. All supervisors will be familiar with parallel process in supervision, a process where unconscious material, which has its origins in the relationship between client and counsellor, imposes itself on the relationship between supervisee and supervisor. Most supervisors welcome such parallel phenomena as the resulting dynamics provide a more direct way of experiencing the counselling process than second-hand reporting by the counsellor. Indeed, the parallel process can also work in reverse where the supervisory dynamics are reflected in the counselling relationship (Hawkins and Shohet 2000, Page and Wosket 2001). Yet Jacobs (1996) warns against parallel process becoming a mantra and being found in nearly every supervision session. Despite this, however, Carroll (1999:151) asserts that the parallel process is worked out when 'workplace counsellors will do to their supervisor what the organisation has done to them. Effective supervisors will pick this up and work with it rather than take it personally or blame the counsellor.'

> Kate is a counsellor working in a large national company where she has worked for the last 25 years, only latterly fulfilling a counsellor role. In supervision with David she explores the issue of 11 clients from the same call centre coming to see her because of their stress levels at work. They maintain that the organisation will not listen to their concerns regarding their working conditions and all feel that they will go off on sick leave very soon. Working for the same organisation, Kate is very aware that the culture within the centre is abusive and that there is a high attrition of staff. She expresses the wish to go and talk to the clients' line manager (she has the permission from all of them) to 'make him listen and see sense'.
>
> Within the supervisory session, David explores the advantages and disadvantages of this action with her and finds that he is being heard less and less. She said 'you haven't said I can't do it, so I will!' It seems that Kate is determined to pursue a course of action that will lead to her being abused as her clients had been. Therefore, it was not until the parallel process was uncovered and the precipitous action was averted that Kate understood what influence the organisation was having upon the supervisory process.

In this case study both Kate's and David's experience of working in organisations was vital in stopping the destructive spiral. Kate was then able to work on ways in which she could support her clients whilst they found other employment. Thus the influence of organisational culture is pervasive and can go unnoticed if a supervisor is not vigilant. However, it takes time for a supervisor to gain knowledge of the cultural influences on the client work in order to identify parallel processes. They must first know how the supervisee works before they can identify unusual behaviour patterns in the supervisee's presentation of their work.

Help counsellors build working models for understanding counselling within organisations

Carroll (1999) is clear that a 'purist' approach to counselling may not be the best way to work in an organisational context where the client's needs and also the needs of the organisation may not fit into traditional patterns for delivery of the service. Carroll (1996:122) outlines a model showing the relationships between counsellor, client and the organisation. Similarly, Towler (1999:182) outlines his model of the 'three-cornered contract' where the provider of supervision is external to the organisation. Models like these are useful in helping the counsellor and supervisor to conceptualise their relationship with the organisation. Indeed, as Page and Wosket explain, a model of supervision

> articulates both what is going on and also how it is done. It embraces both methodology and objectives, and enables practitioners to locate themselves in the process by mapping out the terrain or territory. An effective model is clearly understandable and can be readily put into practice and adapted to the demands of the situation and the needs of its users.
>
> (Page and Wosket 2001:30)

The model of supervision within organisations that I am presenting can be applied to all types of organisation and adapted both to in-house and external supervision. It is important to recognise the different dynamics embedded in each supervisory position, while also recognising the similarities that belong to all supervision work in a variety of settings:

- securing the supervisory position
- contracting for the supervisory work
- engaging in the supervisory process
- making relationships work within the organisation
- reporting back to the organisation
- evaluating, assessing and accrediting the supervisory work
- Terminating the work and making new beginnings.

The organisation and its culture encompass this process, influencing the counselling and supervision work and its culture. Therefore, there is a need to embrace and understand the processes that are involved in beginning, engaging in and ending the supervision work within different organisational contexts. If the beginning processes are loose, this will influence the efficacy of the subsequent work and similarly, if there are no policies or procedures for working within the organisation, clients and their counsellors will be cast adrift in a culture of anarchy. A model of supervision in organisations needs to be adaptable to very diverse settings and types of counsellors, but most of all it needs to encompass the needs of all parties in the working alliance, including those of the supervisee's line manager. Supervisors working with this model need to believe that they can be effective in helping counsellors to live and work at the interface between themselves and the organisation whilst still maintaining ethical practice.

Evaluate, with counsellors, how counselling can be a vehicle for understanding and facilitating organisational change and transition

Carroll is aware here of the need for counsellors and supervisors to begin to think differently in order to act differently. He outlines the mindset changes needed from:

- Individual thinking to organisational thinking
- Individual assessment to assessment in context
- Interpersonal relationships to systems relations
- Uni-role involvement to multi-role involvement
- A counsellor to being a counselling consultant
- Setting up counselling to integrating counselling into the workplace

(Carroll 1999:153)

Supervisors in my research study endorsed this (Copeland 2000a), indicating that their role, whether in-house or external, was to educate or act as an agent of change within the organisation. One supervisor was sure that most organisations did not know what they were buying when they started a counselling service. However, another maintained that the supervisor was in a position to say things that others could not say and they could have a different perspective from the one espoused by the organisation. Yet the supervisor was still working through the supervisee to effect change within the organisation rather than working directly with the supervisee's line manager. Therefore, the supervisor's position as educator and agent of change for the organisation is one that could make sense when:

- The organisation has little understanding of the counselling and supervisory process.
- The organisation was open to the change process and actively sought feedback from the counsellor and supervisor.
- The supervisor has a flexible approach to the supervisory process.

Therefore, it is important that the supervisor is aware of the functions and tasks involved in the supervisory role, especially when it is embedded within an organisational setting. However, to engage in the functions and tasks of supervision successfully within this organisational setting, both supervisor and supervisee will also need a competent level of skills to manage the process effectively.

SKILLS

Carroll (2001) maintains that the skills of organisational counsellors include the ability to hold in tension and in some relief polarities that emerge from

- the needs of the individual versus the needs of the organisation
- the values of counselling versus the values of business
- the role of counselling versus taking on other roles
- the need to look after individuals and the needs of groups.

In an organisational context a supervisee needs to develop other skills that will enable them to communicate and work effectively with their line manager and colleagues in a multi-disciplinary team. If they are to be a fully functioning member of a team within an organisation they will need to engage in

- negotiating
- asserting themselves
- mediating
- managing group dynamics
- mentoring
- coaching.

Some counsellors will already have these skills that have been transferred from previous work situations. Others will need to acquire them, perhaps through the supervision process. Other counsellors may state that these skills are unnecessary for their role as engaging in dialogue with colleagues concerning their work would endanger the confidentiality of their clients.

However, even if counsellors have the extra skills to work within the organisational context there is also a need for them to have an attitudinal mindset that sees the organisation as an exciting place to work.

Rachel is the first staff counsellor to be employed in a large commercial organisation. Over the first three years of her work she has built up a busy practice mainly by word of mouth. However, she has always known that her role could be as an agent of change within the organisation and so over the next year she strives to make herself known within each department so that all employees, including managers, are aware of her role. She was a personnel officer in her previous working life and so she understands how organisations function and can identify organisational culture clearly. With this knowledge she has an enthusiasm for the change process. She is also aware that in her role as counsellor she has knowledge about the effectiveness of organisational systems that could be useful to the organisation. Therefore, she already has the mindset and the skills that will enable her to seek opportunities to negotiate and mediate on behalf of her clients to effect change within the organisation. This will not be an easy task. However, she will be energised and challenged by the work.

In the case study above, Rachel is well placed to influence organisational change. However, she will need to work closely with her supervisor to ensure that she remains ethical in all her dealings with managers within the organisation.

CONCLUSION

When engaging in the supervisory process within an organisational context, the tasks, functions and skills take on an extra dimension that, in effect, appears to make the process more complicated. The work in the supervisory dyad needs to encompass the organisation with all its complexities. The tasks and functions that are explored in many texts on supervision are expanded to include the organisational dimension, especially the organisational culture and the part the supervisee's line manager plays within that culture. Supervisors are encouraged to explore these extra dimensions with their supervisee to enhance the work both for the client and subsequently the organisation. New skills will be needed for this work to be successful, skills that could have been acquired in another work role or skills that need to be learnt as the supervisor's role expands alongside the counsellor's role. With the expanded role for both counsellor and client come new responsibilities.

Responsibilities of the supervisee

- Expanding their attitudinal mindset to include the organisational dimension of their work
- Acquiring the extra skills that will enable them to work more effectively within the organisational setting
- Maintaining ethical practice, whilst communicating more widely within interdisciplinary teams

Responsibilities of the supervisor

- Ensuring that the tasks and functions of the supervisory process include the expanded organisational context of the work

- Acquiring the skills needed to work more effectively within the organisational setting
- Ensuring that they understand organisational culture and its possible impact on the counselling process

Responsibilities of the line manager

- Listening to feedback from both counsellor and supervisor
- Acting on that feedback to the best of their ability
- Being open to the educative process in order to learn more about the counselling and supervision process

Reporting back to the organisation

> Supervisors who have an agreed contract with the organisation and do not report incompetent practices identified in counsellors during supervision, may find themselves legally responsible for the effects of the counsellor's incompetence on the employee's psychological well-being.
>
> (Tehrani 1996:271)

INTRODUCTION

Chapter 8 discussed the importance of the supervisory relationship and the need to establish trust and openness was seen as essential. This type of relationship is doubly important when organisations require supervisors to report back on the work in progress. Accountability within the counselling profession has increased dramatically within the last decade. Counsellors working within organisational settings are often required to provide statistical information for their line managers. This means that there is a need for them to account for the efficacy of the service, so justifying to the accountants the money spent. Similarly, supervisors are finding themselves in the position of having to account, to the organisation, for their work with their supervisee. This can often feel threatening for both parties in the working alliance. As noted in Chapter 5, supervisors find employment within organisational contexts in a variety of ways, either formally or informally.

If they have been employed formally through applying for a job advertisement and then through the open interview process they will know what to expect in terms of their accountability to the organisation. They will have been well acquainted with policies and procedures and so able to make an informed decision about whether they accept the post. However, if the supervisor has been employed informally, through their supervisee, they may be unaware of the reporting procedures that are evolving within the organisation, to improve accountability for all employees. This may produce ethical and professional dilemmas that will need to be addressed with both the supervisee and their line manager. (Some organisations split operational line management from professional line management in cases where the operational line manager is not a member of the counselling profession. In cases such as these the professional line manager will be the person who liaises with the supervisor. The professional line manager then liaises with the operational line manager. Needless to say this means that communication systems are more complicated than when this split does not occur.) As supervisors engage in training for their work, awareness grows of the need to be ethical, yet accountable, both to the organisation and to the counselling profession for the work that they do.

In this chapter the purpose of the supervisory report will be discussed, what information is needed within it and how that can be communicated to management.

THE PURPOSE OF A SUPERVISOR'S REPORT TO THE ORGANISATION

When considering whether to engage in a reporting back process with their supervisee's organisation, it is important for the supervisor to be clear about the purpose of the report. External supervisors who have been employed directly by the organisation may find that the organisation sees supervision as one of the few safeguards they have from litigation (Tehrani 1996). Therefore, they will be expected to take some responsibility for reporting on the competence of the counsellor and also to have oversight of the well-being of the employees using the service. In employing a supervisor to carry out such tasks, the organisation needs to be sure that the supervisor is competent. Tehrani (1996) asserts that despite the fact that counselling supervision is an obligatory professional requirement as defined by BACP, the standards of competency for supervisors to undertake supervisory work are not clear. This also applies to the standards for supervision work set by the BPS. This means that organisations that employ counselling supervisors are in a difficult position. They will need to safeguard the ethical practice of both counsellors and supervisors. This makes a report essential within the supervisory process. Yet I have talked with supervisors who have been asked to provide a report for their supervisee's organisation without any indication of how the report would be used. This leaves the supervisor and their supervisee with a dilemma, how much of their practice do they reveal?

Hilary is a counsellor within a college of further education. Her case load is well above the recommended level for the hours that she works. However, when writing the supervisory report together, she was reluctant to include the information about her case load being too high. She was new to the organisation and did not think that her line manager would understand. He was not a counsellor and there was a culture of over-work within the college. Hilary was afraid that the information would be used against her in some way.

In this scenario it is essential for Hilary's supervisor to know how the report will be used. She needs to be sure that it will not form part of the organisation's appraisal process, or used to withhold salary increases that are linked to productivity. Indeed, clarification about the purpose of any report requested is essential to avoid any misunderstandings between supervisee and their line manager. Conflict between these two parties over many issues was a relatively common dilemma reported by supervisors (Copeland 2000a). Line managers were seen to be unsupportive by 35 per cent of respondents in this survey of supervisors. This was especially prevalent in industry, health and educational settings. When interviewed, supervisors also noted that even within counselling agencies, managers did not always have an understanding of the counselling and supervisory process and therefore, given this information, supervisors need to be careful when reporting back to such organisations. The opportunities for misunderstanding are legion. However, a supervisor's report for a trainee counsellor to their training organisation is common practice and this aspect of reporting back will be addressed more fully in Chapter 10.

Therefore, the purpose of the supervisor's report is to provide information about:

- the statistical data on regularity of supervision sessions and the type of issues discussed
- the therapeutic effectiveness of the counsellor
- the administrative effectiveness of the counsellor
- the counsellor's ethical/professional practice
- the constraining influences of organisational culture on the therapeutic work
- the counsellor's effective use of supervision
- the training needs of the counsellor.

Some or all of these purposes will be useful information for the organisation. They can be used to enhance the counsellor's professional effectiveness in their role. Additionally, they can be used to enable the organisation to make changes that will be beneficial to their employees' psychological health. However, to remain ethical, the supervisor and counsellor will need to be clear about the type and extent of information divulged. Each of these purposes will be explored in the next section in order to elicit the extent of the information that can be given in each category whilst still keeping the appropriate client work and organisational issues confidential. It is useful to first explore the relevance of naming the report appropriately.

NAMING THE REPORT

When instigating a reporting procedure within an organisation the relevance of the name of the report needs to be discussed as this can carry hidden messages both to the writer(s) and also to the recipients. Therefore, it is useful to consider a number of titles for the report and the subsequent messages they will give.

Supervisor's report

In naming the report the supervisor's report it will be assumed that the supervisor has written it and so has ownership of it. This will give the message to the supervisee and also the organisation that the report, even when it is jointly signed by both parties, is the supervisor's professional opinion about the supervisee's competence and fitness to practise within the organisation. Therefore, the organisation will need to think carefully about the purpose of the report before giving it this title.

Joint supervisor and supervisee report

By using the word 'joint' report there is an indication that this will be written in a collaborative way between both the parties and so will contain joint opinions about their work together. This will mean that the organisation is aware that the report is written jointly and is an amalgamation of both their perspectives on the effectiveness of the supervisory process. When giving this name to the report, the organisation will be signalling their wish that the information is about the process and effectiveness of the supervisory work rather than solely concerned with supervisee competence.

Personal and professional development report

Naming the report a personal and professional development report means that the organisation is ensuring that the counsellor is growing and developing through their work within the organisation. This sounds supportive and will mean that any training needs highlighted by the report will need to be addressed by the organisation. It may not mean that the organisation gains information about their responsibilities to ethical practice with clients. However, if the counsellor is accredited by BACP, it may be duplicating the annual work done to gain re-accreditation.

Professional summary report

When the report is entitled a professional summary report it indicates that the organisation needs to be aware of the counsellor's professional practice. It will need to outline the efficacy of the counselling work and their ability to use supervision effectively. With such a title, it might mean that some organisational issues are ignored, e.g. the difficulty of working: for a low salary, on a split site, with poor working conditions, with a hostile organisational culture, with no time set aside for administration, and so on.

Professional appraisal report

When the word 'appraisal' appears in the title of a report it can be very misleading for counsellors and supervisors. In Chapter 2 the appraisal process and its link to a management function was discussed and therefore does not sit easily with the counselling supervisory process. However, in some organisational contexts, where the supervisor has a dual role as supervisor/manager, this title for the report could be apt. It would mean that the supervisor was reporting back on case work/professional work as well as the administrative part of the work. It would also mean that professional training needs were highlighted.

By exploring a selection of possible titles for the report, it will be important for the organisation, in consultation with the supervisor and their supervisee, to decide on a title that accurately reflects the purpose of the report.

WHAT IS REPORTED BACK?

When attending to the purpose of the supervisory reports there is a need for the supervisor and the counsellor to negotiate the extent of the information to be supplied to the organisation. If the counsellor feels vulnerable, the information in each category will be minimal. However, if they perceive that there is a real need to educate their line manager, this report will be the catalyst for discussions. For those counsellors who have a line manager who is familiar with counselling, the supervisor's report will serve to confirm discussions that have already taken place on the issues being reported. Indeed for those organisations that provide separate line management supervision and clinical/professional supervision, the information required will need to be divided up between the two supervisors accordingly.

The advantages and difficulties of combining or separating line management supervision and clinical/professional supervision have been discussed earlier in Chapter 3. If the roles are separated the managerial supervisor will have responsibility for the statistical information, the administrative effectiveness of the counsellor, information about the constraining influences on the therapeutic work that originates from organisational culture and the identification of the counsellor's future training needs. It could also be argued that they would need to know something of the counsellor's ethical/professional practice and their therapeutic effectiveness. However, this can only be ascertained if the line manager is also a practising counselling supervisor. Therefore, when the roles of management and clinical practice/ professional supervisor are split careful consideration needs to be given to who reports back which piece of information. In such cases there appears to be a danger of duplication. Nevertheless, this may be preferable to a supervisee feeling stymied and unable to be open in the supervisory process when the roles are combined.

Statistical information

Organisations can ask supervisors for a statistical report on their supervisee. This will mean that they request written information either monthly or biannually on:

- the date and time of the supervisory session
- how long the session lasted
- how many cases were discussed in the session
- what type of client issues were discussed
- what type of organisational issues were discussed.

In requesting such information a supervisee's line manager can present the information in statistical form to auditors within the organisation. This will enable them to ensure that supervision has taken place and for a requisite amount of time. It will also provide information about how many cases can realistically be explored in the time available and also the nature of the client issues that occur. Additionally, it will alert the management to organisational issues that may need their attention. Such statistical information will ensure that management is accountable for the time and money spent on supervisory services to their counsellors. However, they may need more detailed information to be accountable, not just to the company auditors, but also to the profession.

Information about the therapeutic effectiveness of the counsellor

This type of information may be needed by an organisation as a form of staff appraisal. The supervisor and their supervisee will need to write this part of the report in non-counselling language if the supervisee's line manager is not a counsellor and so does not have the knowledge to evaluate the counsellor's work themselves. Therefore, the counsellor and supervisor will need to agree the kind of detail that might be useful in this part of the report. First, there will be a need to comment on the counsellor's ability to make a clear and accurate assessment of a client's needs or at least formulate initially what a client may need from the counselling process. Second, the counsellor's competence in building a therapeutic relationship with the client needs to be evaluated. Third, comments on the counsellor's skills and use of a range of effective interventions is needed in order to evaluate practice. Finally, there is a need to be clear about the theoretical framework from which the counsellor is working in order to demonstrate congruence between theory and practice. As noted in Chapter 10, supervisors are similar in evaluating their supervisee's therapeutic effectiveness in this way (Gilbert and Sills 1999). However, they may be unfamiliar with divulging this information to a third party. This section of the report will enable supervisees to become more reflective practitioners. However, there will need to be a high level of trust in the supervisory relationship for therapeutic effectiveness to be discussed openly. This type of relationship is discussed in Chapter 8.

Information about the administrative effectiveness of the counsellor

A counsellor's effectiveness in keeping records is essential to an organisation, especially in an increasingly litigious world. There is a need for a supervisor to be aware of the kind of records a supervisee keeps and how confidentiality is maintained within the organisation. In this part of the report there is an opportunity for both supervisor and supervisee to educate the organisation if too much information is required in client case notes or if the record-keeping system is not sufficiently confidential. Increasingly, record keeping within organisations is becoming an issue for line managers. They are responsible for managing a service where complaints could be made against their counsellors. Therefore, there is a need for them to ensure that counsellors' records are accurate and written in a way that are accessible to a lay person in the event of them being requested by a court of law. They may need to complete short case history forms, risk assessment forms, short case notes on individual sessions and finally forms that provide statistical information about duration of the counselling, etc. In some counselling agencies or departments this type of information may already be accessible to the counsellor's line manager as part of their managerial function. Some organisations do separate managerial supervision and clinical supervision and so in such instances this part of the supervisors report would not be necessary. However, if a counsellor is effective with their administrative tasks, their supervisor and their line manager can be confident in their ability to be publicly accountable for their practice. Nevertheless, there is also a need for supervisors to ensure that their supervisees are practising ethically and organisations need to be reassured about this fact.

The counsellor's ethical/professional practice

Part of a supervisor's responsibility is to ensure that their supervisee maintains ethical practice in accordance with the ethical codes of practice outlined by their professional association. However, this responsibility can be more difficult to discharge when the supervisee is working in an organisational context. As noted in Chapter 3, the organisational culture can have a detrimental effect as counsellors try to work ethically. If the organisation only pays lip service to issues around client confidentiality, this can mean that the counsellor may struggle to maintain ethical practice. However, supervisors can help their supervisees to become more proficient in ethical problem management within an organisational setting. By working systematically through ethical dilemmas with them, supervisors have information concerning their ability to practise ethically and professionally. This information can then be recalled for reporting purposes when necessary. Additionally, this information, when contained in a report, can be a way of educating the organisation about the ethical and professional norms of the counselling profession.

Similarly, this part of the supervisor's report can address issues of dual roles within the organisation. Sometimes counsellors are required to combine their role as counsellor with that of a trainer, manager, nurse, chaplain, etc. This can cause difficult boundary issues that can be complicated to manage. The supervisor can highlight these issues in their report.

Although there may be resistance to reporting on the ethical and professional aspects of the therapeutic work, the supervisor's accountability to the organisation and to the profession is clearly stated in ethical codes of conduct. Therefore, to provide the organisation with reassurance about the professional quality of the counselling work seems to be a reasonable request.

Information about constraining influences on the therapeutic work that originate from the organisational culture

For some organisations one of the purposes of the report may be to elicit information about the organisation that cannot be found elsewhere. For some supervisees, the dilemmas that they face will originate from the culture of the organisation. As discussed in Chapter 3, organisational culture can have a detrimental effect on all employees, including the counsellor. Yet each department within a large organisational setting can have its own mini-culture. The constraining effects of any mini-culture on clients will become evident when more than one client talks about it in their counselling sessions with the same counsellor. Each client may be unaware that the other is saying the same thing about the organisational culture; the counsellor will be the guardian of this information and this information could be useful for organisational change.

Elizabeth was in such a position when counselling four individual clients from the same department in a large commercial organisation. All clients were being bullied by their manager and were finding it very stressful. Two of them were off work with stress and the other two were considering leaving the organisation.

The information that Elizabeth has concerning the bullying manager would be useful to the organisation. If the bullying behaviour of the manager was eradicated it would enable employees to be retained or prevent sickness absence. This would be especially significant in an organisation that prided itself on having a culture of learning and development. However, the difficulty of disclosing this information, whilst still maintaining client confidentiality, is a dilemma. When discussing this issue with her supervisor, Elizabeth will need to work out a strategy for enabling this information to be disclosed for the benefit of both her clients and the organisation. Information like this could not go in a supervisor's report until it was no longer confidential client material. One strategy would be for Elizabeth to gain her clients' permission to address the issue of bullying with their line manager. An alternative strategy would be for Elizabeth to empower all the clients to address the issue with the manager, either individually, or more ideally, as a group. Finally, if all other strategies failed, Elizabeth may be able to gain the clients' permission to pass on the information to higher management within the organisation. This would mean that the bullying behaviour could be tackled if the management chose to do so. The example from the scenario with Elizabeth is a very specific example of information about adverse management practices gained by the counsellor and taken to supervision. However, sometimes counsellors will gain information about the organisational culture that is of a more general nature, yet nevertheless would be useful to the organisation, especially in time of significant organisational change.

Steve worked as a counsellor in a commercial organisation that was down sizing quite dramatically. He was seeing clients who were distressed at this move and fearful that they would be next for redundancy. However, there were no effective mechanisms in place to disseminate proposed information concerning who would be next on the list.

In this scenario Steve was able to write this information in the joint annual supervision report in a general way. This enabled managers to devise a system that enabled employees to learn about forthcoming redundancies more quickly and therefore partially alleviate the high stress levels evident in those workers who might be affected.

Whilst it is generally regarded as useful that organisations gain information about the constraining influences of the organisational culture on the therapeutic work, it is very difficult to remain ethical whilst enabling that information to be in the public domain.

The counsellor's effective use of supervision

When an organisation is paying for the counsellor's supervision it is important to know that the process is being used effectively. However, the supervisor, supervisee and their line manager may have different views about what constitutes 'effective' use of supervision. Many line managers, especially if they are not counsellors themselves, see supervision as their safeguard from litigation. Yet there is a possibility that they do not understand the counselling supervision process fully and are not therefore able to comment on whether the counsellor is using supervision effectively. For this they will need to rely on the supervisor's judgement. When discussing the definition of supervision in Chapter 1, it was noted that there was a high possibility that a line manager might see the process as hierarchical and similar to the supervision function as understood in a commercial setting. Even within the care sector there can be a different understanding of the supervision process. It may be more about case management than effective therapeutic intervention. Wiener and colleagues (2003) indicate that in medical settings, supervision may be synonymous with 'not coping'. This could also be true of the uniformed services. Therefore, line managers need to have at least a rudimentary understanding of the process and need to be assured that the process is working effectively to protect the clients and their organisation.

Effective supervision means that the supervisory relationship needs to be open and trusting, as noted in Chapter 8. This openness in turn means that there is no fear of bringing the difficult dilemmas to supervision. No client, therefore, will be neglected within such a process. Nevertheless, 'effectiveness' to both supervisor and supervisee might mean something different. For some supervisors, the counsellor's effective use of supervision will mean that they come prepared for the session and report back on the effectiveness of the client work in subsequent sessions. For other supervisors the counsellor's effective use of supervision will mean that the counsellor is creative and spontaneous in supervision, using themselves in ways that are not conventional, but accessing the material that is at the edge of their awareness. Additionally, it means that counsellors are supported by their supervisor when both personal and professional issues are difficult.

For counsellors, their own perception of their effective use of supervision may be influenced by what their supervisor expects of them, especially if they are quite inexperienced in the profession. They may expect the supervisor to guide them towards effective use of the supervision time. However, if the counsellor is experienced, both parties will want to negotiate how they work together. This will mean working towards a mutual understanding of what effectiveness means to both of them. When this type of working relationship is established, they will be able to negotiate around the content of the report.

There may also be some supervisory dyads that resent having to report back on the supervisee's effective use of supervision. To them it could indicate a lack of trust by the organisation. Other dyads, however, will view it as an opportunity to educate the line manager about the supervisory process itself and how it works effectively. This will indicate the collegiate rather than hierarchical nature of the relationship and its openness to unconscious processes that will inform the work. It will also mean that the reflective process that is necessary when writing the report, will ensure that both parties increase their skills of reflection.

To identify the supervisee's future training needs

The supervisor's report is also an opportunity for the supervisee to identify their future training needs and formally communicate these to their line manager. In organisations where the line manager is a counsellor, this channel of communication will not be necessary. But in organisations where counselling is being provided for employees, the line manager will need help to identify these training needs accurately. If communication channels are open and clear between the counsellor and their line manager, this section of the supervisor's report will not be needed. When supervisors were asked to identify common dilemmas encountered in supervision they cited problematic relationships between counsellors and their line manager as very common (Copeland 2000b). If the report requested by the organisation is vague as in Figure 9.1, it leaves the supervisor and supervisee feeling unsafe and confused about what to write. So the need for a formal channel of communication for this information is clear. It is even more vital with the on-going need for continual professional development for counsellors and the commitment of employers to this process.

All parties in the working alliance need to be sure that the information reported back to the organisation is for the benefit of everyone in that alliance including the organisation itself. It would be unethical to collect information just for the sake of it. Both supervisor and supervisee need to be sure that the information will be used to enhance all aspects of the therapeutic work and to help to enhance organisational culture. A sample report form can be found in Appendix 4.

HOW DO WE REPORT BACK?

Once an organisation has made the decision to ask their supervisors to report back on the supervisory process it needs to be established how this will be achieved. Whether the process is informal or formal, it needs to be clear and agreed by all parties in the working alliance. When a counsellor is in training it is fairly standard practice that a supervisor writes a joint learning statement, with the counsellor, about their work together. Generally, this is requested by the training organisation. However, once a counsellor is

To bring our system in line with others in the organisation we have devised this
form for supervisors to complete.

Progress so far since last review:

Supervisee initials:

Supervisor's name:

Signed: _____   Date:

                     Supervisor

Figure 9.1 Supervision review sheet

qualified that procedure is not usually carried over into the employing
organisation.

When an organisation does decide that it wants feedback from the supervisor or alternatively, the supervisor decides there is a need to report back to
the organisation, there is a need to decide how to do this so that ethical
standards are maintained. Tripartite meeting will enable all parties in the
working alliance to negotiate procedures. The supervisory dyad can decide
that they want control over the type of information that is revealed to the
organisation. Alternatively, the supervisee's line manager can decide what
information they need from the supervisor. If there is an impasse over the
type of information needed by the organisation and the mechanisms for

disseminating it, the supervisor will need to decide how far they can go in meeting the needs of the organisation.

Research (Copeland 2000a) has found that where reports were required within an organisation, they were either verbal or written. Written reports were more common within counselling agencies than in any other type of organisation. Nevertheless, anecdotal evidence suggests that reporting back by the supervisor to the supervisee's employers is not widespread. However, training courses for supervisors are raising awareness of the need for accountability, not only to the profession, but also the employing organisation. Exploration of written and oral systems will help all parties in the working alliance to decide which type will suit their purposes.

Formal, written supervisor reports

A system of formal, supervisor reports is more likely to be instigated by the organisation, especially if it is a counselling agency, than by the supervisor. Nevertheless, once the decision has been made that written reports are to be provided by the supervisor, the shape and frequency they take needs to be agreed by supervisor, supervisee and the organisation. Yearly, written reports are often produced by supervisors of trainee counsellors and are required by the training institution. Similarly, the organisations where managers have a good understanding of the counselling and supervisory process negotiate with the supervisor to report back annually. The last section explored the purpose and content of this report. However, the mechanics such as the date the report is due and whether there will be any feedback from the line manager once they have read it, need to be finalised. From my own experience, I know that when I have written a joint report with the supervisee for an organisation, I would have appreciated a response by the line manager, indicating that they had read it and were responding to the action points. Without this response there is the feeling that the report is disappearing into a black hole and is of no use whatsoever.

Therefore, all parties in the working alliance need to be sure that they are in agreement with the timing of the report and what will happen when it is received. This will mean that there has to be a well-established relationship between all parties and a good line of communication in the supervisory rhombus. However, the line manager will have to decide what action they will take if a supervisor refuses to write such a report. Will they tell the supervisee to find another supervisor? Or will they meet the supervisor to try and persuade them to co-operate? The answer to questions such as these will depend on whether the line manager understands the processes that are being reported on and believes that such a report is necessary for the organisation's safety from litigation. Similarly, if the supervisor or supervisee does not agree with the reporting back process then negotiations will need to take place in order to come to a compromise. Therefore, formal written reports can be useful for all parties in the working alliance, assuming that everyone is in agreement with their purpose, content and frequency.

Informal, oral supervisor reports

In contrast to formal written supervisor reports, informal, oral reports can fulfil a useful role for supervisee, supervisor and line manager. This type of report is most likely to be used within an organisation where the supervisor is in-house and in contact with the supervisee's line manager easily and frequently. Nevertheless, in such circumstances, there could be a danger of leaking boundaries and unethical practice.

Mandy is a senior counsellor and supervisor in a voluntary counselling agency. She has worked there for over a decade. She is concerned about the time-keeping patterns of one of her supervisees. She voices these concerns to the centre manager. Between them they plan a course of action to help the supervisee to become clearer about her time boundaries and in doing so they hope to help the supervisee with her practice, whilst unwittingly breaking boundaries themselves.

In the above scenario, in long-established organisations with a stable staff, it is easy for in-house counsellors and supervisors to break the boundaries of confidentiality within every day conversation. Therefore, if this informal type of report is to be used, as with the formal written report, the purpose, content and frequency of the report needs to be clarified with all parties and the agreed boundaries kept. Leaking out small pieces of information frequently will lead to unethical practice. Within counselling agencies informal reporting procedures could be common and confidentiality agreed within the agency rather than between working dyads. However, as with all good communication systems, everyone, including the clients, will need to be aware of the limits to the confidentiality agreement. Care needs to be taken so that this process is not too cumbersome with clients.

Informal reporting systems can work well, especially if there is a good working relationship between all parties. A three-way meeting between supervisor, supervisee and their line manager would be the most open way for an informal, oral report to be executed. A trusting relationship between all parties is essential and ways to establish this have been discussed in Chapter 8. However, if the power dynamic is unbalanced and favours any one member of the triad, the oral report will be less useful. Supervisors who have been part of this process have sometimes viewed it as directly relating to the organisation's appraisal system and therefore not found it very helpful (Copeland 2000a). Appraisal systems can be constructive (Copeland 1988), but any association with the report and the line management function could be viewed in a negative manner. However, if everyone is in agreement with the purpose of the report and there is trust in the relationship it can work to everyone's advantage. The important element in this system is that the supervisor and supervisee agree what will be said before the meeting with the line manager so that there are no surprises. Similarly, the supervisee will need to be sure that their line manager is well briefed about the counselling and supervisory processes.

Increasingly, there is debate in the field of counselling, especially in workplace and health-related organisations, whether the results from CORE evaluations should be incorporated into the reporting back process. Indeed, any form of client evaluation of the effectiveness of counsellor, in any organisational context, is information that can be used to measure performance. However, it does need to be viewed with caution by the supervisor and these outcomes will need to be considered in conjunction with the client work as a whole. This process, as with formal report writing, is time consuming and needs discussion, by the organisation, concerning possible fees for this task.

PAYMENT FOR REPORTS

The decision whether to pay a supervisor for the formal written or informal oral report is a difficult one. Where resources are scarce organisation will be reluctant to pay any extra fee for this work. When this happens a supervisor may feel exploited by the organisation, especially if the report requested is lengthy and time consuming to complete. Similarly, a supervisee might feel annoyed at having to take precious supervision time to discuss a report that is requested by the organisation. However, if the report is seen as an integral part of the supervisory process rather than a 'bolt on' task, resentment will disappear and the report can be compiled as an on-going evaluative process that is an integral part of the work as seen in Chapter 10. Therefore, there will be no need for the supervisor to request an extra fee for the work. When viewed like this, a supervisor will value the evaluative work needed and both parties will find learning within the process.

CONCLUSION

It can be seen that there are both formal and informal mechanisms within organisations, for a supervisor to report back to the supervisee's line manager on the supervisory process. Whatever mechanism is used, there is a need for clarity in understanding the purpose of the report, the type of information that is needed within it and how this information will be communicated to the organisation. When this clarity is found, the possibility of ethical boundaries being broken will be rare.

Responsibilities of the supervisor

- Ensuring that they are clear about the purpose of the report
- Clarity around who will have access to the report
- Negotiating with the supervisee and their line manager the extent of the information to be supplied to the organisation
- Agreeing what information can be divulged in the report concerning the supervisee's therapeutic effectiveness
- Reporting back to the organisation on the effectiveness of the record-keeping system within the organisation
- Educating the line manager about the ethical dilemmas that arise when a counsellor has a dual role within the organisation
- Educating the line manager about the exact nature of the supervisory process

Responsibilities of the supervisee

- Educating the line manager, through the report, about record-keeping systems
- Educating their line manager about the exact nature of the supervisory process
- Identifying their future training needs and reporting back to their line manager clearly about these needs

Responsibilities of the line manager

- Ensuring that the statistical information requested from the supervisor is used by the organisation respectfully
- Acting on any organisational issues that are identified in the report as needing attention, for example poor/unethical accommodation
- Ensuring that record-keeping system for client work is confidential and fit for its purpose
- Clarifying issues that originate from the organisational culture
- Ensuring that, as far as possible, the future training needs of the supervisee are met
- Devising a mechanism by which the reporting back procedure is carried out for all parties

Chapter 10

Evaluation, assessment and accreditation

Issues of assessment and accountability towards training organisations or employing organisations need to be clearly set out at the beginning of the supervisory relationship.

(Jenkins 2001:36)

INTRODUCTION

Part of the reporting back process as discussed in Chapter 9 will involve some evaluation or assessment of the supervisory work. However, there are various ways that these processes can be achieved. During the last decade, supervisor training courses have sprung up to meet the demands of supervisors for training that will enable them to be more effective within the role. In the early 1990s training courses were not generally formally assessed or validated. This has now changed considerably. Nation-wide, courses are validated by universities or validation consortiums that seek to standardise supervision training. However, the restrictions that such standardisation imposes is not welcomed by everyone in the profession. Hawkins and Shohet (2000:123) note that

whilst we welcome the growth in research, training and accreditation in the field of supervision we become increasingly concerned that the joy of continual learning can be overshadowed by the need to fulfil externally generated requirements, and the anxiety this provokes.

Yet perhaps, despite the anxiety that formal assessment engenders, it is necessary if organisations are to have a benchmark when employing counselling supervisors. Institutions offering courses leading to a certificate or diploma in supervision are producing practitioners who understand the theory and practice of supervision and who have become proficient reflective practitioners. So they are attractive to employers who understand the world of formal qualifications and their currency.

Similarly, employers are expecting supervisors to be accredited as a supervisor by their professional association or at least be eligible for and working towards accreditation. Professional bodies such as the British Association for Counselling and Psychotherapy (BACP) are in a position to accredit counselling supervisors, giving them a status within the profession that can be recognised by those outside the field. How else can employers determine the effectiveness of the supervisors they seek to employ if they have no professional benchmark by which to assess effectiveness of their work?

Finally, evaluation has always been an ongoing part of the supervisory process, both on a micro and macro level (Holloway 1995, Carroll 1996, Hawkins and Shohet 2000, Gilbert and Evans 2000, Page and Wosket 2001). On the micro level, within the supervisory relationship, both parties are continually evaluating the work from session to session. On a macro level work is evaluated on ending the supervisory relationship to prepare for movement to another supervisor or for engaging with another supervisee. The outcomes of the evaluation process are useful to employers as statistical information, measuring the effectiveness of the supervisory process for both the supervisee and also for the organisation.

The responsibilities embedded in the evaluation process within supervision will be explored in this chapter. The assessment and accreditation processes for supervisors will also be addressed in relation to their effectiveness as training and development tools and their currency with prospective employers.

THE EVALUATION PROCESS FOR SUPERVISORS

The dictionary definition of 'evaluate' is 'to assess; to determine the value carefully' (Pearsall 2002). So immediately we have the word 'assess' linked with evaluation. This can cause confusion between evaluation which is an informal process between two or more parties and assessment which is one party assessing the competency of another. However, evaluation in supervision is a process that is informal and involves both parties in the working alliance. It is a two-way process that involves both supervisor and supervisee giving feedback to one another about the efficacy of their work both session by session and at the termination of their contract. Hawkins and Shohet (2000:124) maintain the importance of this process happening 'within a direct form of relationship and not by the examination of paperwork by a distant and unknown committee.' This is at the heart of the evaluation process. The openness with which two people can communicate with one another is the key to the usefulness of evaluation. Even when a third party, the supervisee's line manager, is involved with the evaluation, the process can still happen within that direct form of relationship.

For Page and Wosket (2001:145) evaluation in supervision 'provides the opportunity for the supervisor and the supervisee to determine the value of the supervision experience and consider any implications for change. The focus here is mutual evaluation of the co-operative enterprise, not assessment of the supervisee.' Here they are discussing the evaluation that takes place from session to session in the supervisory dyad and the emphasis is on the development of their supervisory process. There may be the need to change aspects of the work. Additionally, there could be identification of the need for more ongoing training for the supervisee. The identification of training needs will also be of concern to the supervisee's line manager.

Carroll (1996) also acknowledges that evaluation is an essential feature of effective supervision but notes the lack of clarity about how it is carried out. He sees the process as being between the supervisory dyad and the purpose is to improve the supervisee's practice. Like Page and Wosket, he emphasises the collaborative nature of the process and the skills needed by the supervisor in giving feedback and also the importance of having a clear format for this work. However, the very formality of this process would indicate that it appears to be more like assessment than an informal evaluation between supervisor and supervisee.

Within this process there will be two levels of evaluation happening; the supervisor will be enabling the supervisee to evaluate their work as a counsellor and the supervisee will be helping the supervisor to evaluate the effectiveness of the supervisory process. Additionally, on a third level the supervisee's line manager will need to evaluate the competence of the supervisor in this working alliance. In reality, however, this third level of evaluation rarely happens, especially if the line manager is not a counsellor or supervisor and has little knowledge of how to measure competence in this profession.

Level 1: Evaluation of the supervisee's work

It was noted earlier that a good, collaborative relationship is at the heart of the evaluation process. Within an organisation it may be useful for line managers to see evaluation as having similarities with the appraisal process. This will help them to understand, to some degree, what happens when the supervisor and their supervisee evaluate their work together. However, the appraisal process, especially if it is hierarchical rather than triangulated, has a power dynamic that is not necessarily present within the supervisory dyad especially if both parties are experienced practitioners. This equality within the relationship enables practitioners to evaluate 'how they are doing' with openness and without judgement. If the relationship is one of supervisor and trainee counsellor, however, there is a power dynamic as one person is more experienced than the other and responsible for feedback to the training organisation concerning the competence of the trainee. The supervisor can seek to balance the power by gradually enabling the supervisee to develop their own internal supervision processes. As noted in Chapter 9 on reporting back to the organisation, there are different aspect of the supervisory processes that will be evaluated. These include the therapeutic effectiveness of the counsellor, their administrative effectiveness, their ethical and professional practice and their effective use of supervision. All of this statistical information will be useful for the organisation so that the efficacy of the counselling service is established.

However, there are particular issues that an organisation, in tandem with the supervisor, will need to address if they are to take their responsibilities as an employer of trainee counsellors seriously. Izzard (2003) in a small scale research project, identified trainee placement organisations with the following issues:

- Loose boundaries, particularly over confidentiality
- Placements which were also the trainee's place of work in which they had conflicting roles with clients
- Placements who provided inappropriate clients, where the client group was very disordered
- Placements where the clients were not voluntary or were removed from counselling without notice.

(Izzard 2003:38)

When placements are providing inappropriate training environments for trainee counsellors it will be impossible for a supervisor or a line manager to evaluate the trainee counsellor's level of competence until such issues have been resolved. A trainee counsellor will be battling to remain ethical and professional if any of the above issues are not rectified. Additionally, it will mean that the supervisor has to tackle such issues if the organisation does not take on the responsibility. Therefore, supervisee competence, especially at trainee level, will be inextricably linked with the efficient management of the organisation. Within the evaluation process, supervisors can be useful to the organisation if they can organise a tripartite meeting with their supervisee and the line manager to address the type of issues that Izzard outlines above.

Level 2: Evaluation of the supervisor's work

Hawkins and Shohet (2000:108) emphasise the importance of the supervisor evaluating themselves through a self-assessment questionnaire which outlines the following aspects of the supervisory process to be evaluated:

- knowledge
- supervision management skills
- supervision intervention skills
- personal traits or qualities
- commitment to own ongoing development

- for group supervisors
- for senior organisational supervisors.

Here the emphasis is on the competence of the supervisor within their role.

Gilbert and Sills (1999:168) also note the importance of supervisor training for the evaluation process. They use a checklist under the two headings of the relationship dimensions and the professional role. These two checklists are comprehensive and could easily be used by supervisor and supervisee together to evaluate their work and to enable supervisors to identify their own future learning objectives. They also indicate that effective performance along the dimensions outlined would be a good indicator that the supervisor was ready for accreditation. Additionally, Gilbert and Sills outline questions for a short supervision review which include:

- What was our contract and have we met it?
- What have you found most useful from your supervisor?
- What do you want more of from your supervisor?
- What do you want less of from your supervisor?
- What is the next developmental edge for you?

(Gilbert and Sills 1999:169)

Therefore, when the supervisory dyad evaluates their work together, they are, in essence, evaluating their own competence and effectiveness in their respective roles. It will be reassuring for a line manager to know that this mutual process is occurring and that it will benefit the organisation in demonstrating competent workers. This information will need to be reported back to the organisation in some form in order for it to be in the public domain, however, it cannot always be assumed that both parties are competent. If the supervisee is not working to the level of competence needed for the organisation, the supervisor will have the responsibility of working with the supervisee to increase their competence level either through more external training or diversifying their experience to other client groups. If these strategies have no effect on competency levels, the supervisor will need to work with the line manager to decide on the best course of action for both the supervisee and the organisation. This may mean that the supervisee's contract is not renewed.

Similarly, the supervisor may not be competent in their work with the supervisee. Both the supervisee and their line manager will be able to identify this by the work that takes place within the supervision sessions and also by the quality of the reports submitted to the organisation by the supervisor. The manager could recommend that the supervisor engage in training for their role if it is skills and knowledge that are lacking. However, if the relationship between the supervisor and their supervisee has broken down irrevocably, the manager will have to terminate the supervisor's contract.

Level 3: The line manager's evaluation of the competence of both supervisee and their supervisor

The evaluation process needs to be open to the supervisee's line manager within the organisation. The line manager may not be interested in the refinement of the supervisory process itself through the evaluation process, they will, however, be interested in any outcome that involves the professional development of their employee or any outcome that has a monetary implication for the organisation. For example, a line manager will need to fund courses or give study time to the counsellor for their continuing professional development whether they are already accredited as a counsellor with BACP or a similar organisation, or working towards that accreditation. Additionally, although it is a rare occurrence for a line manager to assist supervisors with their training, especially within the commercial sector, a line manager could authorise payment for supervision training. This will be a more likely occurrence if the supervisor is working with more than one supervisee within the same organisation. A line manager may also want to have a tripartite meeting with the supervisee and their supervisor to ascertain whether the supervisory process is effective and to elicit training needs. It will also be an opportunity for the manager to gain feedback about how the service can be developed for the benefit of the clients.

Such open communication may be frightening for any of the parties in the working alliance. The counselling and supervision work is carried out in private, and for it to be open to public scrutiny, often by a manager who is not from within the profession and therefore open to misunderstanding, can lead to less openness. If this happens, there is the possibility of an allegiance forming between the supervisor and their supervisee that can become collusive and 'against' the organisation. This is not helpful to the organisation in general or the clients that form an integral part of that organisation. However, openness is at the heart of the evaluation process for all parties in the working alliance and through this openness a line manager can establish a benchmark of competence for both their counsellor and supervisor.

Therefore, the evaluation process is an informal tool for all parties in the working alliance to appraise their work together on a continual basis. Conversely, a formal assessment process is also very important within that alliance, to indicate to those people both inside and external to the profession and the employing organisation, that both practitioners are competent.

THE ASSESSMENT PROCESS FOR SUPERVISORS

The word assessment has the capacity to strike fear into the heart of even the most effective supervisor. The dictionary definition of assess is 'to rate; to valuate or estimate amount, worth, etc.' (Pearsall 2002). It is the fact that an independent party, other than yourself, is assessing your effectiveness as a supervisor or a supervisee and passing judgement upon the work that causes the fear. The other person or persons may be known to you as your tutor(s) on a training course. They will look at your work and deem it fit or unfit for the award in question. Course tutors will be charged with the task of assessing both written and practical assignments and an external examiner will have the task of ensuring that the standard of the tutor's marking is fair and consistent with standards nation-wide. Even when being assessed by a peer group alone, as on person-centred courses, there is a fear of exposing your work only to find that it is not yet assessed as competent. However, the notion of assessment by peers may be less daunting as there is an equality of power within the 'student' role.

Even within such a formal process, the relationships between trainee and trainee, tutor and trainee and tutor and external examiner can ease the fear and tension within this procedure. If trainee and tutor engage in open dialogue about the work for assessment then the fear of being judged subsides. Similarly, if the external examiner and tutor engage with openness and mutual respect, the whole process becomes diffused with a sense of equality, where the notion of judgement is weakened. However, if professional standards are to be maintained this process is a necessary evil.

More informal assessment of a supervisor's knowledge and skill is made when they formally apply for a post as a supervisor within an organisation as outlined in Chapter 5. Here the supervisor will need to fill in an application form and write a letter of application, outlining their experience and skills as a counsellor and supervisor. If the information in the application form and letter meet the job description and person specification the applicant will be invited for an interview. Once again they will be assessed on their suitability for the post. Here, another person(s) is assessing their level of competence for the role within that organisation. This informal assessment process is a common one when gaining a post within an organisation, however it will be less familiar to counselling supervisors who are accustomed to gaining supervision work through 'word of mouth'.

A supervisor is increasingly charged with the guardianship of professional standards and ethics and therefore has a duty to be as effective as they can in a rapidly changing world. In organisations a line manager, especially if they are not part of the counselling profession themselves, will need to have some standard by which to measure the effectiveness of the counsellor and the supervisor they are appointing. In this way a certificate or diploma will be a familiar award to them.

As with the evaluation process, there will be two formal levels of assessment of the competence of the counsellor and supervisor. The line manager will also need to make their own assessment of the competence level of those they employ.

Level 1: Assessment of the supervisee's work

The independent assessment of the supervisee's work is more usually associated with the assessment of a trainee counsellor. Izzard notes that

> The unique position of the trainee embarking on clinical practice makes the work of supervision different, in many respects, from that of supervising experienced counsellors. The complexity of relationships with the training course, the placement agency where clinical work occurs, and the student him or herself, together with the particular developmental crises and vulnerabilities of the trainee, and the presence of assessment of the trainee's skill all call for a particular clarity in establishing the limits of responsibility and agreeing explicit contracts.
>
> (Izzard 2001:75)

The assessment process is complicated and the supervisor will have to be involved in some way. This might be on an informal basis in the form of a joint learning statement written by both supervisor and supervisee that is then presented to the training organisation. Ideally, it will also be presented to the training placement where the supervisee is working as a counsellor. This will enable the training placement to be aware of the strengths and limitation of the trainee's knowledge and skills as a counsellor at that point in their training. If a joint learning statement is not presented to the training placement by the supervisor or the trainee counsellor, the organisation will need to formulate their own system to assess the trainee's competence.

The supervisor cannot escape this responsibility, and there is a need for openness between both parties in order that the supervisee can celebrate their strengths but also be prepared to work on their areas for development. Nevertheless, for the supervisee, fear is still ignited by the assessment process. Challenges are often more loudly heard than the support that is also given, as anxiety mounts around being judged to be incompetent by the profession (Carroll 1996). Therefore, the skill for both supervisor and supervisee in this assessment process is in making it collaborative and regular so that there are no surprises in the final joint report. This is where the assessment process is clearly linked to an on-going evaluation process.

When supervising experienced counsellors, formal assessment may not be an issue for the dyad. Nevertheless, the supervisor will be involved in any accreditation process for the supervisee as a counsellor. Whilst this is not strictly assessment, there is the need for the supervisor to give feedback to the accreditation body about the competence of the counsellor or supervisor. The supervisor is required to make judgements about the required level of competence of the practitioner.

Level 2: Assessment of the supervisor's work

The formal assessment of the supervisor's work takes place on training courses. It was noted earlier that training courses for supervisors are increasing. A decade ago such courses were not formally assessed but provided a forum in which supervisors could practise their skills and discuss professional and ethical issues, so enhancing their work with supervisees. Increasingly, training courses for supervisors are formally assessed and validated by a university or awarding body consortium. As a result, supervisors are required to undergo formal assessment of both their written and practical supervisory skills. This is carried out by tutors, external examiners and peers on the course. The very nature of this assessment process means that there are criteria by which competence can be measured. The criteria are by no means universal, differing from institution to institution. However, they follow a general pattern agreed by the profession, but sometimes varying according to the theoretical underpinnings of the course. They provide a professional training for supervisors based on assessment of

- theoretical understanding of supervision
- personal and professional development as a supervisor
- written casework
- skills development.

Success in gaining an award in supervision will provide an employer with the minimum criteria for successful selection for interview. It will enable line managers, who are not also counsellors, to draw up the job description with essential and preferred criterion for the post of counselling supervisor. Yet, to date, there is no requirement in the profession that supervisors have any training for the role. To a line manager who is not in the profession, this may seem strange. In the profession, as noted earlier, the position of supervisor is increasingly important for the maintenance of ethical standards. Life-long supervision is required by BACP for all their practising counsellors, yet this role can be undertaken by supervisors who have had no training for it.

Therefore, it is necessary for minimum standards of competence to be set for the role of supervisor within the counselling profession. Gaining a certificate or diploma in supervision will enable all professionals, in different fields of work, to recognise this type of award as relevant to the role. However, this type of award can only be gained by undergoing formal assessment processes however daunting they are. At the moment, formal academic qualifications are not essential (though desirable) to the BACP accreditation process for supervisors. Therefore, it is to that process we now turn.

THE ACCREDITATION PROCESS FOR SUPERVISORS

The dictionary definition of 'accredit' is 'to give credit or authority to' (Pearsall 2002) and the word 'authority' holds within it all the weight of responsibility that goes with the role. Most professional associations connected with counselling and psychotherapy accredit their practitioners in some way. Certainly the BACP accredit its counsellors, supervisors and trainers. Increasingly more members are taking this accreditation process seriously as possible government registration looms on the horizon. However, this is a paperwork process that is carried out at a distance and after formal training and assessment have taken place to gain a professional qualification in counselling and psychotherapy. It could be seen as the final professional recognition for practitioners who have finished their training and also gained some experience in the field.

Some practitioners see the accreditation process as stifling creativity and taking autonomy away from individual counsellors to work in ways that are innovative. Alternatively, it is viewed as a creative learning process in collaboration with a fellow professional. The very act of producing the required paperwork for BACP requires dialogue and the evaluation process outlined earlier. Far from being an automatic process, it becomes reflective, creative and energising. Hawkins and Shohet (2000) are clear that when this process balances support and challenge within a healthy relationship, the danger of institutionalised authority will be diminished. In an increasingly litigious world the accreditation process is necessary as part of a standardising process. How else would an employer, looking for a competent counsellor, supervisor or trainer, begin to identify a practitioner who would be effective, ethical and also meet their organisation's needs? It could be argued that word of mouth might accomplish this task just as easily. However, if a manager has no knowledge of the profession they need the profession to provide the 'gold' standard for them.

BACP (2000) has developed criteria for the accreditation of counselling supervisors that seek to assess the supervisor's fitness to practise. These include a requirement that the supervisor:

1   has current membership of BACP
2   abides by their framework for good practice
3   is a BACP accredited counsellor
4   has undertaken 600 contact hours with clients over three years.

These criteria require the supervisor to provide evidence of their competence in a variety of ways, from written witness statements given by supervisees and perhaps their line manager, to case studies or tape recordings and evaluation of actual supervision sessions. Therefore, although the skills to be assessed are not actually named, it is assumed that they will be evidenced by fulfilling the specific criteria. Evidence of supervisor training or a programme of learning with a supervisor is also needed for successful accreditation, indicating that BACP takes the view that training is essential for supervisors. This is to be applauded, proving that the concept of learning supervision skills through 'supervising as you were supervised' approach is outmoded. Supervisors can no longer rely on working with their supervisees in the same way that their own supervisor worked with them.

Increasingly, managers who are required to pay for their counsellor's supervision will find it necessary to enquire about the supervisor's level of competence. Accreditation by a professional body such as BACP will be one way of ensuring competence in the role. If a supervisor is already employed by an organisation, the line manager can enquire about the accreditation process and find out if the supervisor is working towards accreditation. As a standard by which the profession measures competence, any accreditation process is not infallible, nevertheless, the process is a way of ensuring that counsellors, trainers and supervisors have a minimum standard of skills, knowledge and aptitude with which to practise ethically. Therefore, the accreditation process must indicate an increased professionalism for supervisors as the guardians of ethical standards. However, the small numbers of accredited supervisors to date indicates that there is more work to be done to find a process that is attractive to all supervisors and gives line managers a standard of excellence.

There may be other methods of giving line managers a standard of excellence in supervision, other than the accreditation process. For many counsellors, a diploma in counselling is an employer's standard for counsellors entering the profession and being seen as competent to practise. For supervisors, a certificate or diploma in supervision could also be that standard of competence. It would indicate a level of training for the role. However, the accreditation of such courses by the professional bodies responsible for counselling and supervision seems to be a long way off. Until that day occurs, supervision training courses will remain variable both in their length, scope and depth of skills training. For employers, they are some indication of the competence of a supervisor, but are very far from the definitive standard of excellence needed by employers and the profession.

CONCLUSION

All parties in the working alliance have a responsibility to each part of the evaluation, assessment and accreditation process. The line manager will never know how they can be of use in all these processes if they are not educated about their necessity and how they are carried out. Similarly, the supervisor needs to take responsibly for their own levels of competence in evaluating and assessing the supervisee and their work. If both these processes happen, the supervisee will be enabled to engage with their clients in a competent and clear way, being held by the organisation and its communication systems.

Responsibilities of the supervisee

- Ensuring that they are open to the whole evaluation process with their supervisor
- Being as open as possible with their supervisor about what they want more of and what they want less of within the supervision process
- Enabling their line manager to understand the evaluation process within supervision
- Ensuring that meetings can take place between themselves, their line manager and their supervisor
- Feeding back to their line manager information about their training needs that arise as a result of the evaluation process.
- Ensuring that they are competently trained for the role of counsellor
- Their own ongoing professional development
- Engaging openly in the assessment process
- Giving their line manager feedback about their ongoing professional development training needs
- Their own accreditation process with the relevant professional body
- Providing the relevant material and feedback to enable their supervisor to engage with the accreditation process
- Providing their line manager with information about the accreditation process and its importance

Responsibilities of the supervisor

- Ensuring that the evaluation process is conducted in an atmosphere of respect
- Being open to the evaluation of themselves within the supervisory process
- Ensuring that they can attend three-way meetings within the supervisee's organisation
- Ensuring that they attend to any training needs identified by the evaluation process
- Ensuring that they are competently trained for the role of supervisor
- Giving feedback to the supervisee about their on-going development as a counsellor
- Ensuring their attendance at the tripartite meetings within the organisation
- Their on-going professional development
- Their own accreditation process with the relevant professional body
- Providing the supervisee's line manager with information about the accreditation process and its importance

- Being respectful of the supervisee's material needed for the accreditation process
- Keeping any organisational information confidential when engaging in the accreditation process

Responsibilities of the line manager

- Attendance at meetings called by the supervisory dyad concerning the efficacy of the supervision process
- Understanding the role of evaluation within the supervisory process
- Ensuring that the supervisory relationship within the dyad is sound
- Understanding any assessment processes that counsellor and supervisor are undertaking
- Ensuring that they appoint adequately trained supervisors
- Attending tripartite meetings with counsellor and supervisor
- Being open to feedback about the organisation and its culture and the impact that has on the counselling and supervisory processes
- Ensuring that both counsellor and supervisor are encouraged to apply for accreditation with the relevant professional body
- Understanding the accreditation process
- Facilitating the process whenever possible

Chapter 11

Endings and new beginnings in supervision

> Endings in human relationships activate different issues for different people, growing up, separation, abandonment, loneliness, dependency, self worth, choice, and most of them raise issues of loss.
>
> (Carroll 1996:112)

INTRODUCTION

Ending a supervisory relationship when an organisation is involved is not a straightforward process. When searching the literature for material on endings in supervision there appears to be a dearth of information. This is in direct contrast to the wealth of information on endings in counselling. It is almost as if there is a collusion amongst writers to concentrate on beginning and maintaining the supervisory relationship whilst excluding endings in supervision altogether. Yet a good ending in supervision is vital if new beginnings are to be fruitful for all parties in the working alliance. Some professional organisations (e.g. BACP) recommend that counsellors change their supervisor approximately every three years to avoid collusion creeping into the relationship. However, this is not mandatory and anecdotal evidence suggests that counsellors are reluctant to change their supervisors if the relationship is working well for both parties. Nevertheless, there are some circumstances that will mean a change of supervisor is desirable and even perhaps inevitable. A supervisor may die, retire or move geographical area. Similar circumstances may also happen to a supervisee. There may also be cases where both supervisor and supervisee decide that they are no longer able to fulfil each other's needs within the supervisory relationship.

Additionally, an organisation may change a supervisee's arrangement for supervision for various reasons. So, inevitably during a counsellor's career, there will need to be an ending of the supervisory relationship. If the organisation has formally employed the supervisor, the ending process will also be formal and it is useful for the organisation to encourage the out-going supervisor to be part of the selection process for the new supervisor.

The reasons for endings in supervision and the emotional impact they have on the dyadic relationship will be addressed in this chapter. Additionally, the practicalities of ending, for all parties in the working alliance, will be discussed in relation to the processes needed for making satisfactory endings and new beginnings, especially within an organisational context.

WHY DOES A SUPERVISORY RELATIONSHIP END?

There are many reasons why the supervisor, supervisee or the organisation ends a supervisory relationship. Inskipp and Proctor indicate the following reasons for change:

- Reaching a new stage of professional development – signalled by fresh training, new ideas etc.
- A new stage of personal development, signalled by noticing you require a different balance of support and challenge
- A different client group with whom you may want more expert help
- A changed job which may bring different demands and challenges
- Developing collusion – a merging of perspectives and blind spots between you and your supervisor – which may be signalled by a feeling of almost cosy safety
- Moving locality or your supervisor retiring
- You may have heard of a group and feel the urge for more inter-action with your colleagues in your supervision
- If you are in a group, you may, for any of the reasons above, think that one-to-one supervision would now meet your needs better
- Becoming aware of serious mismatches between you and your supervisor – in basic assumptions, theoretical framework, interactive style. These may be signalled by increasing feeling of being unheard, or misunderstood when you try to raise issues, or a reluctance on your part to even try.

(Inskipp and Proctor 1995:85)

In addition to these reasons for ending a supervisory relationship, an organisation may terminate a supervisor's contract because they decide:

- To change from group to individual supervision or vice versa.
- The supervisor is no longer willing to report back to the organisation.
- The supervisor does not have the competencies necessary for the organisational aspects of the role.
- The supervisor is unwilling to engage in tripartite meetings with the supervisee's line manager.
- The supervisor's fees are too high for the organisation.

- The supervisor is unwilling to engage in a single role rather than dual role capacity within the organisation.

Therefore, it can be the supervisor, the supervisee or the organisation that terminates the supervisory work.

Supervisor or supervisee moves geographical area

When one party in the working alliance moves geographical area the relationship can often end. It does not necessarily have to end, however, as supervision can be carried out on the telephone (Copeland 2003) but for some supervisors and their supervisees this is not always a viable option. Therefore, the supervisory relationship will need to end and the supervisee will need to find a new supervisor so that there are no gaps in their supervision. A number of years ago I was in this position when I moved from Cheshire to Yorkshire to take up a new job. I needed to end with a number of supervisees because it was impossible to fit them into a busy schedule and at such a geographical distance. With each one of them I felt sad at ending our working relationship. We planned for those endings carefully to ensure that there were no gaps in their supervision. Yet for me, those endings, although sad, did involve new beginnings and they also produced new opportunities. When there are not formal contracts with organisations to terminate the ending processes are simplified. However, the supervisor needs to trust that the supervisee will inform the organisation that they are entering a new supervisory relationship.

The supervisor retires

When a supervisor retires it often means that this is an event that has been anticipated for a while. New supervisory relationships may even start with this knowledge in place. However, although there may be sadness at the proposed ending, both parties know that it is circumstances rather than individual choice that makes the ending inevitable. Therefore, the ending can be planned and carried out professionally. When a supervisor retires, perhaps after a long and satisfying career as a counsellor, supervisor and maybe also a trainer, it is a time for celebration of that career and also a time for them to recharge their batteries and undertake a completely new beginning. They may want to try acting, write a novel or travel the world. This change will spark different feelings in both parties and these need to be acknowledged and worked with to ensure a satisfactory completion of their work together. When an organisation is involved, they too will be aware of the impending retirement. They may have employed the supervisor directly for many years and need to acknowledge their long working association in some way. This can mean the termination of a formal contract. In such cases a supervisor will need to give the required period of notification and it would be useful for them to be involved with the selection of a new supervisor.

The supervisor dies

A supervisor's death can be sudden or expected but either way it will mean the end of a relationship that has been important to the supervisee. There may have been a delay in finding out the news of the death and perhaps a funeral missed. Therefore, for a supervisee, finding a new supervisor in such sad circumstances can be difficult. New beginnings too will be fraught with unfinished business especially if the previous supervisor's death has been sudden. If the supervisor dies suddenly, the supervisee may need to start quickly with a new supervisor, whilst still grieving for the previous relationship. Therefore, the new supervisor will need to be much more sensitive than usual to the needs of the supervisee at this formative stage of their relationship. However, for the employing organisation, when a supervisor dies, especially if it is a sudden death, there will be the need to find a replacement supervisor quickly. The supervisee will need supporting and the organisation needs to ensure that the clients are protected. An emergency solution might be for the supervisee to be supervised by a colleague within the organisation until a satisfactory replacement can be found. Alternatively, telephone supervision is an option. Whatever the solution when a supervisor dies, it is the responsibility of the organisation to find a replacement, or to assist the counsellor in this process.

The supervisee has finished their period of training

Sometimes when a supervisee finishes their period of training to be a counsellor, they seek to change supervisors or the supervisor seeks to finish working with the supervisee. There can be many reasons for seeking this change. A supervisor might have felt that they were willing and able to support the supervisee during their training but no longer wanted to continue the struggle with a supervisee with whom they had little rapport. Similarly, a supervisee might have chosen a supervisor who was supportive during their training but who no longer meets their need for challenge as a fully trained counsellor. Whoever seeks to terminate the working relationship, the ending will only be amicable if both parties agree that the ending is necessary. Difficulties can arise when one party wants to end the working relationship and the other does not. This can happen at any time in a supervisory relationship, however it can be especially traumatic for the supervisee if their training and their supervisory relationship are terminated at the same time.

When an organisation continues to employ a counsellor after their training has finished, it is necessary for them to be aware of their responsibility to ensure that the counsellor chooses another supervisor quickly. The counsellor may need help with this process. Alternatively, the counsellor will need to inform the organisation of the need to employ, contract and pay the new supervisor. The organisation will be unaware of the need for this process if the training institution has been responsible for choice and payment of the supervisor previously.

The supervisee wants a different working relationship or set of skills than those provided by their current supervisor

At any time in a counsellor's career the counsellor may want a different working relationship or set of skills than provided by their current supervisor especially as they become increasingly experienced in their work. They may want more personal challenge in the relationship than the current supervisor is able to provide. They may also want a different theoretical perspective on their client work that cannot be provided by their current supervisor. Changing the organisational setting for their work may also be a factor. This could mean that they seek out a new supervisor who has experience of working in a similar setting, which as seen in Chapter 4 can be an advantage for the supervisee. The counsellor may also be undergoing a period of great personal change and decide that part of this change is moving out of their comfort zone and changing supervisors too. Similarly, a supervisor and their supervisee may be aware that they have both reached the end of their productive working relationship. There could be a mutual agreement to move on.

An organisation may also decide that their counsellors need to change supervisors when time-limited work is introduced for clients. If managers are conversant with the needs of their counsellors regarding the supervision process, they will be able to employ a supervisor who can support and challenge the counsellors whilst, additionally, providing a service to the organisation. Nevertheless, their first responsibility is to the counsellor and their clients. Within this process, too, there is need for the counsellor to be fully involved at every step of the employment process.

Supervision boundaries become problematic

In some situations supervision boundaries can become problematic for a variety of reasons. Perhaps the supervisor has a dual or triple role within the organisation and feels that they need to relinquish the group supervisory role in order to maintain clear boundaries. Similarly, a counsellor trainer may choose to give up their supervisory role within a course as it causes divided loyalties when assessing students' work. Additionally, a supervisor may choose to stop supervising a particular supervisee when their social circles collide and professional boundaries become too difficult to maintain. For a supervisor to maintain ethical practice may mean making the difficult decision to terminate the work. Boundary issues need to be managed when they occur in organisational settings. It is important that the supervisory relationship is ended if it is also coupled with a managerial role. Similarly, if a counselling and/or a training role is involved, such dual or triple roles need to be terminated to clarify boundaries. Termination of one or more role, which may include the supervisory role, needs to involve negotiations with all those it affects.

The supervisory relationship is becoming collusive

Ethically, changing supervisor every three years is often advised to avoid a collusive relationship. As supervision is mandatory for all counsellors who are members of BACP, there could be the temptation to stay with one supervisor throughout a person's counselling career. This means that ethical practice is maintained through the required supervision and the counsellor remains within their comfort zone in terms of the relationship that has been established over considerable time. However, the danger with long-term supervisory relationships is that they become too familiar and so can lack the challenge required to enhance counselling practice. As discussed in Chapter 8, a sound relationship is at the heart of good supervision. When this is established there can be a reluctance to make changes that end such a relationship. Indeed, there are practitioners who dispute the need for change at all. Nevertheless, when there is an acknowledgment, by both parties, that change is needed to effect growth for the counsellor, there will be a readiness to terminate the relationship. For some organizations the onus will be on the supervisee's line manager to instigate change when collusion is identified. However, it is more likely that the supervisory dyad itself will decide that the relationship has become cosy and needs to change.

Long-term illness of the supervisor

When a supervisor is incapacitated by a long-term illness there are specific issues involved with ending the relationship. There may be difficulties in making the decision about ending permanently or simply using another supervisor as a temporary measure for the duration of the illness. Either way, the supervisee will need to ensure that they do not have any gaps in the supervision of their clients. It will also be the organisation's responsibility to help the supervisee with this process. There could be another counsellor within the organisation whose supervisor would be prepared to take on the supervisee, on a temporary basis. There may also be the opportunity for peer supervision for a short period. Group supervision within the organisation might also be an option. However, if the counsellor is the only one in the practice, they will need to fill the gap quickly, informing the organisation of the temporary or permanent change. This can mean that an organisation needs to arrange a contract of employment quickly when a new supervisory relationship is begun.

At the end of a probationary period for the supervisory relationship

It is common practice for supervisory relationships to begin with an agreement to have a probationary period of anything between three and six months. This enables both parties to find out if they can work together productively. Some relationships end after this probationary period. This may be because one or both parties are not satisfied that the relationship will work. There are many reasons for this occurrence. A supervisor can find that the supervisee is not competent as a counsellor and so they are not willing to be responsible for a practitioner who may attract complaints from clients. Additionally, a supervisor can find that their theoretical orientation is not compatible with that of their supervisee. Many supervisors who I have trained have shown that differing theoretical orientations do not necessarily impede the supervisory relationship. Nevertheless it can sometimes happen, especially if the supervisee is a trainee or a very inexperienced counsellor. A supervisor can also find that the organisational context of their supervisee's work does not provide clearly defined boundaries for ethical practice. If the supervisee is unwilling to relinquish the work in this organisation, the supervisor will have no alternative but to terminate the supervisory relationship at the end of their probationary period.

At the end of a probationary period a supervisee may decide to terminate their work together. Again, as with the supervisor, this can be for numerous reasons. The supervisee might decide that they are not getting what they want from the relationship. They may have the need for more support or challenge or for the supervisor to have experience of working with a similar client group or within a similar type of organisational culture. They may also require the supervisor to have the ability to supervise their supervision work, a task for which not all supervisors are sufficiently trained or experienced. Additionally, they may find that the supervisor is difficult to engage with because of insurmountable transferential issues. Inskipp and Proctor, when writing about the development of the counsellor in supervision, address this issue

> One-to-one interactions that are experienced (or anticipated) as authoritative can be very re-stimulating of old relationships for us. Parent, teacher, boss may be the models we bring, and our earlier experiences of such authority figures when we were young and relatively powerless may not have been good. As in counselling, so in supervision, it is possible to find ourselves feeling surprisingly childish – and transferring emotions to our supervisor as if she were an authority figure from our past. In other

words, experiencing a transference situation that may be disempowering
– or illuminating! Becoming aware of this possibility enables us to use it
and learn from it.

(Inskipp and Proctor 1995:29)

A situation such as this occurring within the probationary period may be
worked with or, alternatively, could be so disempowering that the supervisee
has no alternative but to end the relationship. However, it will still be material
to be explored in the supervisee's own therapy. Ending the relationship can
often be a more difficult task if there is a power imbalance within the relationship, especially if the supervisee is a trainee or very inexperienced. In such
situations it is useful for the organisation to become involved. The supervisee's line manager can be instrumental in helping them to end the relationship
amicably by a tripartite meeting in which the difficulties are raised and
discussed before the termination takes place.

When the supervisory relationship breaks down

When a supervisory relationship breaks down there needs to be an ending of
the work together. There are many reasons why such a relationship can break
down. When a supervisor is allocated to a supervisee within an organisational
setting then the relationship can be difficult from the outset. The supervisor
may resent not having a free choice of supervisor within the organisation.
Research shows that this is often a cause of dysfunctional supervisory relationships (Copeland 2000a). Within a voluntary organisation, one supervisor
found that their supervisee would have liked to choose their own supervisor.
Similarly, this supervisor would also have liked the opportunity to choose
their own supervisees from within the organisation. From my own experience,
when supervisees are not given free choice of their supervisor, then it takes
hard work and a great deal of time to establish a relationship that is productive and trusting. Sometimes it is an impossible task despite the good will that
is displayed on both sides. However, it is only usually within an organisational
context that supervisors are allocated to supervisees, mainly for pragmatic
or financial reasons. When an organisation employs one supervisor there is
a need for consultation about their supervisory needs before an appointment
is made.

Supervisory relationships can break down even when both parties have
actively chosen one another. Maybe the supervisee finds it difficult to
acknowledge that they are unfit to practise for some reason, resulting in the
supervisor having to make the difficult decision to terminate their work with a
counsellor who they know is practising unethically. Similarly, a supervisee
may know that they need to terminate their work with a supervisor who is
cavalier with time boundaries. These examples assume that it is only one
party in the supervisory relationship that is unhappy with their work

together. When this is so it is far more difficult to end than if the agreement to end is mutual. If there have been tripartite meetings between the supervisor, supervisee and their line manager, there is an opportunity for the line manager to act as mediator between the other two parties. However, it will take a skilled manager to broker a deal that leads to an amicable ending.

The organisation will not pay the supervisor's increased fees

When the organisation is involved with the payment of the supervisor's fees, disputes can occur that may lead to the termination of the supervisory contract. As discussed in Chapter 6, supervisors can be paid by the organisation either directly or indirectly through the supervisee. If the supervisor has a contract with the organisation for their supervisory work it means that they have a direct line of communication for negotiating an increased fee. This is an ideal scenario because the supervisee does not have to be involved with the negotiations and the supervisor can use their personal power to affect the necessary change. However, if the supervisor has no direct communication with the counsellor's line manager they will have to rely on the supervisee to negotiate a fee increase. If this is not forthcoming the supervisor will have to decide whether to terminate their work with the supervisee. This decision can be very difficult to make, although on economic grounds there may be no alternative. The supervisee could decide to make up the difference in fee but this still leaves the supervisor with the knowledge that the organisation does not value the work they do with the counsellor. This situation is less likely to occur if the supervisor has a professional contract of employment, with terms and conditions of service clearly outlined, including when the pay scale will be reviewed.

The organisation views the supervisor as incompetent

If the organisation is employing the supervisor directly they need to be sure that they are competent and continue to be for the duration of their employment. This can seem like an unlikely scenario, especially if the counsellor's line manager has little understanding of the role of the supervisor and even less understanding of the competencies needed to fulfil that role. Nevertheless, in some organisations, especially counselling agencies, line managers do have a full understanding of the supervision process and will be aware of the responsibilities they need their supervisors to undertake. In these organisations, an employer has the right to terminate employment if the employee is not working to a satisfactory standard. This is where the supervisor's contract with the organisation, as discussed in Chapter 6, plays a vital part in the ending of the supervision work. There are many reasons why an organisation may seek to end its contract with a supervisor. Perhaps the supervisor is no longer engaged in continuing professional development, or maybe the feedback from the supervisee indicates that there is a lack of challenge in the relationship. Whatever the case, it might mean that the organisation terminates the supervisor's contract and so both parties in the supervisory relationship have to make an ending to their work. However, this is a last resort for an organisation and not a decision that would be taken lightly because of the effect on the supervisee and their work.

The organisation now needs a supervisor who is also competent in running groups

Similarly, the organisation can decide that it is going to change the supervision provided within the organisation, from individual to group supervision. This means that the current supervisor needs to be competent in facilitating groups in order to continue with the contract. The supervisor may not want to continue working for the organisation under these changed conditions and so decides to terminate their work with the organisation. Whoever decides that the supervisory relationship needs to end and for whatever reason, there will be emotional realities and practicalities to be dealt with. Additionally, when an organisation is involved, or instrumental in engineering the ending, there will be a third party to consider within the ending process. The contract will need to be terminated and new ones negotiated.

There are many reasons why supervisory relationships end. Whether the ending is welcomed or feared, there will be practical issues to address for supervisor, supervisee and the organisation.

THE PRACTICALITIES OF THE ENDING PROCESS

All supervisors, as counsellors themselves, will be familiar with the ending process with clients. They will know how to make a good ending and, whenever possible, will plan for the ending in a systematic way. Yet I have met many supervisors who say that although they are good at endings with clients, their endings with supervisees are less than clear. Perhaps this accounts for the lack of writing on the subject. However, the practicalities of ending a supervisory relationship need to be clearly addressed by all parties in the working alliance.

Money issues

When ending a supervisory relationship there may be many issues, especially over payment, that need to be resolved amicably if an organisation is involved. If the supervisee is responsible for paying the supervisor and does so on a monthly basis there should be no problems in this area when the relationship ends. The supervisee will just pay the supervisor, as normal, on the last session. However, if an organisation is involved, decisions will need to be made, hopefully at the beginning of the supervisory relationship, as to whose responsibility it is to inform the organisation about the termination of the work. The key once again lies with the supervisory contract. This may be a tripartite contract with the supervisee, the supervisor and the organisation. Alternatively, the contract may just exist between the supervisor and their supervisee, as outlined in Chapter 6. Within either contract there needs to be an indication of whose responsibility it is to inform the organisation about the termination of the work so that payments cease. This could be payment that goes directly to the supervisor or alternatively it could be paid to the supervisee who then pays the supervisor. However this payment occurs, communication of information needs to be swift and accurate after the termination of the work, to avoid over-payment by the organisation and the inconvenience to the supervisor of having to return unearned cheques. This is especially relevant if the supervisor is contracted for a specific number of sessions with a training organisation. This has happened to me on one occasion and it severely tested my honesty! However, it is more common practice for supervisors to invoice an organisation for individual session and therefore over-payment at the end of a contract would not occur. Nevertheless, it is important that a supervisor invoices an organisation swiftly on termination of the work, before another supervisor starts, to avoid confusion with the accounts department. When there is a risk that the organisation will cease to exist, either through insolvency or lack of charitable funding, it is important for the supervisor to ensure that they will be paid at the end of their contract. So again prompt invoicing is essential.

Money issues, although rarely discussed in public, are important to a supervisor and can generate uncomfortable, unresolved feelings if they are not dealt with swiftly. Communication is the key to amicable settlement of such matters.

Is it really an ending?

Some endings in supervision can be misleading and there may be some doubt as to whether it really is a permanent ending to the work. This can happen when a supervisee decides to have a break from their practice for a while. There are a number of reasons for this. They might be suffering from a stress-related illness, or there is a lack of clients within their organisation at any one time. Similarly, the supervisee may decide to take an extended break from counselling to travel for a while or visit relatives in a remote part of the world. In cases such as these there needs to be clear understanding concerning the contract for the supervisory work, is it actually suspended rather than permanently ended? In cases such as these there can be a temptation to assume that the work will continue and therefore, a formal ending is not made. In the event of the supervision not continuing in the future, it means that no formal ending will ever be made. This situation can provide a dilemma for all parties in the working relationship. Do they formally end or not? Each supervisory dyad will find the answer to this dilemma, nevertheless, it seems pertinent to assume that a formal ending is necessary to ensure that new beginnings can be made satisfactorily with another supervisor in the future. When a formal contract is made with an organisation it will provide clarity through ending the work, even temporarily, so that another contract can be begun at a future date.

Ending with trainees

When ending with trainee counsellors, the supervisor needs to take special care to ensure that they are prepared for trainee requests to carry on with the supervisory relationship when their course has ended. Many supervisors have said to me that they were unprepared for such a request having assumed that their trainee would want to change supervisors after their training had finished. For trainees, the supervisory relationship is often a real support within training that can be stormy and life changing. Therefore, there is a tendency to want to hold on to the relationship whilst they are encountering the strong emotions that ensue at the end of a course. For this reason, supervisors need to prepare their response to any request for a continuation of the relationship. Alternatively, if a supervisor is expecting the relationship to continue after the end of their supervisee's training, they could be surprised by a request for an ending. Either way, a supervisor needs to anticipate what they feel would be the best course of action both for them and their supervisee.

Anecdotal evidence suggests that sometimes supervisors are not prepared to continue with the supervisory work as a trainee becomes a fully qualified counsellor. They find themselves in that situation by default because they have not thought through the ramifications for their relationship, caused by the ending of the course. As noted earlier, the organisation can also be instrumental in deciding whether a supervisory relationship continues after a counsellor's training is finished. Once the link with the training institution has been severed, the organisation can instigate a new supervisory regime involving internal supervisors. Alternatively, the organisation can insist that the counsellor finds a supervisor who is sympathetic to the organisation's aims and client group. In many geographical areas, where counsellors are plentiful, an organisation can pick and choose the counsellor they employ and the terms of that employment can include a stipulation concerning the arrangements for supervision. This can mean an enforced ending for the trainee counsellor, even when the supervisory relationship was good.

Therefore, planning, well in advance, is important for supervisory relationships with trainee counsellors. The supervisor is in a position to help them to decide what they need from supervision in the future and who can fulfil that role. However, it could also be the organisation that helps the counsellor with this decision, hopefully with their full negotiation and support.

Ending as a tutor/supervisor

The ending in this supervisory relationship as a tutor/supervisor is often an ending with a group rather than an individual trainee. Nevertheless, it still needs to be managed carefully and this is where the organisational context of the work is also highlighted. The group tutor/supervisor needs to be aware of the dynamics of a trainee finishing their work within the organisation appropriately. The ending will need to be foreshadowed with clients early enough for them to work through the therapeutic ramifications of the work that has been done and maybe the work that is still to do in the future. The tutor/supervisor needs to hold the therapeutic frame whilst also noting the parallel process of their own ending with the group. For some trainees the end of the supervisory group may be a relief as it means the end of the course and entry into the professional world as a fully qualified counsellor. For others, this ending will mean the end of work with a supportive group of peers and tutor/supervisor that will be difficult to replicate in the world outside the course. The polarisation of each position will need to be held by the supervisor and acknowledged with support and challenge. The tutor/supervisor themselves will have feelings about the ending of the relationship with the group. The group may have been a challenge to manage, and therefore the ending will be a relief. Alternatively, sadness may be an emotion experienced at the ending of a productive group relationship. Whatever feelings are around, the tutor/supervisor will have the skills to model a good ending in a way that leaves all trainees ready to face their professional life with confidence, having experienced a good ending in group supervision.

THE EMOTIONAL IMPACT OF ENDING A SUPERVISORY RELATIONSHIP

Gray (1993) indicates that managers are afraid of the affective side of organisational life. Yet endings are inevitable in all areas of employment, whether planned or unplanned, welcomed or feared. The management of the emotions that are generated by endings also needs to be respected and acknowledged. When redundancies are announced within an organisation they are often the catalyst for using counsellors to enable people to talk about their emotions and plan for the future. So the ending of a supervisory relationship will generate an emotional response that cannot be ignored. Usually it is left to the supervisory dyad to manage these difficult endings, however, the supervisee's line manager can also be involved with the ending if they have been part of the tripartite meetings throughout the supervisor's contract.

Sadness

Sadness is often associated with endings in general and the ending of a supervisory relationship is no exception for some supervisors and supervisees. If the relationship has been strong and empowering, both parties will be reluctant to part. The parting could be enforced by some of the reasons explored above and so the sadness will be deep. When there has been clear transferential relationship, the sadness can be overwhelming. If this relationship started when the supervisee was a trainee counsellor and continued after the end of the training programme, the bond will be deep and difficulty experienced in acknowledging the end. In managing the end, both parties in the working alliance need to talk about how they would like it to be. There may be a difference in how they manage endings in their own lives. If the supervisee tends to avoid them, the supervisor needs to ensure that time is reserved for this purpose. This will enable the supervisee to learn a new way of managing their sadness when ending relationships and so have an impact on their future endings with clients. Similarly, if the supervisor can acknowledge their own sadness at the ending of the relationship, they will be modelling a way of being that is helpful to their supervisee. I know that I have been moved to tears by many endings in my supervisory relationships and this has been cathartic whilst also being empowering.

When organisations have been instrumental in the ending of the supervisory relationship, the line manager will need to have a tripartite meeting so that feelings can be expressed before new supervisory relationships are begun. Yet sadness is not the only feeling that is experienced on the ending of a supervisory relationship. However, it may be easier to acknowledge than other emotions.

Relief

Relief at the ending of a supervisory relationship is not always easy to acknowledge especially if it is only experienced by one party in the working alliance. Perhaps the supervisor is relieved to be finishing with a trainee counsellor who has been difficult to engage openly in the process. For example a trainee may be changing from a profession where they were not expected to reveal their feelings. A nurse in the accident and emergency department of a busy city hospital is not expected to show their feelings whilst working. This will mean that, as they make the transition to qualified counsellor, they need to shift their awareness from suppression to internal awareness of their emotions and consequently, external expression of them. This is not an easy task for the trainee, and will also mean that the sessions are difficult for the supervisor. Therefore, the supervisor will be relieved at the ending of the relationship.

Similarly, a supervisee can be relieved when the decision to end a supervisory relationship is made. However, it is not an emotion that is easy to express as it can imply dissatisfaction in the relationship. Perhaps it is easier for the supervisor to help the supervisee to express the relief felt rather than vice versa. In approaching this emotion it will be helpful to voice the positives in the relationship so that the relief can be heard more readily. The relief can be about practical details such as ending a long arduous journey to the supervision or the difficulty that boundary issues played in the work. In such cases relief is more easily expressed than when the relationship has been difficult and there has been very little attempt to acknowledge the problems. In such cases, especially if the relief is on the part of the supervisor, perhaps the relief will not be voiced. This will mean that an opportunity for learning is lost by both parties in the working alliance. In supervision for supervision, a supervisor can explore ways in which relief can be voiced in a non-destructive way that enables learning to take place, celebrating strengths and exploring ways to develop practice more fully.

When an organisation is involved in enabling the supervisee to choose their own supervisor, the supervisee will be able to express their feelings of relief to their line manager but it will be more difficult to express them to their supervisor. However, it is important for a supervisee's line manager to be aware of any difficulties within the supervisory relationship. This will enable them to discuss how to manage the ending in a positive, but hopefully honest, way. It will also enable the line manager to avoid similar difficulties when choosing a new supervisor.

Anger

Anger will be around for either party in the working alliance when one person wants to end the relationship and the other would rather continue the work. This may echo the anger felt when ending previous relationships both personal and professional. It is necessary to facilitate the acknowledgement of the feeling in order for both parties to move on in ending the relationship. It may be possible for the person ending the relationship to instigate and facilitate the expression of anger in the other party. Alternatively, especially within an organisational context, it will need a third person to mediate in this ending process and help both supervisor and supervisee to hear one another. The supervisee's line manager could be that third person if they were willing to be part of this process. However, they could also have feelings about the ending of the supervisory relationship, especially if they would prefer the supervisor to continue with the work. They may be angry that the supervisor has broken their contract with the organisation because of a breakdown of relationship between themselves and the organisation. Once again, it is necessary for the line manager, as the representative of the organisation, to either mediate between two parties or alternatively, have a tripartite meeting where all parties can express their anger freely. This is a responsibility that an organisation cannot avoid.

For some organisations, the change in supervision arrangements and the organisation's part in this process will need to be acknowledged and time given for the ending process. When line managers are not counsellors there can be a lack of understanding of the importance of this ending process. Nevertheless, it is their responsibility to facilitate the expression of feelings that are around when a supervisory relationship ends either because it has reached its natural conclusion or because it no longer serves the purpose for which it was intended.

Celebration

The celebration that can take place at the end of a supervisory relationship can be a very positive experience. It marks the ending in a distinctive way and is the launching pad for a new beginning with another supervisor. The celebration of the supervisee's learning and development is essential to mark as is the skill and experience of the supervisor. In engaging in the celebration of the work done, both parties are making the ending clear. This celebration may be marked by sharing a meal together or exchanging gifts after reviewing the work, the high and low spots, the beginnings together and prospective new beginnings with another supervisor. If the organisation has been closely involved with the supervisor, celebrating the work done within that context would also be appropriate.

NEW BEGINNINGS

When a supervision contract ends there will inevitably be a new beginning within an organisation. If the contract with the supervisor has been formal, the ending will also have a structure to it. This means that supervisor, supervisee and their line manager will all be involved. If the ending has been amicable, it is possible that the outgoing supervisor will have the opportunity to help with the process of choosing a new supervisor. Not all supervisors will want to be part of this process, however, if they do their experience will be invaluable to the organisation. They can help the line manager to write the advertisement, job description and person specification. They could also be involved with the interviewing process, if it was carried out formally. If the process is informal, their advice would be useful. It could be noted that the supervisee would also be able to fulfil this function.

Rose's research (2001) into counsellor perceptions of supervisory roles in a managed primary care counselling service served this purpose. She began her study when a supervisor appointed by the organisation left and a new one had yet to be appointed. She was eager to establish what each of the counsellors within the counselling service needed, hoped for and feared in the appointment of a new supervisor for both individual and group supervision. As a result she found eleven aspects of the supervisor's role in the setting to be important for the counsellors. These included: expert, member of a system, valuing at a professional level, containing, creative, being in a comfortable relationship, educator/mentor, reflective practitioner and challenger. These results were relayed to the line manager who used them as information when choosing the new supervisor. Not every organisation has the luxury of a research project to inform them about future supervisory needs, however, it is a model that would be useful to use, even in an informal way, as a developmental tool for supervision in organisations.

As new beginnings in supervision are forged, so past experiences inform new choices. This process is vital if there is to be development in how organisations use their supervisors, not just as a resource for the individual supervisee but also for the whole organisation.

CONCLUSION

It is acknowledged that endings in supervision are an important part of the supervisory process. Counsellors and supervisors who avoid making a formal ending in supervision will undoubtedly be poor at endings with their clients. Similarly, organisations that do not involve themselves with the ending of a supervisory relationship will probably find that there are aspects of the counselling service that would benefit from closer management. Supervisors could be helpful in giving information to the organisation concerning all the processes involved in supervision which will include the ending of the relationship.

Responsibilities of the supervisor

- Ensuring that the ending with their supervisee is planned and managed professionally
- Informing the supervisee's line manager that the supervisory relationship is being terminated
- Invoicing the organisation promptly for the final session(s) of supervision
- Involving themselves in a tripartite meeting with the supervisee and their line manager in order to discuss points for development in the future with a new supervisor
- Producing a joint report with their supervisee, for the organisation, on the supervisory work
- Offering to involve themselves with the selection of a new supervisor for the organisation

Responsibilities of the supervisee

- Ensuring that they plan and manage the ending with their supervisor professionally
- Informing their line manager that their relationship with their supervisor is ending
- Ensuring that there is no gap in their supervision when one relationship comes to an end and a new one starts
- Involving themselves in a tripartite meeting with their line manager and their out-going supervisor
- Producing a joint report for the organisation, with the supervisor, on the supervisory work

Responsibilities of the line manager

- Ensuring that any contractual arrangements are concluded professionally, including final payments to the supervisor
- Involving themselves in a tripartite meeting with the supervisor and their supervisee to celebrate successes and detail areas for development
- Ensuring that any written report requested from the supervisor and supervisee is completed

Conclusion

In this book I have advocated that it is important for supervisors to become more proactive in helping their supervisees to work effectively within the organisation. Part I initially explored the role of the counselling supervisor within post-modern organisations. The clarity needed in defining the role is discussed in order to ensure that the organisation knows what knowledge and skills the supervisor can offer both to their supervisee and also in time, to the wider organisation. Part II outlined the dilemmas around managing the cultural fit between counselling and supervision and the organisational culture in which they reside. This has given voice to the need for supervisors to be culturally aware, both of their own professional cultural norms and, additionally, of the diverse cultures that exist in different types of organisations. Managing the cultural fit is challenging. However, the challenge needs to be faced if the supervisory process is to be effective. In Part III, systems are explored to enable supervisors to become formally employed and therefore more involved with their supervisee's organisation. Managers are also challenged to find ways of working with the tripartite relationship between themselves, their counsellor and the supervisor. If formal systems are in place to facilitate communication between all parties within this supervisory rhombus, both the client and subsequently the organisation will benefit. First, the clients will be held within a safe environment where ethical practice is maintained and second, communication systems will ensure that the supervisor is valued by the organisation and their knowledge and skills are acknowledged and used more widely for the benefit of the organisation. Consequently, for this to happen the supervisor, supervisee and their line manager will need to be aware of the extent of their responsibilities in this formal system (see Appendix 5 for a composite list of the responsibilities of all parties in the working alliance).

However, in writing this book I have become more acutely aware of the need for the standardisation of supervision competencies. Supervisors have very little guidance concerning national standards that indicate the minimum level of competence to practise. At the time of writing, BACP are re-writing their accreditation processes for supervisors. Yet the poor uptake of this award in the past has suggested that supervisors do not readily see the need for this type of recognition for their work. Line managers employing supervisors within organisations need to have some way of measuring effectiveness in supervision, counselling supervision costs are high and organisations may not be getting value for their money.

Training courses in supervision have expanded over the last decade. However, the length, content and standards expected of course participants varies greatly across the UK. Some courses last for one academic year and yet others only last for a week-end or are a short module within another award. Additionally, the name of the award, either certificate or diploma, is no indication of its value for supervisors in knowledge and skill acquisition. There is an urgent need for the accreditation of supervisor training courses to ensure, as with counsellor training, that a minimum standard of practice is achieved by all supervisors across the UK. In the counselling profession the role of supervision is given great importance for maintaining ethical standards yet there is no mandate for supervisors to be trained. Some employers are becoming aware of the need for supervisors to be trained, other are not. Therefore, until there is a common standard and a recognised need for training courses that address all aspects of the supervision process, including the organisational context of the work, supervision will remain a relative mystery to some employers. I do not want to paint too bleak a picture as I know that there are supervisors who are trained and competent, working diligently to uphold ethical standards and supporting their supervisees who are often working in very difficult conditions of employment. However, this is no excuse for complacency, supervision needs to continually develop and grow in order to be the force for change that it can become within organisational contexts. Supervisors, supervisees and their line managers need to embrace their responsibilities within the organisational context of their work and strive to create systems of open communication to ensure that they are all working together for the benefit of the organisation and the clients within it.

Therefore, from small beginnings, by the formal employment of supervisors and the development of tripartite meetings and reporting back procedures, supervisors can gradually begin to take on a more active role, working organisationally as well as individually. In many different types of organisations other employees would find supervision very beneficial too. Talking to a lawyer recently confirmed that when she was engaged in distressing, emotional work, having the benefit of supervision afterwards would alleviate the need to take the distress home. This could also apply to all workers in services such as the prison service and probation work to name but a few professions where great emotional demands are made on employees. Therefore, although the emphasis in this book is on supervision for counsellors, supervisors could also be effectively used for all those professionals who are stressed by the emotional demands of their work. A gradual approach to the more widespread use of supervisors within organisations is needed if they are unfamiliar and wary of the supervision process and the knowledge and skills that supervisors possess. The supervisor will need to gain the trust of managers and to work hard to develop a higher profile within the organisation. When this is achieved they will be in a position to be consultant, mentor, coach and supervisor to the organisation itself.

Appendix I

North Umbria Health Care Trust
Psychology Department
£27–£31K pa, pro rata

Part time (16 hours per month)

A Counselling Supervisor is required to supervise eight experienced counsellors working for the Primary Health Care Trust in four different GP surgeries within the Eastley–Helliton area.

You will be responsible for providing individual supervision for two hours a month to eight counsellors. You will work with each counsellor in their individual surgeries and a reasonable travel allowance will be paid.

You will have a recognised counselling training, considerable counselling experience and be accredited by BACP or equivalent professional organisation.

You must work within an ethical framework or code of conduct. Supervision training and at least three years' experience as a practising supervisor is essential.

You will be required to report back to the Psychology Department about attendance, professional practice and organisational issues for statistical purposes.

For further information or to request an application form
and a detailed job description, please contact
Joanne Hollinsworth on 061 462907

Appendix 2

Application form for post of: Counselling Supervisor

Name		Date of birth
Address	Telephone: mobile day evening	
Date of application		
Items marked * require photocopy evidence		
Counselling Please indicate your main style of counselling:		
* Are you accredited as a Counsellor yes/no Supervisor yes/no		
By whom?		
Are you working towards accreditation?	yes/no	
With whom?		

* Counsellor training		
1. Details:		
Duration	No. of hours	Qualification:
2. Details:		
Duration	No. of hours	Qualification:
3. Details:		
Duration	No. of hours	Qualification:
Counselling experience		
1. Details:		
Dates		Average number of clients/week
Type of counselling/clients		
2. Details:		
Dates		Average number of clients/week
Type of counselling/clients		
3. Details:		
Dates		Average number of clients/week
Type of counselling/clients		

What is your average number of sessions per case?	
Do you regard your counselling as short term?	yes/no
Current Counselling Supervisor:	
Name:	
Address:	
Duration of counselling supervision	Hours
Frequency of counselling supervision	
Style of counselling supervision	Individual/Group/Peer
May we contact your Counselling Supervisor for a reference?	yes/no
* Supervision training	
1. Details:	
Duration	Number of hours
Qualifications	
2. Details:	
Duration	Number of hours
Qualifications	

3. Details:	
Duration	Number of hours
Qualifications	
Have you recent experience in supervising individuals?	yes/no
Dates	Hours/month
Supervision of supervision	
Current supervision supervisor:	
Name:	
Address:	
Duration of supervision of supervision	Hours
Frequency of supervision of supervision	
Style of supervision of supervision	Individual/Group/Peer
May we contact your supervision supervisor?	yes/no
General	
To which codes of ethics and practice do you adhere?	
Do you have £1,000,000 professional indemnity insurance?	yes/no

Have you ever worked in a commercial organisation?	yes/no
Which organisation?	
In what capacity?	
Signed:	Date:

(Adapted from the Post Office Consultative Support/Supervision Network Application Form.)

Appendix 3

INDIVIDUAL SUPERVISION CONTRACT

This Agreement is made on the 1st day of September 2004 between SCW and . . . . (the Supervisor).

   SCW wishes to make use of the Supervisor's services to supervise the counsellors in its employment.

1. Duration

- The Agreement will commence on 1st September 2004.
- The Agreement will continue in force until the second anniversary of the commencement date when it will expire automatically.

2. Supervisor's Obligations

- All work to be performed under this contract will be executed in an efficient and appropriate manner to the reasonable satisfaction of SCW.
- If the Supervisor fails to carry out properly any part of the work as detailed in the contract the defects or omissions will be remedied by the Supervisor within a reasonable period of time in accordance with the contract and with no additional charge other than as may be agreed in writing by SCW.

3. Supervisor's Standards

- All supervisors will be properly qualified, trained and experienced in accordance with the Supervisor's selection criteria as described in the Appendix 3:2.
- Supervisors are to use SCW's reporting forms.

4. Monitoring and Inspection

- All Supervisors are to complete an application form providing evidence of their training, experience and professional supervision.
- SCW will seek validatory references from the Supervisor's own counselling and supervision supervisors.

5. Fees and Expenses

- Subject to SCW being satisfied as to the quality and manner of the performance of the services provided, SCW will pay the Supervisor the fees at the time stated in the contract, within 45 days of the receipt of an invoice. Invoices should be submitted using the agreed Claim Form and clearly indicate the period for which the payment is due.
- SCW will pay reasonable out of pocket and travelling expenses incurred by the Supervisor. Details of travel and other expenses must be supported by receipts.
- The fees for the provision of individual supervision will be at the rate of £40–£45 per hour for individual supervision sessions. There shall be no increase of fees within a period of 12 months from the date of the previous increase or the date of this contract (whichever is the later) provided nothing is different as provided in Appendix 3:1.
- The Supervisor will be liable to account to the Inland Revenue for all taxes on fees paid to the Supervisor and to the relevant authorities for any National Insurance or other statutory contributions.

6. Confidentiality

- The Supervisor shall not disclose to any third party any personal information relating to the counsellors at SCW.
- The Supervisor will not disclose any information relating to SCW and its business.
- Personal information regarding SCW counsellors will remain confidential within the limits laid down by the British Association for Counselling and Psychotherapy, information regarding the competency of each counsellor to undertake their work, their training needs and organisational issues which may affect the quality of their work will be communicated to the counsellors' line manager by the Supervisor.
- The Supervisor will ensure that disclosure of information by them to any person will comply with the provisions of the Data Protection Act (1984).

7. Termination

- Either party may, by giving 30 days' notice in writing, terminate this agreement if the other party committed a substantial breach of any of the terms of this agreement.
- Either party may, by giving 30 days' notice, terminate this agreement forthwith.
- Where SCW considers there to be a sufficiently serious breach of Clauses 2 or 3, the contract may be terminated forthwith.
- Any termination shall be without prejudice to any rights which have accrued up to the day of termination or which shall accrue thereafter.

8. Variations

- If at any time SCW wishes to undertake any reasonable alteration or addition to, or omission from, the tasks set out in the Agreement, it will notify the Supervisor in writing, the Supervisor will, within 14 days, provide a written statement of the amount by which such variations would increase or decrease the time taken to perform the service and the cost of the service and such other information as SCW may require.

9. Facilities to be Provided

SCW shall arrange for the Supervisor to have access to premises as is necessary to enable the Supervisor to fulfil their obligation under the contract.

10. Liability for Personal Injury and Damage to Property

The Supervisor will be liable for any personal injury or death or any loss of or damage to property arising as a result of any act of omission on the part of the Supervisor relating to this contract and shall indemnify SCW against any loss, costs or expense incurred by SCW as a result of such act or omission.

11. Conflicts of Interest

If at the time of signing the contract, or at any time during the existence of this contract, any actual or possible conflict of interest between the work undertaken in this contract and any other activities of the Supervisor exists or may exist, the Supervisor must inform SCW without delay. If SCW will decide that a conflict of interest does exist, then SCW may require the Supervisor to cease such other activity or activities. If the Supervisor fails to do so at the earliest reasonable opportunity, then SCW may terminate this contract in the terms contained hereunder.

12. Signatories

Signed and agreed on behalf of SCW Signed and agreed by Supervisor

Date: Date:

APPENDIX 3.1: INDIVIDUAL SUPERVISION SERVICES PROVIDED TO SCW

Supervisors provide supervision as defined in the most recent BACP Ethical Framework. This supervision needs to reflect the organisational context in which the activity is provided. It is therefore required that the Supervisor formally contract with both the supervisee and the organisation.

APPENDIX 3.2: SELECTION CRITERIA FOR SUPERVISORS

Criteria for supervisors:

- Must be BACP accredited or UKCP registered or BPS chartered counselling psychologist.
- Need to have experience of organisational counselling.
- Evidence required of indemnity insurance plus appropriate academic qualifications and experience. (All should be detailed on Curricula Vitae.)
- Need to have experience and be positive about working with short-term intervention.
- Remuneration is usually around £40–£45 per hour.

(Adapted from the Contract Agreement between Counselling Supervisors and the Post Office.)

Appendix 4

SUPERVISOR'S/SUPERVISEE'S PROFESSIONAL REPORT TO THE ORGANISATION

One Supervisor's Report is required for every six months of practice for Supervisees working towards accreditation and yearly for those who are accredited. The Report should be discussed with the Supervisee and submitted to their line manager. The Supervisee needs to keep a copy. The production of these reports should be incorporated within the normal Supervision session.

Name of Supervisee:

Name of Supervisor:

Period covered by this Report:

Frequency of supervision:

Length of supervisory session:

Type of client issues discussed:

Please describe the Supervisee's abilities and/or qualities in the following areas, outlining particular strengths and areas for development.

The Therapeutic Effectiveness of the Counsellor

- Contracting, planning and boundary management:

- Developing a therapeutic relationship:

- Skills in therapeutic interviewing/intervention:

- Theoretical framework from which counsellor is working:

The Administrative Effectiveness of the Counsellor

- Record keeping:

The Counsellor's Ethical/Professional Practice

- Applying ethical principles:

- Reviewing and evaluating:

Constraining Influences on Therapeutic Practice

- Organisational culture:

- Management styles:

Counsellor's Effective Use of Supervision

- Case management:

- Presentation as a professional colleague:

- Professional communication – written and verbal:

Supervisor's summary about the Supervisee's strengths and recommendations for future training and development:

Supervisee's comments on the Supervisor's report:

Supervisor's signature: _____

Date: _____

Supervisee's signature: _____

Date: _____

(Based on ATOS ORIGIN's Employee Health Services Supervisor's Professional Development Report.)

Appendix 5

THE RESPONSIBILITIES OF THE SUPERVISOR, SUPERVISEE AND THEIR LINE MANAGER

Securing a supervisory post

Supervisee

- Working with their line manager to devise an advertisement, job description and person specification for the post
- Ensuring that their line manager understands the supervisory process and if necessary providing the line manager with a facts sheet on the supervisory process
- Ensuring that the line manager is aware of the rates of pay expected by supervisors
- Understanding what they want from their supervisor in terms of knowledge, experience, skills and personal qualities
- Ensuring that the supervisor has understanding of different organisational settings and their culture

Supervisor

- Understanding the organisational culture of the work
- Understanding the contract nature of the work including their responsibility/accountability to the organisation
- Ensuring that they have a full understanding of the reporting procedures required by the organisation
- Managing boundaries between themselves, the supervisee, line manager and any other colleagues within the organisation
- Ensuring that ethical practice is maintained within the boundaries of the organisation
- Ensuring that consultative support is available for this work

Line manager

- Advertising for a suitable supervisor
- Appointing an appropriate supervisor for the organisation
- Understanding the supervisory process
- Consulting with the supervisee about the appointment of a supervisor
- Communicating with the supervisor and supervisee over ethical and practical organisational issues whilst, at the same time, maintaining confidentiality
- Contracting with the supervisor for an annual or biannual report about the effectiveness of supervisory work
- Terminating a supervisor's contract where appropriate

Contracting for the supervisory work

Supervisor

- Educating the supervisee and the line manager about the content of the formal supervisory contract with the organisation if all parties agree on a formal type of contract
- Negotiating the finer details of the formal contract with the supervisee's line manager
- Signing the formal contract and abiding by the details within it
- Negotiating the details of an informal contract if that is more acceptable to all parties
- Adhering to the contract of employment whether informal or formal

Supervisee

- Educating their line manager about the type of contract needed by their supervisor
- Keeping themselves informed of the contract between their supervisor and the organisation
- Keeping the supervisor informed of any organisational issues that might affect either their own or their supervisor's working contract
- Adhering to their own contract of employment

Line manager

- Understanding the nature of the supervisory contract needed by the supervisor
- Making decisions about the type of supervisory contract needed by the organisation
- Drawing up the supervisory contract

- Negotiating with the supervisor before finalising the contract
- Keeping all parties in the working alliance informed about the contracts
- Updating of the contract of employment on a regular basis

Relationships within the supervisory rhombus

Supervisor

- Developing a sound collaborative relationship with the supervisee
- Developing a clear line of communication with the supervisee's line manager
- Ensuring that, if they hold a dual role within the organisation, the boundaries of each role are kept when engaging with their supervisee
- Becoming an agent of change within the organisation

Supervisee

- Developing a sound collaborative relationship with their supervisor
- Enabling the line manager and the supervisor to set up lines of communication

Line manager

- Enabling the supervisee to choose their own supervisor or when this course of action is not possible, consult the supervisee on the kind of supervision they need
- Ensuring that they do not have a dual role of supervisor and line manager
- Organising regular tripartite meetings between themselves, the supervisee and their supervisor

The heart of the supervisory work

Supervisee

- Expanding their attitudinal mindset to include the organisational dimension of their work
- Acquiring the extra skills that will enable them to work more effectively within the organisational setting
- Maintaining ethical practice, whilst communicating more widely within interdisciplinary teams

Supervisor

- Ensuring that the tasks and functions of the supervisory process include the expanded organisational context of the work
- Acquiring the skills needed to work more effectively within the organisational setting
- Ensuring that they understand organisational culture and its possible impact on the counselling process

Line Manager

- Listening to feedback from both counsellor and supervisor
- Acting on that feedback to the best of their ability
- Being open to the educative process in order to learn more about the counselling and supervision process

Reporting back to the organisation

Supervisor

- Ensuring that they are clear about the purpose of the report
- Clarity around who will have access to the report
- Negotiating with the supervisee and their line manager the extent of the information to be supplied to the organisation
- Agreeing what information can be divulged in the report concerning the supervisee's therapeutic effectiveness
- Reporting back to the organisation on the effectiveness of the record-keeping system within the organisation
- Educating the line manager about the ethical dilemmas that arise when a counsellor has a dual role within the organisation
- Educating the line manager about the exact nature of the supervisory process

Supervisee

- Educating the line manager, through the report, about record-keeping systems
- Educating their line manager about the exact nature of the supervisory process
- Identifying their future training needs and reporting back to their line manager clearly about these needs

Line manager

- Ensuring that the statistical information requested from the supervisor is used by the organisation respectfully
- Acting on any organisational issues that are identified in the report as needing attention, for example poor/unethical accommodation
- Ensuring that record-keeping system for client work is confidential and fit for its purpose
- Clarifying issues that originate from the organisational culture
- Ensuring that, as far as possible, the future training needs of the supervisee are met
- Devising a mechanism by which the reporting back procedure is carried out for all parties

Evaluation, assessment and accreditation

Supervisee

- Ensuring that they are open to the whole evaluation process with their supervisor
- Being as open as possible with their supervisor about what they want more of and what they want less of within the supervision process
- Enabling their line manager to understand the evaluation process within supervision
- Ensuring that meetings can take place between themselves, their line manager and their supervisor
- Feeding back to their line manager information about their training needs that arise as a result of the evaluation process
- Ensuring that they are competently trained for the role of counsellor
- Their own ongoing professional development
- Engaging openly in the assessment process
- Giving their line manager feedback about their ongoing professional development training needs
- Their own accreditation process with the relevant professional body
- Providing the relevant material and feedback to enable their supervisor to engage with the accreditation process
- Providing their line manager with information about the accreditation process and its importance

Supervisor

- Ensuring that the evaluation process is conducted in an atmosphere of respect
- Being open to the evaluation of themselves within the supervisory process

- Ensuring that they can attend three-way meetings within the supervisee's organisation
- Ensuring that they attend to any training needs identified by the evaluation process
- Ensuring that they are competently trained for the role of supervisor
- Giving feedback to the supervisee about their on-going development as a counsellor
- Ensuring their attendance at the tripartite meetings within the organisation
- Their on-going professional development
- Their own accreditation process with the relevant professional body
- Providing the supervisee's line manager with information about the accreditation process and its importance
- Being respectful of the supervisee's material needed for the accreditation process
- Keeping any organisational information confidential when engaging in the accreditation process

Line manager

- Attendance at meetings called by the supervisory dyad concerning the efficacy of the supervision process
- Understanding the role of evaluation within the supervisory process
- Ensuring that the supervisory relationship within the dyad is sound
- Understanding any assessment processes that counsellor and supervisor are undertaking
- Ensuring that they appoint adequately trained supervisors
- Attending tripartite meetings with counsellor and supervisor
- Being open to feedback about the organisation and its culture and the impact that has on the counselling and supervisory processes
- Ensuring that both counsellor and supervisor are encouraged to apply for accreditation with the relevant professional body
- Understanding the accreditation process
- Facilitating the process wherever possible

Endings and new beginnings in supervision

Supervisor

- Ensuring that the ending with their supervisee is planned and managed professionally
- Informing the supervisee's line manager that the supervisory relationship is being terminated
- Invoicing the organisation promptly for the final session(s) of supervision

- Involving themselves in a tripartite meeting with the supervisee and their line manager in order to discuss points for development in the future with a new supervisor
- Producing a joint report with their supervisee, for the organisation, on the supervisory work
- Offering to involve themselves with the selection of a new supervisor for the organisation

Supervisee

- Ensuring that they plan and manage the ending with their supervisor professionally
- Informing their line manager that their relationship with their supervisor is ending
- Ensuring that there is no gap in their supervision when one relationship comes to an end and a new one starts
- Involving themselves in a tripartite meeting with their line manager and their out-going supervisor .
- Producing a joint report for the organisation, with the supervisor, on the supervisory work

Line manager

- Ensuring that any contractual arrangements are concluded professionally, including final payments to the supervisor
- Involving themselves in a tripartite meeting with the supervisor and their supervisee to celebrate successes and detail areas for development
- Ensuring that any written report requested from the supervisor and supervisee is completed

References

Arnold, J., Cooper, C. L. and Robertson I. T. (1995) *Work Psychology: understanding human behaviour in the workplace*. London: Pitman Publishing.

Bimrose, J. and Wilden, S. (1994) 'Supervision in careers guidance: empowerment or control?', *British Journal of Guidance and Counselling*, 22(3):379–383.

Bond, T. (1990) 'Counselling supervision: ethical issues', *Counselling*, 1(2):3–45.

Bordin, E. S. (1979) 'The generalizability of the psychoanalytic concept of the working alliance', *Psychotherapy Research and Practice* 16(2):252–260.

British Association for Counselling (BAC) (1988, 1990, 1996) *Code of Ethics and Practice for Supervisors of Counsellors*. Rugby: BAC.

British Association for Counselling and Psychotherapy (BACP) (2000) *Counselling Supervision Accreditation*. Rugby: BACP.

British Association for Counselling and Psychotherapy (BACP) (2002) *Ethical Framework for Good Practice in Counselling and Psychotherapy*. Rugby: BACP.

Bull, A. (1997) 'Models of counselling in organisations', in Carroll, M. and Walton, M. (eds), *Handbook of Counselling in Organisations*. London: Sage.

Bunting, M. (2004) *Willing Slaves: how the overwork culture is ruining our lives*. London: HarperCollins.

Burton, M., Henderson, P. and Curtis-Jenkins, G. (1998) 'Primary Care counsellor's experience of supervision', *Counselling*, 9(2):122–133.

Carney, P. (2001) 'Supervision, support and surviving complaints', in Casemore, R. (ed.), *Surviving Complaints against Counsellors and Psychotherapists*. Ross-on-Wye: PCCS Books.

Carroll, M. (1995) The Generic Tasks of Supervision: an analysis of supervisee expectations, supervisor interviews and supervisory audio-taped sessions. Ph.D thesis, University of Surrey.

Carroll, M. (1996) *Counselling Supervision: theory, skills and practice*. London: Cassell.

Carroll, M. (1997) 'Counselling in organisations: an overview', in Carroll, M. and Walton, M. (eds), *Handbook of Counselling in Organisations*. London: Sage.

Carroll, M. (1999) 'Supervision in workplace settings', in Carroll, M. and Holloway, E. (eds), *Counselling Supervision in Context*. London: Sage.

Carroll, M. (2001) 'Supervision in and for organisations', in Carroll, M. and Tholstrup, M. (eds), *Integrative Approaches to Supervision*. London: Jessica Kingsley.

Carroll, M. (2003) 'Life coaching: the new kid on the block', *Counselling and Psychotherapy Journal*, 14(10):28–31.

Carroll, M. and Holloway, E. (eds) (1999) *Counselling Supervision in Context*. London: Sage.

Coelho, P. (1997) *The Pilgrimage*. London: HarperCollins.

Cole, M. A., Kolko, D. J. and Craddick, R. A. (1981) 'The quality and process of the intern experience', *Professional Psychology*, 12(5):570–577.

Coles, A. (2003) *Counselling in the Workplace*. Maidenhead: Open University Press.

Coll, K. (1995) 'Clinical supervision and community college counsellors: current and preferred practices', *Counselor Education and Supervision*, 35(2):36–40.

Connor, M. (1997) Mentoring for Medics: an investigation into the outcomes of the doctors' development and mentoring networks in Northern and Yorkshire regions of the NHS. Unpublished research commissioned by the Development Unit of the NHS Executive.

Copeland, S. (1988) Staff Appraisal in Schools and Colleges. Unpublished M.Ed dissertation. Keele University.

Copeland, S. (2000a) People, Power and Pragmatism: an investigation of counselling supervision in organisational contexts. Unpublished M.Phil thesis. University of Birmingham.

Copeland, S. (2000b) 'New challenges for supervising in organisational contexts', in Lawton, B. and Feltham, C. (eds), *Taking Supervision Forward: enquiries and trends in counselling and psychotherapy*. London: Sage.

Copeland, S. (2001) 'Supervisor responsibility within organisational contexts', in Wheeler, S. and King, D. (eds), *Supervising Counsellors: issues of responsibility*. London: Sage.

Copeland, S. (2003) 'Supervision on the telephone: stop gap solution or good time management?', *Counselling and Psychotherapy Journal* 14(8):34–36.

Creese, J. V. (2002) *My Windward Side*. Stockport MBC Community Services.

Cummins, A. and Hoggett, P. (1995) 'Counselling in the enterprise culture', *British Journal of Guidance and Counselling*, 23(3):301–312.

Curtis-Jenkins, G. (2001) 'Counselling supervision in primary health care', in Carroll, M. and Tholstrup, M. (eds), *Integrative Approaches to Supervision*. London: Jessica Kingsley.

Curtis-Jenkins, G. and Einzig, H. (1996) 'Counselling in Primary Care', in Bayne, R., Horton, I. and Bimrose, J. (eds), *New Direction in Counselling*. London: Routledge.

Daloz, L. A. (1999) *Mentor: guiding the journey of adult learners* (2nd edn). San Francisco: Jossey-Bass.

Data Protection Act (1988). HMSO.

Davis, S. (1995) The firm, the boss, his consultant and her morals: an exploration of the one to one interventions for change in senior teams. Unpublished M.Sc dissertation, Bristol University.

De Board, R. (1978) *The Psychoanalysis of Organisations: psychoanalytic approaches to behaviour in groups and organisations*. London: Routledge.

Dodds, J. B. (1986) 'Supervision of psychology trainees in field placements', *Professional Psychology: Research and Practice*, 17(4):296–300.

Drucker, P. (1964) *Managing for Results*. New York: HarperCollins.

Dryden, W. (1985) *Therapist's Dilemmas*. London: Harper and Row.

East, P. (1995) *Counselling in Primary Care*. London: Open University Press.

Edwards, D. (1997) 'Supervision today: the psychoanalytic legacy', in Shipton, G.

(ed.), *The Supervision of Psychotherapy and Consulting: making a place to think*. Buckingham: Open University Press.

Egan, G. (1994) *Working the Shadow Side*. San Francisco: Jossey-Bass.

Ekstein, R. (1964) 'Supervision of Psychotherapy: Is it teaching? Is it Administration? Or is it therapy?', *Psychotherapy: Theory, Research and Practice*, 1:137–138.

Feltham, C. (2002) 'A surveillance culture?', *Counselling and Psychotherapy Journal*, 13(1):26–27.

French, J. R. P. and Raven, B. (1959) 'The basis of social power', in Cartwright, D. (ed.), *Studies in Social Power*. Anne Arbor: Michigan Institute for Social Research.

Gilbert, M. C. and Evans, K. (2000) *Psychotherapy Supervision*. Buckingham: Open University Press.

Gilbert, M. C. and Sills, C. (1999) 'Training for supervision evaluation', in Holloway, E. and Carroll, M., *Training Counselling Supervisors*. London: Sage.

Gray, H. (1993) 'Unscrambling the B-Picture: counselling, consultancy and strategic management', *British Journal of Guidance and Counselling*, 21(2):156–160.

Gubi, P. (2002) 'Practice behind closed doors: challenging the taboo of prayer in mainstream counselling culture.' Paper presented to the Annual Conference of the Society of Psychotherapy Research, Santa Barbara, California, USA.

Hall, R. H. (1991) *Organizations: Structures, processes, outcomes*. Englewood Cliffs, N.J: Prentice-Hall International, Inc.

Handy, C. (1985) *Understanding Organisations*. London: Penguin.

Handy, C. (1993) *Understanding Voluntary Organisations*. London: Penguin.

Harrison, R. (1993) *Diagnosing Organisational Culture*. San Diego, CA: Pfeiffer.

Harvey-Jones, J. (1988) *Making it Happen*. London: Fontana/Collins.

Harwood, D. (1993) 'Organisational consultancy, institutional dynamics and the role of the student counsellor', *British Journal of Guidance and Counselling*, 21(1):53–63.

Hatch, M. J. (1997) *Organisation Theory: modern symbolic and post modern perspectives*. Oxford: Oxford University Press.

Hawkins, P. and Shohet, R. (1989) *Supervision in the Helping Professions*. Milton Keynes: Open University Press.

Hawkins, P. and Shohet, R. (2000) *Supervision in the Helping Professions* (2nd edn). Milton Keynes: Open University Press.

Heisler, J. (1974) *Why Counsellors Resign*. Rugby: National Marriage Guidance Council.

Henderson, P. (1997) Supervision (Supplement 3). Middlesex: Counselling in Primary Care Trust.

Henderson, P. (1999) 'Supervision in medical settings', in Carroll, M. and Holloway, E. (eds), *Counselling Supervision in Context*. London: Sage.

Henderson, P. (2001) 'Supervising counsellors in primary care', in Wheeler, S. and King, D. (eds), *Supervising Counsellors: issues of responsibility*. London: Sage.

Hewson, J. (1999) 'Training supervisors to contract in supervision', in Holloway, E. and Carroll, M. (eds), *Training Counselling Supervisors*. London: Sage.

Hitt, D. (1996) 'The learning organisation: some reflections on organisational renewal', *Employee Counselling Today*, 8(7):16–25.

Holloway, E. (1995) *Clinical Supervision: a systems approach*. London: Sage.

Holloway, E. and Carroll, M. (eds) (1999) *Training Counselling Supervisors*. London: Sage.

Hughes, L. and Pengelly, P. (1997) *Staff Supervision in a Turbulent Environment: Managing process and task in front line services*. London: Jessica Kingsley.

Inskipp, F. and Proctor, B. (1995) *The Art, Craft and Tasks of Counselling Supervision, Part II, Becoming a Supervisor*. Twickenham: Cascade Publications.

Izzard, S. (2001) 'The responsibility of the supervisor supervising trainees', in Wheeler, S. and King, D. (eds), *Supervising Counsellors: issues of responsibility*. London: Sage.

Izzard, S. (2003) 'Who is holding the baby?', *Counselling and Psychotherapy Journal* 14(5):38–39.

Jacobs, M. (1996) 'Parallel process – confirmation and critique', *Psychodynamic Counselling*, 2(1):55–66.

Jenkins, P. (2001) 'Supervisory responsibility and the law', in Wheeler, S. and King, D. (eds), *Supervising Counsellors: issues of responsibility*. London: Sage.

Johnson, P. R. and Indvik, J. (1999) 'Organisational benefits of having emotionally intelligent managers and employees', *Journal of Workplace Learning*, 11(3):84–88.

Kaberry, S. (2000) 'Abuse in supervision', in Lawton, B. and Feltham, C. (eds), *Taking Supervision Forward*. London: Sage.

Kadushin, A. (1976) *Supervision in Social Work*. New York: Columbia University Press.

Kadushin, A. (1985) *Supervision in Social Work* (2nd edn). New York: Columbia University Press.

Katz, J. H. (1985) 'The socio-political nature of counseling', in *The Counseling Psychologist*, 13(4):615–624.

Lammers, W. (1999) 'Training in group and team supervision', in Holloway, E. and Carroll, M. (eds), *Training Counselling Supervisors*. London: Sage.

Landany, N., Lehrman-Waterman, D. E., Molinaro, M. and Wolgast, B. (1999) 'Psychotherapy supervisor practices: adherence to guidelines, the supervisory working alliance and supervisee satisfaction', *Counselling Psychologist*, 27(7):443–475.

Lawton, B. (2000) ' "A Very Exposing Affair": explorations in counsellors' supervisory relationships' in Lawton, B. and Feltham, C. (eds), *Taking Supervision Forward: enquiries and treads in counselling and psychotherapy*. London: Sage.

Lawton, B. and Feltham, C. (eds) (2000) *Taking Supervision Forward: enquiries and treads in counselling and psychotherapy*. London: Sage.

Lee, R. and Lawrence, P. (1985) *Organizational Behaviour: Politics at work*. London: Hutchinson.

Lewis, J., Clark, D. and Morgan, D. H. J. (1992) *Whom God Hath Joined Together: the work of marriage guidance*. London: Tavistock Routledge.

McCarthy, P., Sugden, S., Coker, M., Lamendda, F., Mawer, S. and Renninger, S. (1995) 'A practical guide to informed consent in clinical supervision', *Counselor Education and Supervision*, 35(2):130–138.

McGarvey, R. (1997) 'Final score: get more from your employees by upping your EQ', *Entrepreneur*, 25(7):78–81.

McGowan, B. G. (1989) *Trends in Employee Programs*. London: Routledge.

McLean, A. and Marshall, J. (1988) *Cultures at Work*. Luton: Local Government Training Board.

McLeod, J. (1993) 'Learning from the National Marriage Guidance Council', *British Journal of Guidance and Counselling*, 22(2):163–174.

McLeod, J. (1999) 'Counselling as a social process', *Counselling Journal of the British Association for Counselling*, 10(3):217–222.

McLeod, J. (2000) 'Assimilating Research and Inquiry into the Culture of Counselling.' Paper presented at the 8th Annual International Counselling Conference, Centre for Studies in Counselling, University of Durham.

McMahon Moughtin, M. (1997) *Focused Therapy for Organisations and Individuals*. London: Minerva Press.

Martin, E. (2003) 'Problems and ethical issues in supervision', in Wiener, J., Mizen, R. and Duckham, J. (eds), *Supervising and Being Supervised*. London: Palgrave.

Mearns, D. (1995) 'Supervision: a tale of the missing client', *British Journal of Guidance and Counselling*, 23(3):421–427.

Morgan, G. (1986) *Images of Organisations*. London: Sage.

Page, S. and Wosket, V. (2001) *Supervising the Counsellor: a cyclical model* (2nd end). London: Routledge.

Pearsall, J. (2002) *Concise Oxford English University Dictionary*. Oxford: Oxford University Press.

Peters, T. (1994) *The Frontiers of Excellence*. London: Nicholas Brearley Publishing.

Proctor, B. (1994) 'Supervision: competence, confidence and accountability', *British Journal of Guidance and Counselling*, 22(3):309–319.

Proctor, B. (1997a) 'Supervision for counsellors in organisations', in Carroll, M. and Walton, M. (eds), *Handbook of Counselling in Organisations*. London: Sage.

Proctor, B. (1997b) 'Contracting in supervision', in Sills, G. (ed.), *Contracts in Counselling*. London: Sage.

Proctor, B. (2000) *Creative Group Supervision*. London: Sage.

Proctor, B. (2002) 'Towards an autonomous and accountable profession?', *Counselling and Psychotherapy Journal*, 13(2):36–37.

Rose, S. (2001) Circles within Circles, Wheels within Wheels: a study of counsellor perceptions of supervisory roles in a managed primary care counselling service. College of Ripon and York: Unpublished MA dissertation.

Senge, P. (1990) *The Fifth Discipline: The art and practice of the learning organisation*. New York: Doubleday/Currency.

Shea, C. and Bond, T. (1997) 'Ethical issues for counselling in organisations', in Carroll, M. and Walton, M. (eds), *The Handbook of Counselling in Organisations*. London: Sage.

Sills, G. (1997) 'Contracting and contract making', in Sills, G. (ed.), *Contracts in Counselling*. London: Sage.

Stoltenberg, C. D. and Delworth, U. (1987) *Supervising Counselors and Therapists*. San Francisco: Jossey-Bass.

Sugarman, L. (1992) 'Ethical issues in counselling at work', *Employee Counselling Today*, 4(4):23–30.

Tehrani, N. (1996) 'Counselling in the Post Office: facing up to legal and ethical dilemmas', *British Journal of Guidance and Counselling*, 24(2):265–275.

Tholstrup, M. (1999) 'Supervision in educational settings', in Carroll, M. and Holloway, E. (eds), *Counselling Supervision in Context*. London: Sage.

Towler, J. (1999) 'Supervision in uniformed settings', in Holloway, E. and Carroll, M. (eds), *Training Counselling Supervisors*. London: Sage.

Tudor, K. (1997) 'The contract boundary', in Sills, G. (ed.), *Contracts in Counselling*. London: Sage.

Tudor, K. and Worrell, M. (eds) (2004) 'Person-centred perspectives on supervision', in *Freedom to Practice: person-centred approaches to supervision*. Ross-on-Wye: PCCS Books.

Tune, D. (2001) 'Is Touch a Valid Therapeutic Intervention and Worthy of Consideration in Supervision?' Paper presented to the annual conference of the Society for Psychotherapy Research (International), Montevideo.

Tyndall, N. (1993) *Counselling in the Voluntary Sector*. Buckingham: Open University Press.

Valentine, J. (2004) 'Personal and organisational power: management and professional supervision', in Tudor, K. and Worrell, M. (eds), *Freedom to Practice: person-centred approaches to supervision*. Ross-on-Wye: PCCS Books.

Van Ooijen, E. (2003) *Clinical Supervision Made Easy*. London: Churchill Livingston.

Wallbank, S. (1997) 'Counselling in voluntary organisations', in Palmer, S. and McMahon, G. (eds), *Handbook of Counselling* (2nd edn). London: Sage.

Walton, M. (1997) 'Counselling as a form of organisational change', in Carroll, M. and Walton, M. (eds), *Handbook of Counselling in Organisations*. London: Sage.

Webb, A. (2000) 'What makes it difficult for the supervisee to speak?', in Wheeler, S. and King, D. (eds), *Supervising Counsellors: issues of responsibility*. London: Sage.

Weber, M. (1947) *The Theory of Social and Economic Organisation*. New York: Oxford University Press.

West, W. (2003) 'The culture of psychotherapy supervision', *Counselling and Psychotherapy Research*, 3(2):123–127.

Wheeler, S. (2000) 'Taking supervision forward: a roundtable of views', in Lawton, B. and Feltham, C. (eds), *Taking Supervision Forward: enquiries and trends in counselling and psychotherapy*. London: Sage.

Wheeler, S. (2001) 'Supervisor accreditation: is it time to apply?', *Counselling and Psychotherapy Journal*, 12(2):30–31.

Wiener, J., Mizen, R. and Duckham, J. (2003) *Supervising and Being Supervised*. London: Palgrave.

Williams, D. I. (1992) 'Supervision: a new word is desperately needed', *Counselling*, 3(2):96.

Williams, P. and Davis, D. C. (2002) *Therapist as Life Coach: transforming your practice*. London: W.W. Norton and Company.

Zeus, P. and Skiffington, S. (2002) *The Complete Guide to Coaching at Work*. Australia: McGraw-Hill.

Zinkin, L. (1995) 'Supervision: the impossible profession', in Kingler, P. (ed.), *Jungian Perspectives in Clinical Supervision*. Switzerland: Damion Press.

Index

accountability 3; in contracts 93, 97; to organisation 136; for practice 127; of supervisee 124

accreditation 2, 32, 168–9; BACP criteria for 168–9, 190–1; definition 168; measuring professional competence 169; by professional assessment 160

advertisements 2, 29, 80–1, 143; externally 3–4; internally 3, 79–80

affirmation 125

allegiance 38

alliance 2, 18, 19, 68, 71; working 29, 81, 99, 103–5, 114; tripartite 100, 103, 127

anarchy 138

anger at ending of relationship 186–7

anxiety of assessment 159

appraisal 68, 127; connection to evaluation 161; connection with report 145, 156–7

assessment 32; anxiety of 159; of client needs 148–9; definition 164–5; formal: for supervisee 165; for supervisor 167; informal: for supervisee 165; link to evaluation 126, 160; link to responsibility 124; of supervisee's work 166; of supervisor's work 167

audit 29, 56, 136

authority 4, 27; personal 28–9; of profession 28; of role 27–8

BACP: Complaints Procedure 46–7; criteria for accreditation 168–9, 190–1; Ethical Framework for Good Practice 40, 46

boundaries 1, 33; confidential 30, 31, 95; dilemma 38; multiple 95; of complicated relationships 103, 105, 111; of informal contract 98–9; of the

report 128; overlapping 73, 78; transgression of 113; when ending supervision 176–7; when working with a team 135; with client 123; *see also* contract

bullying 50–1

celebration at ending of relationship 187

change 4; agent of 139; organisational 55, 111, 123, 139–40; of supervisor 173–81

choice of supervisor 107–10

coach 4, 12–15, 22; versus consultant 16

cognitive behavioural model 63

communication 2; between supervisor and line manager 112–13; channels of 110; direct line of 180; four way 114–16; lines of 99; systems 63, 68, 113, 115–16, 117, 144; *see also* language

competence 32, 96; reporting for 144; lack of by supervisor 180–1; in running groups 181; measuring 169; *see also* contracts; reports

confidentiality 12, 14, 77; boundaries of 30, 31, 95; client 30, 57; with contracts 89, 95–6, 98–9; fear of breaking 128, 131, 136; of information 113, 118; limits of 128, 131; policy on 127; statistical information and 56; within a team 127; within auditing of notes 136; within organisation 112

Consultancy Supervision 21

consultant 4, 15–17, 21, 22; as a function of supervision 122; versus coach 16

containment 125

contract 4, 83–101; confidentiality 89, 95–6, 98–9; definition 84; definition of terms 92; dilemmas in 85–7, 95, 110;